BEER HIKING
MINNESOTA, WISCONSIN & THE UPPER PENINSULA

Great Hikes and Breweries from the Twin Cities to the Northwoods

Beer Hiking Minnesota, Wisconsin & the Upper Peninsula
Great Hikes and Breweries from the Twin Cities to the Northwoods

By: Kristen Radaich

ISBN: 978-3-03964-102-4
Published by Helvetiq, Lausanne/Basel, Switzerland
Graphic Design and illustration: Daniel Malak, Jędrzej Malak
Printed in China
First Edition 2026

info@helvetiq.ch

www.helvetiq.com/us
www.facebook.com/helvetiq_usa
instagram: @helvetiq_usa

helvetiq.com

BEER HIKING
MINNESOTA, WISCONSIN & THE UPPER PENINSULA

Great Hikes and Breweries from
the Twin Cities to the Northwoods

TABLE OF CONTENTS

1

INTRODUCTION

ABOUT THE AUTHOR

Kristen Radaich grew up on a farm in northern Minnesota. As a lover of summer, she moved to Arizona in 2007 to soak up the warm sun year-round. It was there in the desert that Kristen discovered a love for both craft brews and rugged trails.

Kristen's appreciation for craft beer expanded as she and her friends began visiting new breweries opening in the Phoenix area. Around the same time, Kristen adopted two pit bulls, Cool Whip and Hercules, who took to hiking like old pros. Soon, her preferred itinerary when hosting friends and family for a visit included a local hike in the Superstition Mountains, then a stop at one of her favorite dog-friendly breweries.

Kristen and her dogs' shared love of outdoor adventures fueled a range of escapades, from day hikes and backpacking trips to multistate road trips that spanned entire summers. They spent years meandering around the Southwest, roaming along the Rocky Mountains into Canada, traversing badlands across the plains, and wandering the forests and lakes of the upper Midwest. Over the years, Kristen has written about these dog-friendly explorations for the GoPetFriendly blog and her own blog, Dogs & Detours.

Kristen's connection with GoPetFriendly led to the opportunity to write about hiking and beer for this book—perfectly timed with a few key life transitions. Cool Whip and Hercules passed away around the time Kristen moved back to Minnesota's Northwoods in 2023, but their adventurous legacy lived on with Lu, a 50-lb, swamp-loving, meatball-shaped rocket ship carefully disguised as a pit bull. This project was Kristen and Lu's first big road trip together, and Lu exuberantly joined in on every dog-friendly hike they explored.

BEER HIKING MINNESOTA, WISCONSIN & THE UPPER PENINSULA

Northwoods, Northland, Up North, North Country, Upper Midwest, Western Great Lakes States—no matter what you call it, this region spanning Minnesota, Wisconsin, and Michigan's Upper Peninsula has a character all its own. Shaped by ancient glaciers that once scraped the land, the landscape is a patchwork of forested hills, bogs, rugged cliffs, and interconnected waterways.

The trails showcased here guide you through prairies flush with native grasses and wildflowers; forests teeming with deer, black bears, and songbirds; wetlands harboring carnivorous plants; and lakes ringing with loon calls. You'll stroll the grounds of a former Schlitz Brewing farm, wind along rivers that once powered flour mills and sawmills, and wander beside abandoned mine pits turned glittering lakes. Each trail tells a story, echoing with the history of both wilderness and industry.

While this guide focuses on the Northwoods as defined by environmental maps, it would be remiss to skip over the outstanding territory many of you will travel through on your journey through these northern Midwest states. The driftless region of southern Minnesota, the vibrant Twin Cities, Milwaukee's urban charm, and the scenic western shoreline of Lake Michigan all offer their own adventures and flavors.

As for the rest of Michigan: Honestly, I could only travel so far before my cats threatened to take over my parents' house and Lu forgot our full-time home. While the mitten of Michigan is a spectacular space worth considering for a future project, I promise you the included territory is overflowing with exciting trails and delicious brews.

From bustling cities to tiny towns, the North Country is home to proud, hardworking people who cherish both their wild spaces and tight-knit communities while still opening their arms to welcome visitors as if they were long-time friends. The brewers revel in crafting beers that celebrate the local flavors of the land—think blueberries, rhubarb, honey, and maple syrup—while still including a diverse selection of ingredients and styles. This isn't the land of bland beer, it's a melting pot of rich porters and stouts, a diverse range of hoppy IPAs, an eclectic mix of saisons and sours, plus nut browns, shandies, old English ales, and more.

So, whether you're a seasoned explorer or a first-time visitor, a beer connoisseur or an occasional sampler, get ready to hit the trails and explore the taprooms across the Midwest's vibrant northern countryside and communities.

CHOOSE THE BEER OR THE HIKE

HIKE LOCATION

REGION

MAP

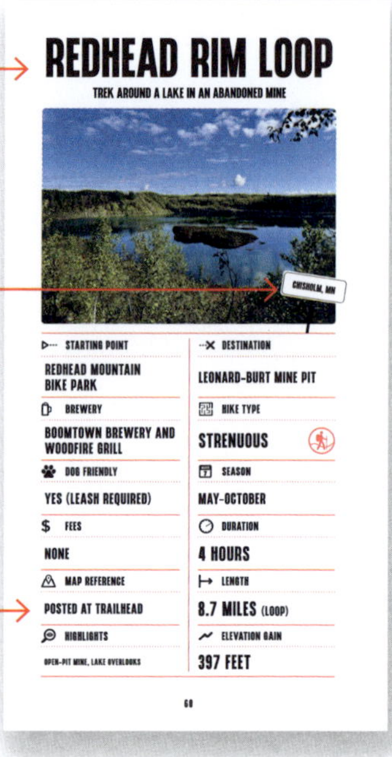

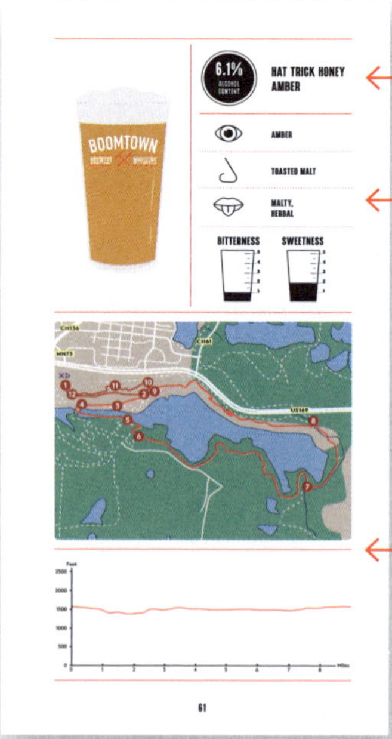

NAME OF THE BEER

INFORMATION ABOUT THE BEER

INFORMATION ABOUT THE HIKE

ON THE HIKES AND HIKE RATINGS

This guide highlights a diverse collection of hikes that showcase the natural beauty of Minnesota, Wisconsin, and Michigan's Upper Peninsula. The trails range from easy riverside strolls and paved pathways to moderate hills and challenging, rocky ascents.

Hike difficulty ratings are based on factors such as terrain, total mileage, elevation gain, and my personal experience and abilities. Your experience may differ, and any one of these hikes could feel easier or more demanding depending on your own fitness level and the current trail conditions.

EASY

Easy hikes are under 4 miles in length and typically feature less than 100 feet of elevation gain. The footpaths are generally smooth and free from tripping hazards like rocks or tree roots.

MODERATE

Most of the routes in this guide are moderate hikes. These generally range from 3 to 6 miles and require 2 to 3 hours to complete. Some moderate hikes may be longer but have gentle terrain, while others are shorter with steeper climbs or trickier footing. For example, the Root River State Trail is 8.3 miles out-and-back on a smooth, paved surface, whereas Eagle Trail spans just 2.4 miles but includes a rocky section that demands careful footing.

STRENUOUS

The strenuous hikes are typically more than 6 miles in length and can feature up to 764 feet of elevation gain. Expect these trails to take 4 to 6 hours to complete. Hogback Mountain is a notable exception—though only 3.6 miles, it has a rocky footpath and a steep ascent that may require a brief scramble.

I completed most of these hikes after a wet spring when heavy rains led to washed-out bridges, muddy or flooded paths, and closed or rerouted trails across the three states. Check current trail conditions and routes before setting out on your adventures as heavy winds, rain, and spring snowmelt can significantly alter trails throughout the region.

Some hikes in this guide require entrance or parking fees. Most permits, such as the Minnesota State Parks vehicle permit, the Wisconsin State Park System vehicle permit, and the Michigan Recreation Passport, can be purchased online before arriving.

A few trails do not allow dogs, and those that do require them to be leashed. Confirm local trail regulations before setting out on your excursion.

Verify your destination's time zone. Most of the hikes fall within the central time zone, but the Upper Peninsula stretches across both the central and eastern time zones. The following hikes are in the eastern time zone: Manistique Boardwalk, Bush Bay, Tahquamenon Falls, Chapel Loop, Mount Marquette Loop, Hogback Mountain, and Mt. Baldy.

ON THE BREWERIES AND BEER RATINGS

Brewery selections were based on several factors, including proximity to the featured hikes, reviews, recommendations from fellow beer enthusiasts, and my own experiences. The list includes different business styles, from intimate, owner-operated establishments to larger breweries with a full team of staff members. Many of the brewers began their journeys with humble homebrew kits in basements or garages but have since transformed a fascinating array of buildings—such as a former Department of Natural Resources (DNR) ranger station—into thriving gathering places for beer lovers. Ultimately, they're united by a passion for craft beer and a love of sharing their expertly brewed creations with others.

The featured beers represent a blend of brewer recommendations, flagship brews, beers that best complemented the hike or season, and some of my personal favorites. While many of these brews are available year-round, some appear only as part of a rotating selection of seasonal and experimental releases. Whether you prefer light and fruity, rich and dark, or boldly sour flavors, you're certain to find a pint that excites your palate. Don't hesitate to sample widely, chat with the beertender for personalized recommendations, and perhaps discover new favorites along the way.

One brewery of note that could not be included is Agonic Brewing Company in Rice Lake, Wisconsin. The brewery and three other businesses in the building were destroyed by a fire in late 2024. I thoroughly enjoyed my conversation with owners Danni Moon and Desmond Benavides and had planned to feature their coffee blonde ale, Dirty Blonde. If Agonic Brewing Company has reopened by the time you head into Wisconsin for a beer hiking adventure, consider exploring a portion of the Ice Age Trail near Rice Lake before stopping by the brewery.

Most of the breweries highlighted in this guide are best reached by car. Enjoy your beer responsibly and never drink and drive. If you're short on time, ask for to-go options, like a growler or a pack of cans, so you can sip these local brews safely at your final destination.

PREPARING FOR YOUR HIKE

Exploring the natural spaces of the Northwoods means embracing unpredictable weather, varied terrain, and spotty cell service. That's why carrying the Ten Essentials is more than just good advice—it's a necessity. Tailor your gear to the hike's length and difficulty, the weather forecast, and your personal needs.

THE TEN ESSENTIALS (PLUS ONE)

Whether you're heading out for a leisurely stroll or a full day's trek, preparation is key to a safe and memorable adventure in the great outdoors. With the right gear, knowledge, and mindset, you'll be ready to enjoy the lush beauty of the North Country. These core items can help you handle emergencies, navigate safely and confidently, and stay comfortable no matter what nature throws your way.

- **Navigation** – Even if you rely on digital maps on a cell phone or GPS device, include a paper map and compass as a reliable backup—and know how to use them. Electronic devices may lose battery faster in low-reception areas, so consider packing extra batteries or a charging pack and cable.
- **First Aid** – Carry a compact first aid kit that can treat minor injuries and manage emergencies on the trail. Review your kit each season to remove and resupply any expired medications.
- **Hydration** – Bring more water than you expect to drink. Hydration needs increase in hot weather and during more demanding hikes. Include a reliable purification system should you need to resupply your water from natural sources.
- **Nutrition** – Pack more food than you plan to consume. Calorie-dense, non-perishable snacks plus an additional day's supply will help support you if your hike takes longer than expected. Dehydrated backpacking meals are an easy and lightweight option for backup food.
- **Skin Protection** – Shield yourself from the sun and insects! Use sunscreen, a hat, sunglasses, and sun-protective clothing to guard against harmful rays. Apply bug repellent and wear long sleeves and long pants to protect against ticks, mosquitoes, and other biting insects.
- **Insulation** – Weather can turn in a heartbeat. Include insulating and rainproof layers to adjust to changing weather and maintain your body temperature. Consider packing an insulating jacket, a rain shell, a hat, gloves, and thermal underwear.
- **Light** – A headlamp or flashlight is essential if you're delayed after dark. Test the batteries before you leave home and pack extras.
- **Tools** – A multi-tool is a hiker's best friend. It's useful for food preparation, fire starting, and emergencies. Look for one that includes a knife, scissors, pliers, saw, screwdriver, and more.
- **Fire** – Waterproof matches, a lighter, or flint can help you start a fire for warmth or signaling. Tinder or fire starters are helpful to bring as well.
- **Shelter** – An emergency bivy or a space blanket will provide protection if you must spend an unplanned night outdoors.
- **Share your plans** – Not something you can pack but just as important: Let someone know your planned route and expected return—a friend, family member, or even park rangers. If you're unable to call for help and fail to report a safe exit, this person can call the proper authorities to initiate a search.

HIKING SEASON

Prime hiking season in the western Great Lakes states runs from May through October. In spring, some trails may be closed due to mud or flooding from snowmelt—check conditions before heading out. Fall can be a busy time on the trails, particularly along Minnesota's North Shore and throughout Michigan's Upper Peninsula, so have a backup plan in case trailhead parking lots fill up. Many trails transition to ski and snowshoe use once the snow arrives, and hiking may be prohibited on groomed paths.

HUNTING SEASONS

Hunting seasons and regulations vary by state, weapon, and species. Educate yourself on local rules and verify trail access prior to embarking on your journey—some trails close during the firearms deer seasons. For safety, wear blaze orange during the fall hunting season.

Minnesota: dnr.state.mn.us/hunting
Wisconsin: dnr.wisconsin.gov/topic/Hunt
Michigan: michigan.gov/dnr/things-to-do/hunting

WEATHER

The upper Midwest is known for its cold and snow, and spring or fall snowstorms are not uncommon. With the arrival of spring, thunderstorms, high winds, and tornadoes become more likely. These weather patterns can leave behind damaged trails and downed trees. While dense forest canopies provide shade on most of the trails included here, heat and humidity present serious concerns during the summer. Always check the weather forecast while planning your trip and again before you set out. Dress for the conditions and pack extra gear to handle whatever Mother Nature has in store.

ADDITIONAL RESOURCES

MINNESOTA

Hiking: Minnesota Department of Natural Resources, dnr.state.mn.us/hiking

Breweries: Minnesota Craft Brewers Guild, mncraftbrew.org
Visitor Amenities: Explore Minnesota, exploreminnesota.com

WISCONSIN

Hiking: Travel Wisconsin, travelwisconsin.com/hiking-report

Breweries: Wisconsin Brewers Guild, wibrewersguild.com
Visitor Amenities: Travel Wisconsin, travelwisconsin.com

MICHIGAN'S UPPER PENINSULA

Hiking: Upper Peninsula Travel and Recreation Association, uptravel.com/outdoors-recreation/trails/hiking

Breweries: Michigan Brewers Guild, mibeer.com

Visitor Amenities: Pure Michigan, michigan.org

North Country Trail Association, northcountrytrail.org
Ice Age Trail Alliance, iceagetrail.org
Superior Hiking Trail Association, superiorhiking.org
Minnesota State Parks, dnr.state.mn.us/state_parks
Wisconsin State Parks, dnr.wisconsin.gov/topic/Parks
Michigan State Parks, michigan.gov/dnr/places/state-parks
Leave No Trace, https://lnt.org/

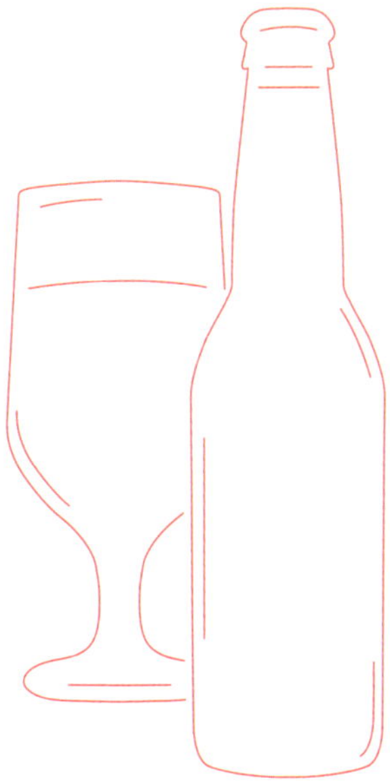

TRAIL ETIQUETTE

Practicing good trail etiquette is about showing respect for the land, wildlife, and your fellow outdoor adventurers. Your actions set an example for others and help protect these natural spaces for generations to come. As interest in hiking continues to grow, it's more important than ever to be a thoughtful and responsible visitor.

Whether you're a seasoned explorer or just starting out, these guidelines will help you minimize your impact, stay safe, and ensure every journey into nature is enjoyable for all.

- Pack out trash. Carry out everything you bring in, including trash. Even biodegradable items, such as fruit peels, can disturb the surrounding ecosystem and may take years to decompose. Bring a trash bag or reusable container to collect your waste and any litter you find along the trail.
- Dispose of human waste responsibly. If you need to go to the bathroom while hiking, go at least 200 feet from trails and water sources. Dig a hole at least 6 inches deep and 4 inches in diameter to bury solid waste. Carry out used toilet paper. Add a simple toilet kit to your hiking pack with a lightweight trowel, toilet paper, a bag for used toilet paper, and hand sanitizer. Alternatively, bring a WAG bag.
- Respect trail boundaries. Stay on designated trails to avoid damaging the surrounding ecosystems. Avoid cutting switchbacks, taking shortcuts, or stepping off boardwalks, which can widen trails and harm plant life.
- Be mindful of trail conditions. If a trail is muddy or damaged, consider turning back to prevent additional damage to the trail and surrounding environment. When encountering the occasional mud puddle on a trail, walk straight through. Stepping around a muddy patch unnecessarily widens the trail and damages vegetation.
- Yield to the right-of-way. Hikers going uphill have the right-of-way as it's harder to regain momentum when climbing. Descending hikers should step aside to give space. Bicyclists yield to both hikers and horses. Hikers yield to horses and should step off the trail on the downhill side. When overtaking another hiker, announce yourself politely and wait for a safe spot to pass.

- Minimize impacts in group travel. Some trails have group size limits to reduce impact—verify with the land managers beforehand. Hike in a single line to avoid blocking the trail when others are present so they can pass unobstructed.
- Preserve the peace. Hike quietly and speak in low voices to preserve the natural sounds and respect others' experiences. A friendly nod or greeting is common trail courtesy.
- Observe wildlife and do not disturb. Do not feed wildlife. Doing so can attract them to humans, which is dangerous for both parties. Use binoculars or a camera zoom to view wildlife. Never approach, chase, or try to touch wild animals.
- Practice responsible pet management. Keep your pets leashed and under control, respecting the space and comfort of other visitors and wildlife. Pack out pet waste to minimize impact on the local ecosystem and keep the trails clean for all to enjoy.

2

MAP & INDEX

MAP

MINNESOTA

1. Cuyuna Lakes
2. Northland Arboretum
3. Deep Portage Bog Walk
4. Lake Bemidji State Park
5. Bass Brook
6. Redhead Rim Loop
7. Tilson Bay
8. Split Rock River Trail
9. Brewer Park
10. Ely's Peak
11. Moose Lake Woodland Trails
12. Sandstone Bluffs Loop
13. Theodore Wirth Regional Park
14. Hyland Lake Park Reserve
15. Pike Island
16. Mill Towns State Trail
17. Root River State Trail

WISCONSIN

18. Chippewa Moraine Circle
19. Sandrock Cliffs

20. Makwa Ziibiins Miikana
21. Lakeshore Trail
22. North Lakeland
23. Catherine Wolter Wilderness Area
24. Raven Red Loop
25. Anvil National Recreation Trail
26. Grandfather Falls
27. Schlitz Audubon Loop
28. Mequon Nature Preserve
29. Kohler Dunes Cordwalk
30. Point Beach Loop
31. Baird Creek West Loop
32. Eagle Trail
33. Lynd Point Loop
34. Lake Mary Plains Pathway

MICHIGAN

35. Manistique Boardwalk
36. Bush Bay
37. Tahquamenon Falls
38. Chapel Loop
39. Mount Marquette Loop
40. Hogback Mountain
41. Mt. Baldy
42. Great Conglomerate Falls

HIKES

HIKE	CITY, STATE	LENGTH	PAGE
Anvil National Recreation Trail	Eagle River, Wi	6.1 miles	176
Baird Creek West Loop	Green Bay, Wi	3.8 miles	212
Bass Brook	Cohasset, Mn	3.0 miles	54
Brewer Park	Duluth, Mn	3.1 miles	78
Bush Bay	Cedarville, Mi	4.6 miles	244
Catherine Wolter Wilderness Area	Presque Isle, Wi	5.3 miles	164
Chapel Loop	Munising, Mi	10.7 miles	256
Chippewa Moraine Circle	New Auburn, Wi	4.7 miles	134
Cuyuna Lakes	Ironton, Mn	5.0 miles	30
Deep Portage Bog Walk	Hackensack, Mn	2.4 miles	42
Eagle Trail	Fish Creek, Wi	2.4 miles	218
Ely's Peak	Duluth, Mn	6.8 miles	84
Grandfather Falls	Merrill, Wi	5.1 miles	182
Great Conglomerate Falls	Ironwood, Mi	6 miles	280
Hogback Mountain	Marquette, Mi	3.6 miles	268
Hyland Lake Park Reserve	Bloomington, Mn	5.4 miles	108
Kohler Dunes Cordwalk	Sheboygan, Wi	3 miles	200
Lake Bemidji State Park	Bemidji, Mn	4.6 miles	48
Lake Mary Plains Pathway	Crystal Falls, Mi	7.1 miles	232
Lakeshore Trail	Bayfield, Wi	9.5 miles	152
Lynd Point Loop	Ellison Bay, Wi	2.4 miles	224
Makwa Ziibiins Miikana	Superior, Wi	6.4 miles	146
Manistique Boardwalk	Manistique, Mi	3.6 miles	238
Mequon Nature Preserve	Mequon, Wi	2.8 miles	194
Mill Towns State Trail	Cannon Falls, Mn	4.6 miles	120
Moose Lake Woodland Trails	Moose Lake, Mn	4 miles	90
Mount Marquette Loop	Marquette, Mi	4.5 miles	262
Mt. Baldy	Eagle Harbor, Mi	6.3 miles	274
North Lakeland	Manitowish Waters, Wi	3.9 miles	158
Northland Arboretum	Baxter, Mn	3.8 miles	36
Pike Island	St. Paul, Mn	3.9 miles	114
Point Beach Loop	Two Rivers, Wi	5.1 miles	206
Raven Red Loop	Woodruff, Wi	4.2 miles	170
Redhead Rim Loop	Chisholm, Mn	8.7 miles	60
Root River State Trail	Lanesboro, Mn	8.3 miles	126
Sandrock Cliffs	Grantsburg, Wi	2.8 miles	140
Sandstone Bluffs Loop	Taylors Falls, Mn	3.2 miles	96
Schlitz Audubon Loop	Milwaukee, Wi	2.3 miles	188
Split Rock River Trail	Two Harbors, Mn	4.8 miles	72
Tahquamenon Falls	Paradise, Mi	5.7 miles	250
Theodore Wirth Regional Park	Minneapolis, Mn	3.2 miles	102
Tilson Bay	International Falls, Mn	3.0 miles	66

BREWERIES & BEERS

BREWERY	BEER	PAGE
3 Sheeps Brewing	Wisconsinitis Cream Ale	201
Adventure Club Brewing	Apostle Bear Brown Porter	153
Alpha Michigan Brewing Company	Brule River Red American Amber Ale	233
Barrel + Beam Brewery	Saison Terre A Terre	269
Bemidji Brewing	German Blonde	49
Bent Paddle Brewing Company	Bent Hop Golden Ipa	85
Black Husky Brewing	Sproose Double Ipa	189
Blackrocks Brewery	Super Deluxe Helles Lager	263
Bloomer Brewing Company	Oktoberfest Lager	135
Boomtown Brewery and Woodfire Grill	Hat Trick Honey Amber	61
Brickfield Brewing	Feelin' Your Oats Ipa	141
Brickside Brewery	Summer Wit	275
Castle Danger Brewery	Maple Märzen	73
Cold Iron Brewing	Drift South Jalapeño Ale	281
Copper State Brewing Co.	We Drink At Dawn! Beermosa Radler	213
Cuyuna Brewing Company	Chocolate Peanut Butter Porter	31
Door County Brewing Company	Vacationland Ipa	219
Earth Rider Brewery	Tap Shack Caribbean-Style Lager	147
East Channel Brewing Company	Old Tru's Ipa	257
Five Sons Brewing	Quail's Irish Red	165
Flatiron Brewing	Czech Up Lager	239
Jack Pine Brewery	Vengeance! Jalapeño Cream Ale	37
Klockow Brewing Company	Bhk Nut Brown Ale	55
Les Cheneaux Distillers	Vera B's Honey Brown	245
Loony's Brew	Drunken Loon Dark Belgian	67
Moose Lake Brewing Company	Morning Haze New England Ipa	91
Peach Barn Farmhouse and Brewery	Silo Sisters Peach Sour	225
Petskull Brewing	Schnitzkygerman Hefeweizen	207
Rendezvous Brewing	Sunny Dream Cream Ale	43
Rocky Reef Brewing Company	Musky Bite Ipa	171
Sawmill Brewing Company	Boom Decker Becker Ipa	183
Some Nerve Brewing Company	Mr. Friendly Oatmeal Cream Ale	159
Sylvan Brewing	Gnarly Old Ale	127
Tahquamenon Falls Brewery & Pub	Black Bear Stout	251
The Fermentorium Brewery	Crispy And The Bois Lager	195
Tilion Brewing Company	Peanut Butter Cocoa Stout With Double Marshmallow	121
Tribute Brewing Company	Blueberry Train Wheat Ale	177
Uncommon Loon Brewing Company	Shapeshifter Ipa	97
Urban Growler Brewing Company	Vanilla Latte Blonde Ale	115
Ursa Minor Brewing	Galactic Face Slap Ipa	79
Utepils Brewing	Ewald The Golden Bavarian Hefeweizen	103
Wooden Hill Brewing Company	Kold Shoulder Kölsch	109

3

THE BEER HIKES

MINNESOTA

CUYUNA LAKES

ENJOY PANORAMAS OVER ABANDONED MINE PIT LAKES

STARTING POINT	DESTINATION
MINER'S MOUNTAIN RALLY CENTER	MINER'S MOUNTAIN

BREWERY	HIKE TYPE
CUYUNA BREWING COMPANY	MODERATE

DOG FRIENDLY	SEASON
YES (LEASH REQUIRED)	MAY–OCTOBER

FEES	DURATION
YES	2 HOURS 30 MINUTES

MAP REFERENCE	LENGTH
POSTED AT TRAILHEAD	5.0 MILES (ROUND TRIP)

HIGHLIGHTS	ELEVATION GAIN
LAKE OVERLOOKS, FALL COLORS	216 FEET

5.0%
ALCOHOL CONTENT

CHOCOLATE PEANUT BUTTER PORTER

DARK BROWN

PEANUT BUTTER, CHOCOLATE

PEANUT BUTTER, CHOCOLATE

BITTERNESS **SWEETNESS**

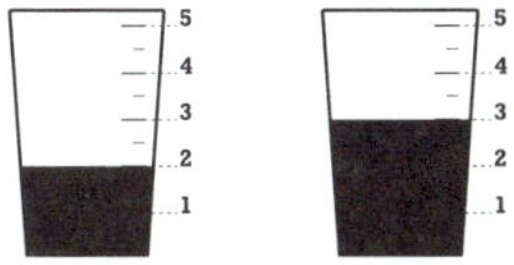

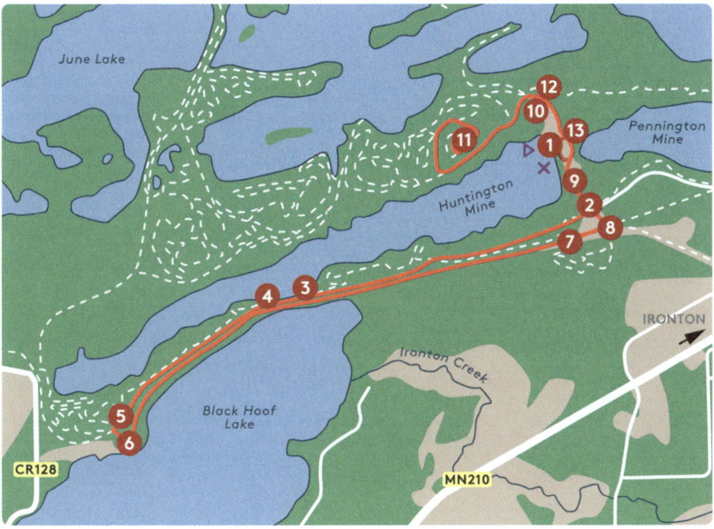

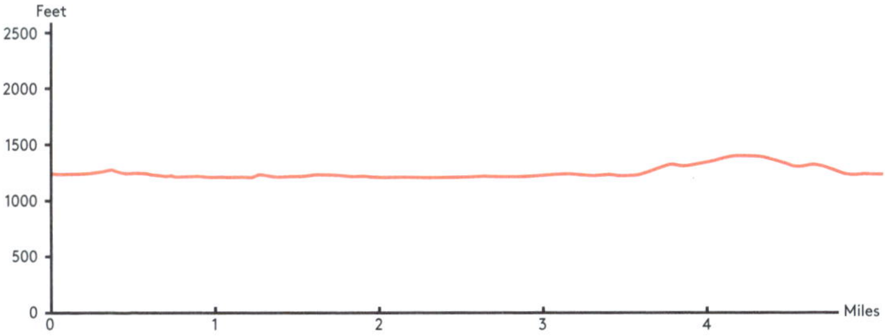

HIKE DESCRIPTION

Mosey down the paved trail along a lake formed in an abandoned pit mine, then power up Miner's Mountain for a bird's-eye view of the sparkling waters below. Posthike, head into town for a tasty pint of Cuyuna Brewing Company's Chocolate Peanut Butter Porter.

Cuyuna County State Recreation Area, established in 1993, includes more than 800 acres of land abandoned by mining companies in the late 1900s. The former open-pit iron-ore mines have since filled with incredibly clear water, and the mountainous rock stockpiles support a range of aspen, birch, oak, and basswood trees that put on a tremendous display in the fall. Cuyuna's extensive mountain-bike trail system (hikers welcome) winds around many of these lakes with switchbacks lacing up and down the rocky hills. The Cuyuna Lakes State Trail, a paved multi-use pathway, also sweeps through this rugged landscape. It offers a more accessible option to explore the region as it stretches eight miles from Crosby to Riverton.

Your adventure begins at the Rally Center, the primary trailhead for the recreation area. You'll step on the Cuyuna Lakes State Trail for a lollipop loop through the thick forest blanketing the land. One mile into your stroll, you'll make a stop at the Huntington-Feigh Mine Overlook. Take a seat on the bench to enjoy a sweeping vista across the lake. After marveling at the immensity of this former mine pit, you'll continue on to pick up the snowmobile trail for the second half of your loop. In the warmer months, this mowed-grass corridor is lined with wildflowers, and you can enjoy beautiful views of Blackhoof Lake.

As you hit the three-mile mark, you'll reconnect with the Cuyuna Lakes State Trail to head back to the Rally Center, but the hike doesn't stop yet. Once you're past the last parking lot, it'll be time to kick it into high gear. You'll hop on the paved road to wind up to the top of Miner's Mountain, rising 200 feet over a half mile. At the summit, you can catch your breath as you take in the incredible scene spread before you. Huntington Mine Lake sits immediately below you. Blackhoof Lake is further to the right. Beyond the Rally Center to the left, you'll see Pennington Mine Lake. Once you've taken pictures and had a water break, you'll amble down the mountain to return to the trailhead.

TURN-BY-TURN DIRECTIONS

1. From the trailhead map, follow the sidewalk south around the parking lot. In 300 feet, cross the road at the crosswalk and turn right onto the paved, signposted Cuyuna Lakes State Trail. In 200 feet, continue straight across the driveway for the boat ramp parking lot.
2. At 0.2 miles, at the junction, turn right to cross the road and continue on the signposted Cuyuna Lakes State Trail. Ignore the next three junctions with dirt trails.
3. At 1.0 miles, at the Huntington-Feigh Mine sign, step off the path to explore the overlook. Marvel at the view, then continue on the paved trail.
4. At 1.1 miles, continue straight, ignoring a dirt trail on the right.
5. At 1.6 miles, continue straight, ignoring another dirt trail on the right. In 250 feet, at the junction with a trail map, turn left onto the wide grassy trail.
6. At 1.7 miles, at the T-junction, turn left to follow the arrow on the orange trail marker.
7. At 3.0 miles, at the junction, continue straight on the wide grassy path.
8. At 3.1 miles, turn left at the junction onto the gravel road to follow the arrow on the Overlook Spur Trail sign. In 350 feet, reach the junction from Step 2. Cross the road and continue straight on the signposted Cuyuna Lakes State Trail.
9. At 3.2 miles, continue straight across the driveway for the boat ramp parking lot.
10. At 3.5 miles, the Cuyuna Lakes State Trail ends. Continue up the hill on the paved road. Ignore all junctions with the dirt trails.
11. At 4.1 miles, reach the top of Miner's Mountain. Explore the vistas, then retrace your path back down.
12. At 4.8 miles, rejoin the Cuyuna Lakes State Trail and continue straight.
13. At 5.0 miles, at the crosswalk, turn right to cross the road and follow the sidewalk back to the trailhead map.

FIND THE TRAILHEAD

From Crosby at 3rd Avenue/Great River Road and Main Street, head south on 3rd Avenue. After 0.2 miles, turn right onto 3rd Street and proceed for 0.7 miles. Continue straight onto 2nd Street for 0.2 miles, then turn right onto County Highway 30/Irene Avenue. After 0.1 miles, turn left onto North Road. Continue for 0.7 miles and then turn left into the parking lot. The trail begins from the trailhead map at the far end of the lot overlooking the lake.

CUYUNA BREWING COMPANY

The town of Crosby was nowhere on their radar when owners Laura and Nick Huisinga first considered opening a brewery. Nick, with a background in science and making vaccines, found he had a knack for the science of crafting beer. After a few years of homebrewing, he knew he wanted to try brewing professionally one day. Then, a mountain-biking trip to Crosby really got the gears turning. He immediately fell in love with the beauty of the area and couldn't wait to share it with Laura and their three kids.

The town was smaller and quieter after the end of the local iron-ore mining. Still, Laura and Nick felt confident that the area's budding network of trails and other recreational opportunities—and a new brewery—were sure to draw people back in. Cuyuna Brewing Company opened in 2017, and Nick still loves brewing beer that people enjoy. Laura enjoys their connection with the growing community and the gathering space they've crafted for all to enjoy.

Cuyuna Brewing Company's Chocolate Peanut Butter Porter is full of flavors thanks to a recipe with a hefty pile of peanuts, two chocolate malts, and cocoa powder. It's a low-alcohol, easy-drinking porter that pairs well with adventure.

LAND MANAGER

Minnesota Department of Natural Resources
Cuyuna Country State Recreation Area
307 3rd Street
Ironton, MN 56455
(218) 772-3690
mndnr.gov/cuyuna
files.dnr.state.mn.us/maps/state_parks/sra00302.pdf

BREWERY/RESTAURANT

Cuyuna Brewing Company
1 E Main Street
Crosby, MN 5644
(218) 866-0914
cuyunabrewing.com

Distance from trailhead: 2.3 miles

NORTHLAND ARBORETUM

ROAM AROUND PINES AND BEAVER PONDS

STARTING POINT	DESTINATION
ARBORETUM TRAILHEAD	BEAVER POND
BREWERY	**HIKE TYPE**
JACK PINE BREWERY	MODERATE
DOG FRIENDLY	**SEASON**
YES (LEASH REQUIRED)	MAY–OCTOBER
FEES	**DURATION**
YES	1 HOUR 45 MINUTES
MAP REFERENCE	**LENGTH**
POSTED AT TRAILHEAD	3.8 MILES (LOLLIPOP LOOP)
HIGHLIGHTS	**ELEVATION GAIN**
JACK PINE FOREST, WETLANDS	60 FEET

4.6% ALCOHOL CONTENT

VENGEANCE! JALAPEÑO CREAM ALE

GOLDEN YELLOW

FRESH-CUT JALAPEÑOS

JALAPEÑO POPPER, MEDIUM HEAT

BITTERNESS

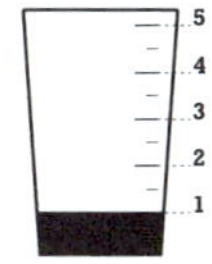

SWEETNESS

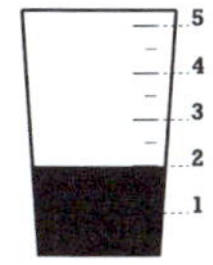

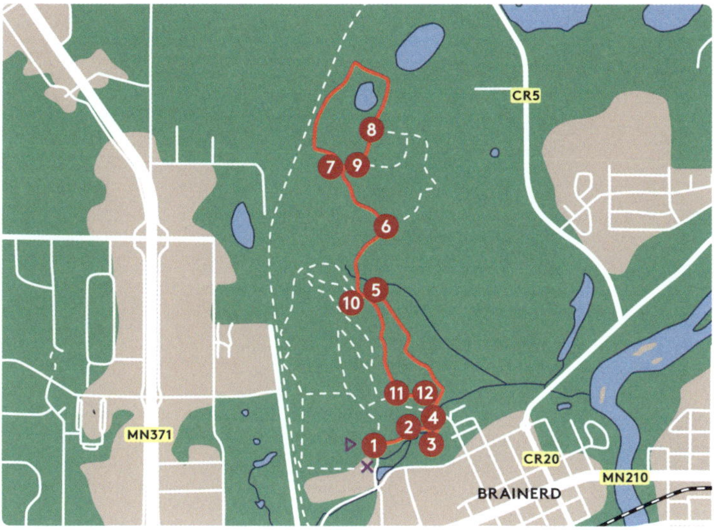

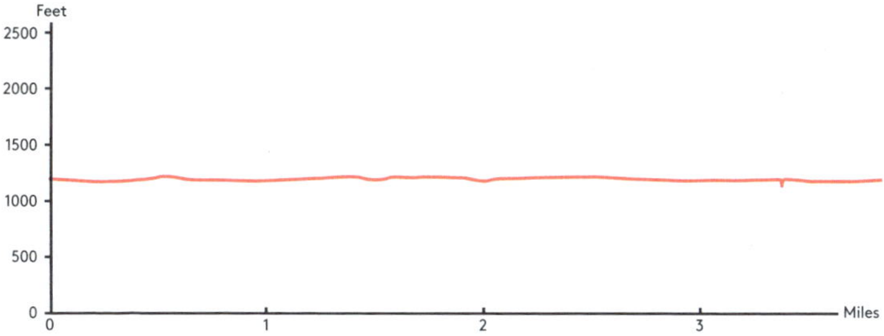

HIKE DESCRIPTION

Stroll forest corridors, garden paths, and wetland loops at Northland Arboretum for a dose of nature between two growing cities. After, taste your way through Jack Pine Brewery's tap list, starting with a cold pint of Vengeance! Jalapeño Cream Ale.

The Northland Arboretum sits on the border of Baxter and Brainerd, preserving more than 400 acres of wetlands, prairie, and forest across both cities. The arboretum boasts an extensive trail system that offers an up-close look at the region's native landscapes.

Your excursion begins with a stroll through the forest along Whiskey Creek. You'll emerge from the trees to a view reminiscent of a Monet painting as the creek flows under a wooden bridge and into a quiet pond. Take in the view of wildflowers and lush marsh grasses as you wander over the Monet Bridge and around the wetland terrain to the

pond's far side. After enjoying the view of the bridge, you'll pick up a two-track dirt road for a couple hundred feet before transitioning onto the Big Ben Trail, a grassy path heading into the forest.

As you work your way up a gentle incline, the landscape transitions to jack pine savanna. Here, the jack pines and prairie grasses thrive in the sandy soil, sediment left from an ancient glacial lake. At the top of the hill, you'll reach an overlook with an expansive view of the savanna spread out before you.

Continuing on the trail, you'll dive back into the thick forest on the North Star Trail. This segment of your journey weaves around wetlands and beaver ponds. You'll pass by the first pond about a mile into your journey and then make a loop around the second a half mile later. Look for evidence of beavers along the way, from the stumps of gnawed-down trees to a dammed-up waterway.

From the wetlands, you'll wind downhill on the Little Ben Trail, a smooth, sandy footpath that dips into the jack pine forest bordering the savanna. It's a tranquil journey from here to the dirt roads, where you'll follow your initial route over the Monet Bridge and back to the trailhead.

TURN-BY-TURN DIRECTIONS

1. From the trailhead map and trail marker 1, walk to the opposite end of the parking lot, through the open gate, and onto the gravel road. In 150 feet, bear right onto the single-track trail, leaving the road behind.
2. At 0.1 miles, continue straight across a two-track dirt road. In 160 feet, turn right onto the wooden bridge.
3. At 0.2 miles, bear left at the fork. In 200 feet, turn left onto the dirt road.
4. At 0.3 miles, the road ends at a T-junction with another dirt road. Continue straight across toward the "Trail Crossing" sign and onto a grassy trail. In 50 feet, bear left at the fork onto the signposted Big Ben Trail.
5. At 0.8 miles, at trail marker 16, reach a junction and a trail map. Bear left onto the signposted North Star Trail.
6. At 1.1 miles, at trail marker 17, bear left at the fork to continue on the signposted North Star Trail.
7. At 1.4 miles, at trail marker 18, bear left at the fork to begin a loop on the signposted North Star Trail.
8. At 2.2 miles, at trail marker 19, continue straight to stay on the signposted North Star Trail.
9. At 2.4 miles, reach the fork from Step 7, closing the loop portion of the North Star Trail. Keep left to retrace your path back to trail marker 17 and then trail marker 16 from Step 5.
10. At 2.9 miles, reach the junction from Step 5. Continue straight onto the signposted Little Ben Trail.
11. At 3.3 miles, reach trail marker 13 and turn left.
12. At 3.5 miles, reach the fork from Step 4. Bear right to retrace your steps back to the trailhead.

FIND THE TRAILHEAD

From Baxter at the intersection of MN-210 and Highland Scenic Drive, head east on MN-210 for 2.6 miles. Turn left at Cypress Drive and proceed for 0.1 miles. At the traffic circle, take the first exit onto Excelsior Road. After 0.3 miles, turn left onto Conservation Drive and continue for 0.2 miles. The road ends at the parking lot in front of the Northland Arboretum Visitor Center. The trailhead map is posted at the parking lot entrance.

JACK PINE BREWERY

When Patrick Sundberg sifted through outdoorsy names for his brewery, Jack Pine stood out as a popular native tree. However, he chose it for more than just its local roots. The jack pine is a serotinous tree, meaning one that needs an environmental trigger to reseed. For the jack pine, fire is the trigger, and it's one of the first trees to sprout after a fire. In a similar fashion, Jack Pine Brewery was the first brewery to open in the area after prohibition.

Patrick opened Jack Pine Brewery in 2013 after 14 years of home brewing and earning a hefty collection of awards. Thinking this would only be a side gig, he started with a scaled-up homebrew system in a space that left little room for growth. The community, however, seemed to have other plans as business grew at a steady pace. Patrick upgraded from his humble beginnings to a three-barrel system and then grew again with a new brewery and taproom in 2017.

Jack Pine Brewery's Vengeance! Jalapeño Cream Ale ignites your senses with the aroma of fresh-cut jalapeños. Its jalapeño-popper flavor goes down easy with a creamy mouthfeel and a medium lingering heat.

LAND MANAGER

Paul Bunyan Northland Arboretum
14250 Conservation Drive
Baxter, MN 56425
(218) 829-8770
northlandarb.org
northlandarb.org/recreation

BREWERY/RESTAURANT

Jack Pine Brewery
15593 Edgewood Drive N
Baxter, MN 56425
(218) 270-8072
jackpinebrewery.com

Distance from trailhead: 2.8 miles

DEEP PORTAGE BOG WALK

A FORESTED STROLL TO PEACEFUL POND VIEWS

STARTING POINT	DESTINATION
DEEP PORTAGE LEARNING CENTER	BOG WALK AND BASS POND

BREWERY	HIKE TYPE
RENDEZVOUS BREWING	MODERATE

DOG FRIENDLY	SEASON
YES (LEASH REQUIRED)	MAY–OCTOBER

FEES	DURATION
NONE	1 HOUR 15 MINUTES

MAP REFERENCE	LENGTH
POSTED AT TRAILHEAD	2.4 MILES (LOOP)

HIGHLIGHTS	ELEVATION GAIN
BOG BOARDWALK, LAKE VIEWS	121 FEET

4.9%
ALCOHOL CONTENT

SUNNY DREAM CREAM ALE

LIGHT GOLDEN HONEY

FLORAL,
SWEET

LIGHT CITRUS,
HONEY,
CLEAN

BITTERNESS

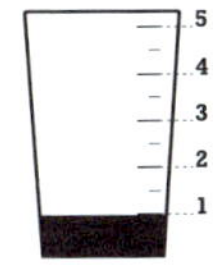

SWEETNESS

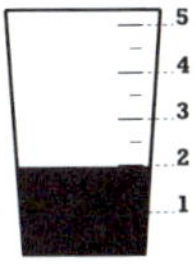

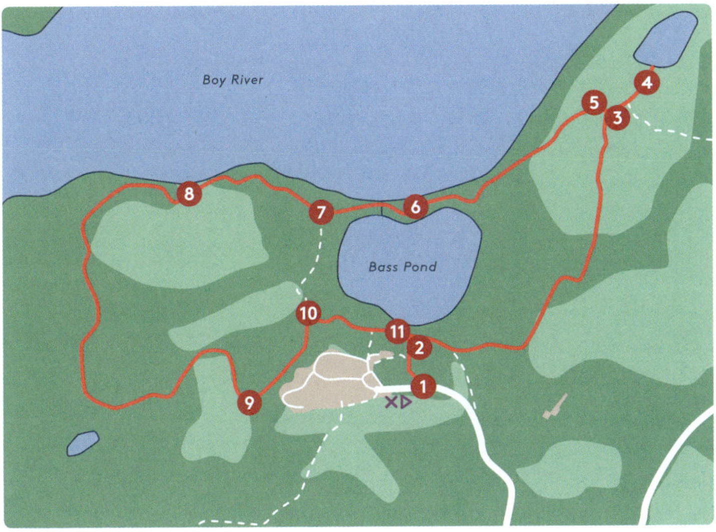

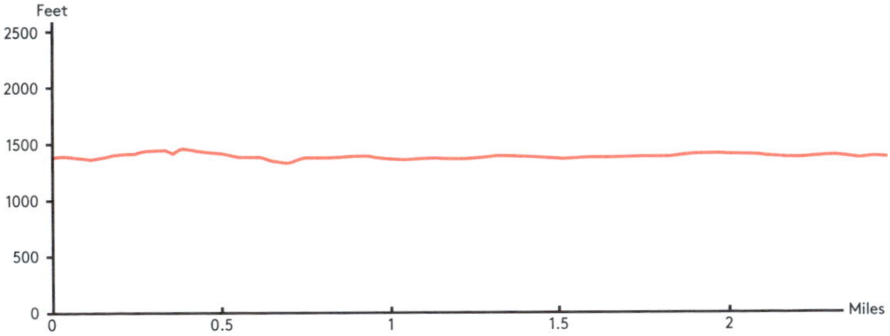

HIKE DESCRIPTION

Seeking serenity? Explore the Deep Portage Conservation Reserve trails, from the bog boardwalk to Bass Pond and beyond. Then head back to Hackensack for a welcoming pint of Rendezvous Brewing's Sunny Dream Cream Ale.

Not far from Hackensack, MN, tucked away down several county roads is a quiet stretch of land dedicated to conservation and education. The 6,307 acres of Deep Portage Conservation Reserve protects bogs, rivers, forests, and a stretch of Big Deep Lake's shoreline. Set in the middle of the reserve's rolling hills is the Deep Portage Learning Center. The learning center provides environmental education programming for school groups, summer camps, and public visitors.

Deep Portage has 11 miles of crisscrossing trails, so you can mix and match trails to suit your level of adventure. In the winter, the trail system transitions from hiking to cross-country skiing and snowshoeing.

You'll start from the trailhead along the main parking area. Right away, you'll see wooden "Bog" signs directing you up the trail. Follow these signs through the wooded hills until you reach the bog boardwalk. Take your time along the boardwalk. Keep an eye out for beavers, ducks, and plants like the carnivorous sundew. Bog water

generally contains few nutrients, so some plants, like the sundew, have adapted to find nutrition elsewhere. Sundews have long hairs with a sticky substance at the end to attract and trap bugs. Once a bug is caught, the hairs curl around it and release enzymes for digestion.

When you're ready to ramble on, you'll retrace your steps back to the previous trail intersection and follow the wooden sign for Bass Pond. From this portion of the trail, you can see Big Deep Lake through the trees to your right. As the trail passes between Big Deep Lake and Bass Pond, follow the trail spur to the left to enjoy a bench with a wonderful view of Bass Pond. Loons, turtles, and beavers are a common sight here. The remainder of your hike takes you deeper into the woods with a few more hills until you circle back to the learning center and the trail you started on.

TURN-BY-TURN DIRECTIONS

1. From the trailhead, take the trail to the right of the map kiosk and follow the wooden signs for "Bog."
2. At 0.1 miles, reach a bench at a viewpoint. Turn right and continue following the bog signs, ignoring trail spurs on both the left and right.
3. At 0.5 miles, at the signposted T-junction, turn right for the bog.
4. At 0.6 miles, reach the bog boardwalk and continue out to the end. Enjoy the bog, then return on the same trail.
5. At 0.7 miles, at the T-junction from Step 3, continue right, following the wooden signs for Bass Pond. Continue straight over the next 0.3 miles, ignoring three trail spurs on the left.
6. At 1.0 miles, turn left onto the 4th trail spur to reach a bench overlooking Bass Pond. Follow the spur until it rejoins the main trail. Continue for 500 feet, going over a small wooden bridge, through a trail intersection, and up a set of steps.
7. At 1.1 miles, turn right onto the paved trail and then left back onto the dirt trail.
8. At 1.3 miles, continue right at the fork, hiking up the hill.
9. At 2.0 miles, turn left at the T-junction.
10. At 2.2 miles, turn right onto the paved trail. Continue for 400 feet, then keep left to transition onto the dirt trail.
11. At 2.3 miles, reach the bench and viewpoint you first encountered in Step 2. Turn right to follow the trail back to the trailhead and parking lot.

FIND THE TRAILHEAD

From Hackensack, drive north on Minnesota Highway 371. After 0.4 miles, turn right onto Woman Lake Road. After 4.7 miles, turn right onto County 46 NW. After 4.6 miles, turn right onto Nature Center Drive NW. Continue for 2.6 miles until you reach the parking lots in front of the Deep Portage Learning Center. The trailhead map kiosk will be on your right as you pull into the dirt parking lot.

RENDEZVOUS BREWING

Sue and Doug Toth started Rendezvous Brewing as a way to create something and give back to the local community. Sue and Doug were ready to move back to Hackensack, but not to retire. They wanted to do something together and chose a brewery because it combined Doug's brewing experience and Sue's financial background. Sue grew up in Hackensack, and the couple had spent a lot of time there as a family enjoying the outdoors, but they'd also seen businesses close around town and wanted to do something to help. Opening Rendezvous Brewing was the first step. Next, Sue and Doug created Rendezvous for a Cause, a series of brewery events designed to highlight local organizations and support their causes. These events range from raising money to update the community tennis courts to raising awareness and funds to support a healthy local lakeshore.

Rendezvous's tap list includes a range of beers, from local favorites to seasonal stars. Their very first brew was Chapter 1 Pale Ale, and it's still on tap today. Another Rendezvous flagship beer is the featured Sunny Dream Cream Ale. This brew uses honey from a local beekeeper. Hackensack happens to be home to the world's largest manufacturer and supplier of beekeeping equipment, Mann Lake Supply. This beer is a sunny, light beer with a deep flavor and a round-mouth feel—a refreshing choice for a post-hike beer.

LAND MANAGER

Deep Portage Learning Center
2197 Nature Center Dr NW
Hackensack, MN 56452
(218) 682-2325
deep-portage.org
deep-portage.org/maps

BREWERY/RESTAURANT

Rendezvous Brewing
112 1st Street South
Hackensack, MN 56452
(218) 675-4200
rendezvousbrewing.com

Distance from trailhead: 12 miles

LAKE BEMIDJI STATE PARK

A PICTURESQUE LOOP TO A LAKE BEMIDJI OVERLOOK

STARTING POINT	DESTINATION
CAMPGROUND PARKING LOT	BOG WALKS
BREWERY	**HIKE TYPE**
BEMIDJI BREWING	MODERATE
DOG FRIENDLY	**SEASON**
YES (LEASH REQUIRED)	MAY–OCTOBER
FEES	**DURATION**
YES	2 HOURS
MAP REFERENCE	**LENGTH**
POSTED AT TRAILHEAD	4.6 MILES (LOOP)
HIGHLIGHTS	**ELEVATION GAIN**
BOG WALKS, LAKE VIEWS	80 FEET

5.0% ALCOHOL CONTENT

GERMAN BLONDE

LIGHT STRAW

CEREAL, MALTY

LIGHT, CRISP

BITTERNESS

SWEETNESS

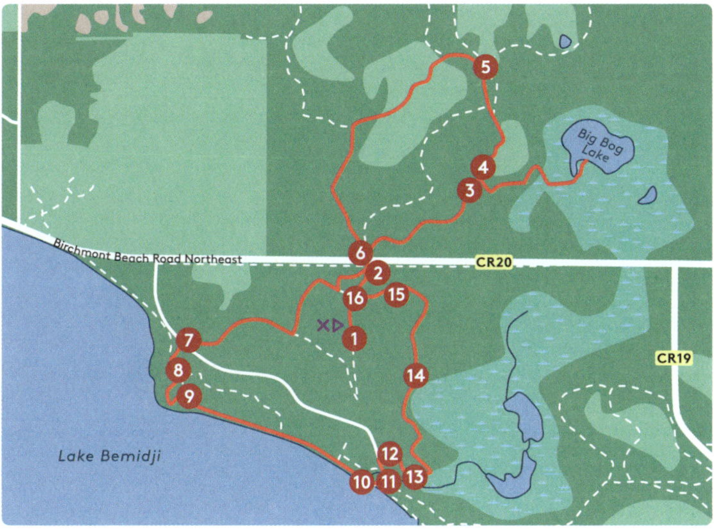

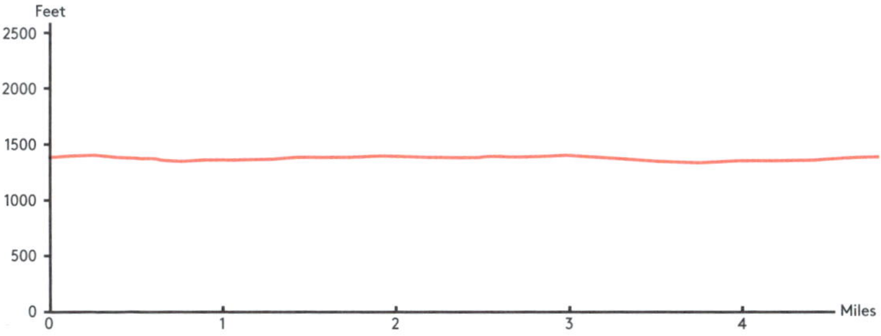

HIKE DESCRIPTION

Catch the view from a high bluff along Lake Bemidji and discover the spacious oak forests, maple groves, and pine bogs that Lake Bemidji State Park has to offer. After, toast your adventure with a crisp pint of German Blonde at Bemidji Brewing.

This excursion through Lake Bemidji State Park takes you across a variety of trail types and landscapes, the combination of which makes this park incredibly interesting. While your hike begins on a dirt road, it transitions to a hiking path and then a wooden boardwalk in less than a mile. The boardwalk leads into the tamarack and black spruce bog surrounding Big Bog Lake. Note the many unique plants and flowers along the walkway, such as lady slippers (Minnesota's state flower) and pitcher plants. At the end of the boardwalk, take in the view of Big Bog Lake. This view gets more colorful in autumn as the tamaracks transition from green to bright yellow. They're one of the only coniferous trees to change color and drop their needles in the fall.

Your next section of the hike takes you on a portion of the Old Logging Trail. You'll notice a significant change as you transition from the smaller, hidden details of the bog to this open and airy section of oaks. This is a wide, mowed-grass path that loops over rolling hills along both old and new logging regions.

As you get close to the lake, the trail narrows and the forest thickens. You'll catch your first view of Lake Bemidji around three miles into the hike from the Rocky Point Trail spur, the highest point around the lake. From here, you'll follow the paved trail down to the shoreline and beach, or in the fall, take the interpretive trail for a colorful walk under the maples. Both trails lead to the beach for more views of the lake. At the far end of the beach, you'll take the bridge over Bass Creek, hike through a small grove of trees, and then cross a second bridge over Bass Creek next to the boat launch. Lake Bemidji is a popular place to fish for walleye, muskellunge, and northern pike.

The final part of your hike winds through another section of bog along the Bass Creek Trail. This two-plank boardwalk weaves through a more deciduous section of trees than the first boardwalk—no two sections of this route are alike! Use caution during wet seasons as portions may be muddy or covered with water. If it's too wet, go straight along the outer edge of the campground.

TURN-BY-TURN DIRECTIONS

1. From the trailhead, head up the road past the cabins on the left. Follow the sign "To Bog and Old Logging Trail" and hike straight through two trail intersections.
2. At 0.2 miles, reach Highway 20. Cross the highway, then continue right on the trail signposted "To Bog Walk Trail."
3. At 0.6 miles, reach a primitive toilet. Turn right onto the signposted Bog Walk Trail. Follow to the end of the boardwalk and return the way you came.
4. At 1.3 miles, reach the toilet again and turn right onto the trail. Continue straight, ignoring a trail spur on the right and then another on the left.
5. At 1.6 miles, reach the signposted Intersection B and turn left. Continue straight until you reach Highway 20, ignoring any trail spurs on the right or left.
6. At 2.4 miles, cross Highway 20. Take the trail on the right and keep right, ignoring two trail spurs on the left.
7. At 3.0 miles, cross State Park Road. Continue on the dirt trail and then turn left onto the paved trail.
8. At 3.1 miles, turn right onto the signposted Rocky Point Outlook spur.
9. At 3.2 miles, turn right onto the paved trail as it follows the shoreline.
10. At 3.7 miles, cross over a wooden bridge and keep to the left.
11. At 3.8 miles, turn left onto the paved trail and cross over another bridge. Continue for 200 feet, then turn right onto the dirt trail at the signposted Intersection R.
12. At 3.9 miles, turn right onto the signposted Bass Creek Trail boardwalk.
13. At 4.0 miles, reach a scenic overlook deck.
14. At 4.3 miles, turn right onto the grassy trail.
15. At 4.4 miles, turn left at signposted Intersection X.
16. At 4.5 miles, turn left at signposted Intersection W. Continue straight back to the trailhead and parking lot.

FIND THE TRAILHEAD

From Bemidji, take MN-17 N/Bemidji Ave N. At the intersection with 23rd St NE, continue north on Bemidji Ave N/US-71. After 3.9 miles, turn right onto Birchmont Beach Road NE. After 1.5 miles, turn right onto State Park Road NE. Follow this road for 0.6 miles to enter Lake Bemidji State Park. Follow the signs for the campground. The dirt parking lot will be on your right at the last loop of campsites. The trailhead is along the road at the front of the parking lot.

BEMIDJI BREWING

Bemidji Brewing opened in 2011 and has since built a core of consistent and available beers. The team aims to brew beers true to style—they like the challenge of brewing to the styles benchmarked by the Brewers Association. While Bemidji Brewing has a wide reach with the distribution of its core beers, the taproom offers a bigger variety. The brewers routinely branch out to try new ingredients and styles to add a twist to the originals, including seasonal beers and taproom exclusives. Bemidji Brewing's German Blonde is one of their flagship beers and has won multiple awards. Its light and bright nature makes it an especially popular choice as visitors stop by after their outdoor adventures.

LAND MANAGER

Lake Bemidji State Park
3401 State Park Road NE
Bemidji, MN 56601
(218) 308-2300
dnr.state.mn.us/state_parks/park.html?id=spk00205#homepage
dnr.state.mn.us/maps/state_parks/spk00205_summer.pdf

BREWERY/RESTAURANT

Bemidji Brewing
211 America Avenue NW
Bemidji, MN 56601
(218) 444-7011
bemidjibeer.com

Distance from trailhead: 7.7 miles

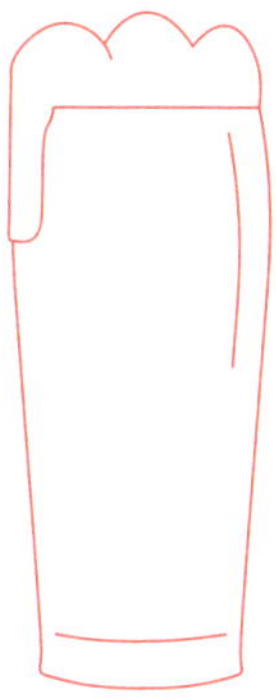

BASS BROOK

CROSS A DAM TO WILDFLOWERS AND RIVER OVERLOOKS

STARTING POINT	DESTINATION
POKEGAMA DAM	RIVER OVERLOOK
BREWERY	**HIKE TYPE**
KLOCKOW BREWING COMPANY	EASY
DOG FRIENDLY	**SEASON**
YES (LEASH REQUIRED)	MAY–OCTOBER
FEES	**DURATION**
NONE	1 HOUR 10 MINUTES
MAP REFERENCE	**LENGTH**
POSTED AT TRAILHEAD	3.0 MILES (LOLLIPOP LOOP)
HIGHLIGHTS	**ELEVATION GAIN**
MISSISSIPPI RIVER, POKEGAMA DAM	62 FEET

5.6% ALCOHOL CONTENT

BHK NUT BROWN ALE

ROASTED BROWN

NUTTY, CHOCOLATE

NUTTY, CRISP

BITTERNESS | SWEETNESS

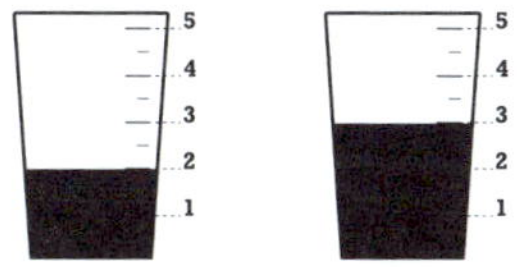

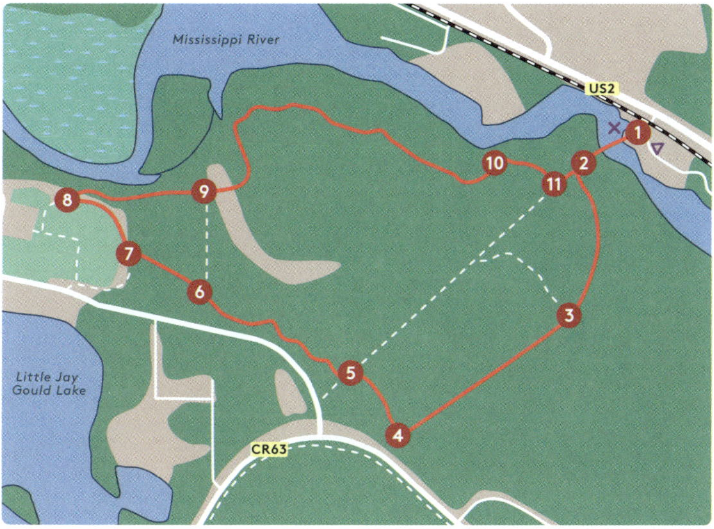

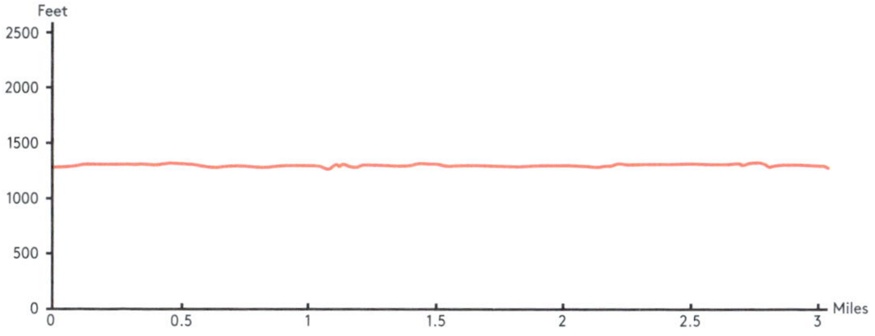

HIKE DESCRIPTION

Get up close and personal with the mighty Mississippi River as you stroll across the Pokegama Dam to roam the quiet trails in the neighboring forest. Then, toast your adventure with a crisp pint of Klockow Brewing Company's BHK Nut Brown Ale.

The Bass Brook Wildlife Management Area (WMA) protects a peaceful patch of forest and wetlands tucked between the Mississippi River and the communities around the Pokegama and Jay Gould Lakes. Across the Mississippi River at the WMA's northeastern side sits the Pokegama Dam Recreation Area. This space offers campsites, picnic areas, fishing access, and a path to the Pokegama Dam, where your adventure begins.

From the Pokegama Dam Recreation Area, you'll set off on a sidewalk leading up to the dam. The current dam is a concrete structure, but it was originally built with wood by the U.S. Army Corps of Engineers in 1885. You'll take a wooden walkway across the dam to the Mississippi River's southern shore. From the walkway, you can look over the edge to the spillway below and the jagged rock outcroppings along the shoreline. Once you've reached land again, you'll step onto a dirt trail leading to the Bass Brook WMA sign and laminated trail map along the forest's edge.

You'll continue into the woods surrounded by a carpet of ferns. In a couple hundred feet, you'll cross a set of railroad tracks and start your clockwise loop around the WMA on a wide, flat path. A few trails cut directly through the property, but you'll keep to the outer trail for your adventure. A mix of wildflowers borders the route—from red columbine to wild roses—with a few thickets of wild blackberries sprinkled in. Hike in the spring to catch the blackberries' delicate white blooms; visit late in summer to treat yourself to the berries. At the far side of your loop, you'll briefly connect with the paved path circling Portage Park. About a quarter of the way around the park, you'll turn back into the forest on a grassy path.

As you traverse the northern portion of the WMA, you'll meander past views both big and small—gaps in the tree line frame river vistas, and a small wetland offers up-close glimpses of wild irises. Heading into the last half mile of your trip, you'll reach a sign with a no-camping icon posted on a tree. Just beyond the sign is a rock outcropping overlooking the river. You can step up to the rocky ledge to survey the view or take a seat on the bench cut into a large log to soak up nature's serenity. When you're ready, you'll continue down the path to a carved wooden trail map and then close the loop back at the railroad tracks. You'll hop over the tracks and then wind back through the ferns and across the dam for one final look at the river to seal your adventure.

TURN-BY-TURN DIRECTIONS

1. From the parking lot, follow the sidewalk up to the Pokegama Dam. Cross the dam and then continue straight on the dirt trail into the signposted Bass Brook State Wildlife Management Area.
2. At 0.1 miles, cross the railroad tracks. In 50 feet, bear right at the fork.
3. At 0.5 miles, continue straight, ignoring the unmarked trail spur on the right.
4. At 0.8 miles, bear right at the fork.
5. At 1.0 miles, turn left at the T-junction. In 100 feet, bear right at the fork.
6. At 1.3 miles, continue straight, ignoring an unmarked trail spur on the left and then another on the right.
7. At 1.5 miles, turn right onto the paved path.
8. At 1.6 miles, turn right onto the grassy path leading into the woods.
9. At 1.9 miles, continue straight at the "Foot Travel Welcome" sign, ignoring an unmarked trail spur on the right.
10. At 2.6 miles, at the no-camping sign, bear left to reach a river overlook and log bench. Enjoy the view, then continue on the main trail.
11. At 2.8 miles, at the T-junction and wooden trail map, turn left. In 200 feet, reach the fork from Step 2. Bear left to retrace your steps over the railroad tracks, back to the dam, and to the parking lot.

FIND THE TRAILHEAD

From the intersection of Highway 2 and Pokegama Avenue in Grand Rapids, head west on Highway 2 for 3.1 miles. After passing the Pokegama Dam Recreation Site sign, turn left into the driveway. In 100 feet, cross over the railroad tracks and then turn right into the parking lot along the Mississippi River. The trail begins at the sidewalk leading to the Pokegama Dam.

KLOCKOW BREWING COMPANY

When Tasha and Andy Klockow set out to open their own brewery, making their own beer was just one of several goals. They also wanted to raise their child in the same type of environment where they had both grown up—somewhere in the Northwoods with a small-town atmosphere and easy access to nature at any time and any season. With that in mind, they looked at Grand Rapids, Minnesota, where Tasha had grown up. Each time they returned to visit, they noticed how the city lacked a brewery of its own, and as brewers, they wanted to change that. For the Klockows, reestablishing their roots here fit everything they wanted and more.

Tasha and Andy opened Klockow Brewing Company in 2017. They keep a wide range of brews on tap but especially like including traditional European-style beers to pair with festivals, like the classic Oktoberfest and Erste Mai, a spring music festival. They enjoy offering events for the whole community—such as Storyteller Sundays, live music, blood drives, brewery yoga, and more—to craft a space where people can connect while also enjoying delicious beer.

Klockow Brewing Company's BHK Nut Brown Ale, named after Andy's dad (his initials), is a medium light-bodied brown ale with a nutty and chocolate aroma. It has just enough hops to balance the sweet-to-bitter ratio and finishes clean and crisp.

LAND MANAGER

Minnesota Department of Natural Resources
1201 East Hwy 2
Grand Rapids, MN 55744
(218) 328-8982
dnr.state.mn.us
cohasset-mn.com/vertical/sites/%7B4DED3294-59E1-4C4A-B675-C7E-6970BA170%7D/uploads/PORTAGE__-_WILD_LIFE_MGMT._-_DNR_-_TRAIL_MAPS.pdf

BREWERY/RESTAURANT

Klockow Brewing Company
36 SE 10th Street
Grand Rapids, MN 55744
(218) 999-7229
klockowbrewing.com

Distance from trailhead: 4.2 miles

REDHEAD RIM LOOP

TREK AROUND A LAKE IN AN ABANDONED MINE

STARTING POINT	**DESTINATION**
REDHEAD MOUNTAIN BIKE PARK	LEONARD-BURT MINE PIT
BREWERY	**HIKE TYPE**
BOOMTOWN BREWERY AND WOODFIRE GRILL	STRENUOUS
DOG FRIENDLY	**SEASON**
YES (LEASH REQUIRED)	MAY–OCTOBER
FEES	**DURATION**
NONE	4 HOURS
MAP REFERENCE	**LENGTH**
POSTED AT TRAILHEAD	8.7 MILES (LOOP)
HIGHLIGHTS	**ELEVATION GAIN**
OPEN-PIT MINE, LAKE OVERLOOKS	397 FEET

6.1%
ALCOHOL CONTENT

HAT TRICK HONEY AMBER

AMBER

TOASTED MALT

MALTY, HERBAL

BITTERNESS

SWEETNESS

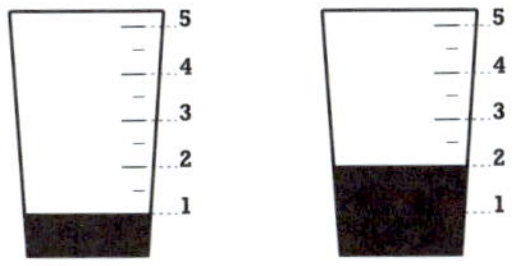

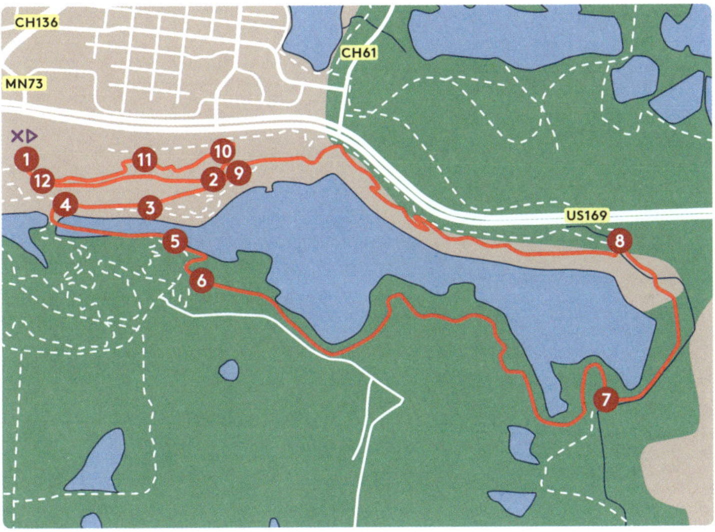

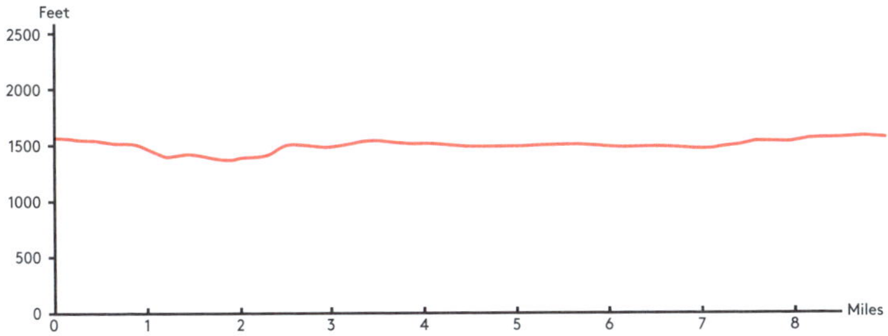

HIKE DESCRIPTION

Hike into an abandoned open-pit mine, then climb up to the rim for picturesque views of this expansive space. Posthike, stop at Boomtown Brewery in Hibbing for a refreshing cold pint of beer.

Minnesota's Mesabi Range, a region rich in iron ore, stretches more than 100 miles from Babbitt down to Chisholm, Hibbing, and Grand Rapids. It's one of the largest iron-ore mining regions in the United States. While you might think of mines as underground tunnels—and that was the case for some iron mining early on—current iron mines operate as massive open pits. One of Minnesota's biggest open-pit iron mines (Hull-Rust, which you can see from a roadside overlook on the way from the hike to the brewery) is over three miles long and nearly two miles wide. Once mining companies abandon a site, nature begins to reclaim the space. Rainwater and snowmelt fill the pits, creating unique lakes, while plants sprout on the piles of red, iron-tinged rocks—remnants of the layers removed during mining. Local cities and community groups also work to improve some of these sites, from building new housing opportunities to creating state parks and recreation spaces.

Redhead Mountain Bike Park at the Minnesota Discovery Center in Chisholm is a perfect example of this. The trails here wind around an abandoned mine pit, zigzagging from the rim down to the accumulated water. Redhead welcomes both mountain bikers and hikers, but keep in mind that bikers have the right of way here and not all trails allow hikers. The trail system is well-marked with names, directional signposts, and numbered intersections.

Your adventure through Redhead begins on the North Star Loop. The trail descends amidst a thick covering of poplar trees, a common choice for mining reclamation efforts due to their fast growth rate and ability to prosper in poor soils. After a mile and a half through a few switchbacks, you'll connect with the Red Hop Trail. This brings you down to the shoreline along the lake where the blue water contrasts beautifully with the red rock of the pit. Take a moment to appreciate the view before you begin the climb back up to the rim. At almost two and a half miles in and halfway to the top of the pit, you'll turn onto the Rim Trail, which circles around the eastern side of the mine pit and provides expansive views of the lake below. You'll briefly connect with a paved path, the Mesabi Trail, which stretches more than 150 miles from the Mississippi River in La Prairie up to the Boundary Waters near Ely. Keep an eye out for the Rim Trail markers to keep you on track until you transition to the High Road Trail for the last mile of your hike. Don't forget to routinely look toward the pit—you can catch views of the lake throughout much of your adventure!

TURN-BY-TURN DIRECTIONS

1. From the trailhead map, follow the gravel path through the gate and immediately turn left onto the signposted North Star Loop Trail. In 100 feet, ignore a spur on the right. In another 200 feet, keep right at the fork to stay on the North Star Loop.
2. At 0.8 miles, reach Intersection 4 and keep right at the fork. In 230 feet, cross the dirt road and immediately turn right onto the signposted Crossfire Trail.
3. At 1.2 miles, at a junction, turn right onto the signposted North Star Loop and continue across the dirt road.
4. At 1.5 miles, at Intersection 8, turn left onto the signposted Red Hop Trail and continue across the dirt road.
5. At 2.1 miles, keep left at the fork.
6. At 2.4 miles, at Intersection 41, turn left onto the signposted Rim Trail.
7. At 4.9 miles, turn left onto the paved path, following the Rim Trail signposts.
8. At 5.7 miles, reach a T-junction and turn left. In 100 feet, turn left onto the signposted Rim Trail.
9. At 7.6 miles, at Intersection 46, turn right to cross the dirt road from Step 2 and then bear right onto the signposted High Road Trail.
10. At 7.7 miles, keep left at the fork to stay on the High Road Trail. In 100 feet, cross a wide dirt road and continue straight.
11. At 8.2 miles, at a dirt road intersection, bear left toward the buildings and the large Exit sign. In 350 feet, turn left onto the signposted High Road Trail.
12. At 8.7 miles, reach the fork from Step 1 and keep right to return to the trailhead.

FIND THE TRAILHEAD

From Hibbing at 6th Street and Howard Street, head east on Howard Street. After 0.6 miles, turn left onto US-169 N and proceed for 5.2 miles. Turn right onto Iron World Road. After 230 feet, continue straight onto Discovery Drive. After 0.1 miles, at the Redhead Mountain Bike Park sign, turn left into parking lot.

BOOMTOWN BREWERY AND WOODFIRE GRILL

Jessica and Erik Leitz opened the Boomtown Woodfire Bar and Grill in Eveleth in 2015. A few years later, they received a purchase invitation for the old, iconic Zimmy's, a tribute restaurant for Bob Dylan, who had grown up in Hibbing (known then as Bob Zimmerman). As soon as they walked in the doors, the overall vibe gave them the sense that the space was meant to be a brewery. Jessica and Erik loved beer, but they weren't brewers, so they put out an ad, and Dennis Holland answered.

With several decades of brewing experience around the country from Ohio to Washington, Dennis brought the knowledge they needed to build a top-notch brewing system and a well-rounded tap list. A few of Boomtown's flagship brews include their Peanut Butter Porter, OREhouse IPA, Tangled up in Blueberry, and Hat Trick Honey Amber. Hat Trick is a balanced amber with a hint of toasted malt and sweetness.

LAND MANAGER

City of Chisholm
316 West Lake Street
Chisholm, MN 55719
(218) 254-7909
ci.chisholm.mn.us
redheadmtbpark.com/trails

BREWERY/RESTAURANT

Boomtown Brewery and Woodfire Grill
531 E Howard Street
Hibbing, MN 55746
(218) 440-1710
boomtownwoodfire.com

Distance from trailhead: 5.9 miles

TILSON BAY

BEDROCK, BAY VIEWS, AND A BOG BOARDWALK

STARTING POINT

TILSON BAY WAYSIDE PARK

DESTINATION

TILSON CREEK BOGWALK

BREWERY

LOONY'S BREW

HIKE TYPE

MODERATE

DOG FRIENDLY

YES (LEASH REQUIRED)

SEASON

MAY–OCTOBER

FEES

NONE

DURATION

1 HOUR 30 MINUTES

MAP REFERENCE

POSTED AT TRAILHEAD

LENGTH

3.0 MILES (ROUND TRIP)

HIGHLIGHTS

FOREST OVERLOOKS, BOG

ELEVATION GAIN

124 FEET

9%
ALCOHOL CONTENT

DRUNKEN LOON DARK BELGIAN

RICH AMBER

BLACK LICORICE, STAR ANISE

BLACK LICORICE, SMOOTH

BITTERNESS

SWEETNESS

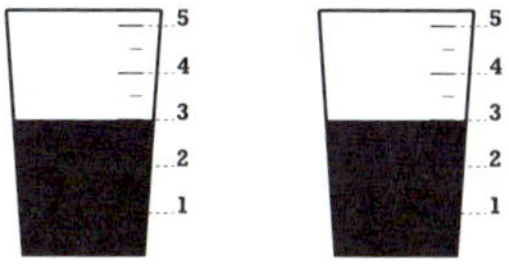

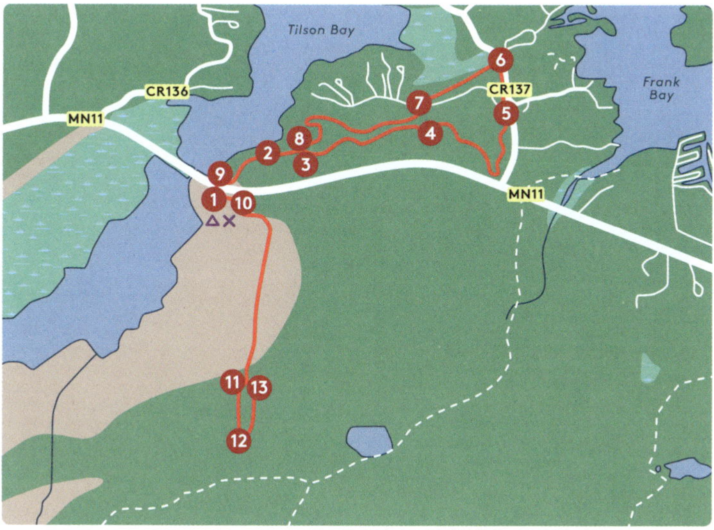

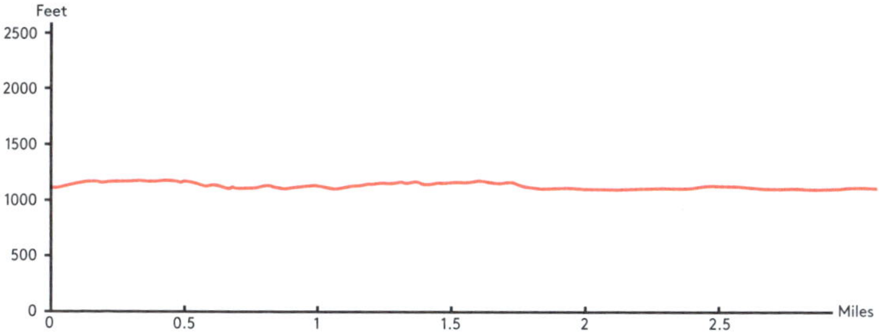

HIKE DESCRIPTION

Dive into Minnesota's northern landscapes on a rocky path winding through the forest along Tilson Bay and explore the neighboring bog via a floating boardwalk. Then kick back and relax at Loony's Brew with a mug of their Drunken Loon Dark Belgian.

Rainy Lake, part of the Minnesota-Canada border, stretches over 60 miles and contains 200 islands. This Northwoods region, which includes the neighboring Voyageurs National Park, is known for water-based adventures like fishing, boating, and canoeing. However, there's still plenty to explore on foot. This route, for example, gets you up close with the forests and wetlands along Tilson Bay on Rainy Lake's southern shoreline.

Your quest kicks off from Tilson Bay Wayside Park and boat ramp, where you'll set out on a lollipop loop through the woods. The path ranges from rocky dirt and exposed bedrock to boardwalks and grassy lanes. Within the first third of a mile, you'll encounter three forks in the trail: The first two are short splits that reconnect, and the third is the start of your loop. Just after the third fork, you'll reach a break in the trees and an overlook with expansive views of the forest below. You can pause at the bench here to soak up the view, then continue back into the forest.

After crossing several sections of exposed bedrock and navigating damp areas via boardwalks, you'll emerge from the trees to cross a gravel road. You'll hike alongside a paved road until you reach a trail map at the one-mile mark and then veer back into the woods. As you skirt through the trees on the edge of the forest, you'll trek up a short but steep and rocky incline. From this elevated position, you'll gain an expansive view of the marsh that spreads out to your right and the lake sparkling in the distance.

You'll cross the gravel road a second time, then the last portion of your loop cruises over a few more mounds of bedrock and past a mossy rock wall. You'll return to the boat ramp—a perfect spot to let any canine hiking partners dip their paws in the bay.

You'll cross the road and pick up the Tilson Creek Bogwalk at the far end of the parking lot. The wooden boardwalk stretches a half mile through the woods and into the bog. Slow your pace to look for small carnivorous plants catching insects with their sticky traps. Pause at the bench halfway to take in the vastness of the bog. If the ground is dry enough at the far end of the boardwalk, you can step off the walkway for a small loop through the forest on the ski trails. Then, back on the wooden platform, you'll make your return trip across the bog to finish your voyage.

TURN-BY-TURN DIRECTIONS

1. From the parking lot, cross the road to the boat ramp and then bear right toward the trail map. Head up the stairs to begin the hike.
2. At 0.1 miles, keep right as the trail forks and then reconnects in 100 feet. In 80 feet, keep right as the trail forks again and then reconnects in another 100 feet.
3. At 0.2 miles, keep right at the fork and trail map to begin a loop.
4. At 0.5 miles, at the trail map, continue straight, ignoring the unsigned spur trail on the left.
5. At 0.9 miles, continue straight across the gravel road and continue to the left of the paved road.
6. At 1.0 miles, at the trail map, veer slightly left to reenter the forest.
7. At 1.2 miles, cross the gravel road, bearing slightly left to pick up the trail at the orange diamond trail marker. In 175 feet, continue straight, ignoring the unsigned spur trail on the left.
8. At 1.5 miles, bear right at the fork to close the loop and return to the boat ramp.
9. At 1.7 miles, reach the boat ramp. Cross the road to the parking lot and continue to the far end of the lot.
10. At 1.8 miles, at the Tilson Creek Bogwalk sign, turn right onto the boardwalk.
11. At 2.3 miles, bear right at the fork and then step off the boardwalk to begin a short loop on the grassy trail.
12. At 2.4 miles, bear left at the fork. In 300 feet, bear left again at the fork.
13. At 2.5 miles, reach the boardwalk again, closing the loop. Keep right at the fork to return to the parking lot.

FIND THE TRAILHEAD

From International Falls at MN-11/Waters of the Dancing Sky Scenic Byway and US Highway 53, head east on MN-11/Waters of the Dancing Sky Scenic Byway and proceed for 8.0 miles. After crossing over Tilson Creek, turn right into the parking lot at the sign for Tilson Bay–Rainy Lake Public Water Access. After parking, cross the road to reach the boat ramp access lot. The trail begins at the trail map on the far end of the lot.

LOONY'S BREW

Owner Matt Kavan was living in Northern California when he decided he was ready for something different. Having grown up in Minnesota and spent time up north where his parents retired, the Northwoods called to him. It's the type of place where people go for vacation, but he wanted to live there full-time. So, when a former fishing resort went up for sale on the shoreline of Rainy Lake, Matt scooped it up. He was ready to expand on his homebrewing skills, and after a year and a half of renovations, he opened Loony's Brew in 2018.

Matt crafted Drunken Loon Dark Belgian as a nod to Belgian Trappist beer, which is brewed by Trappist monks who have been making beer from the same yeast for hundreds of years. The beer also honors the four years he spent living in Belgium. Drunken Loon is a mix of dark malts, coriander, cardamom, grains of paradise, star anise, and rose hips. It's a smooth beer with a bit of a kick.

LAND MANAGER

Minnesota Department of Natural Resources
500 Lafayette Road
St. Paul, MN 55155-4040
(888) 646-6367
dnr.state.mn.us/state_forests/forest.html?id=sft00028#homepage

BREWERY/RESTAURANT

Loony's Brew
3481 Main Street
Ranier, MN 56668
(218) 540-1001

Distance from trailhead: 6.0 miles

SPLIT ROCK RIVER TRAIL

ASCEND A RUGGED AND SCENIC RIVER TRAIL

STARTING POINT	DESTINATION
SPLIT ROCK TRAILHEAD	SPLIT ROCK COLUMN
BREWERY	**HIKE TYPE**
CASTLE DANGER BREWERY	MODERATE
DOG FRIENDLY	**SEASON**
YES (LEASH REQUIRED)	MAY-OCTOBER
FEES	**DURATION**
NONE	2 HOURS 30 MINUTES
MAP REFERENCE	**LENGTH**
POSTED AT TRAILHEAD	4.8 MILES (ROUND TRIP)
HIGHLIGHTS	**ELEVATION GAIN**
WATERFALLS, ROCK TOWERS, RIVER VIEWS	390 FEET

5.7%
ALCOHOL CONTENT

MAPLE MÄRZEN

AMBERY BROWN

TOASTED MALT

MALTY,
MAPLE SYRUP,
CARAMEL

BITTERNESS

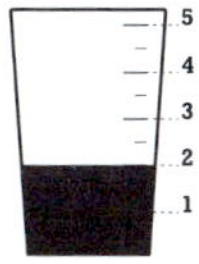

SWEETNESS

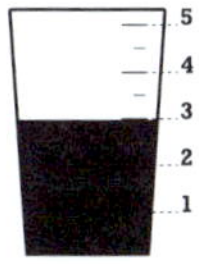

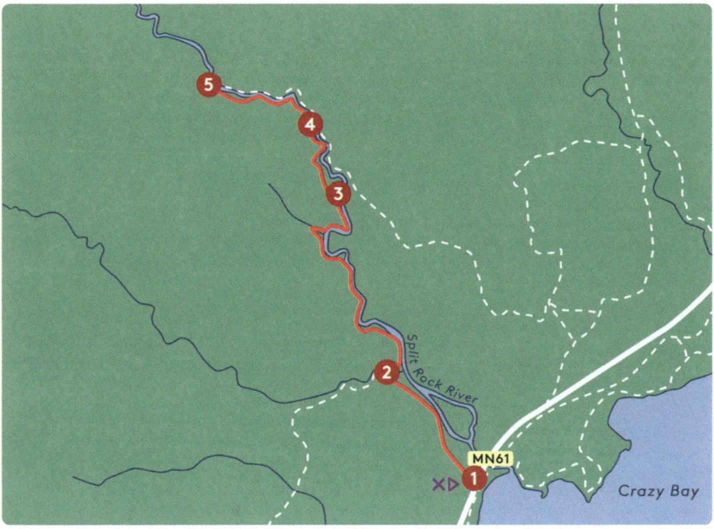

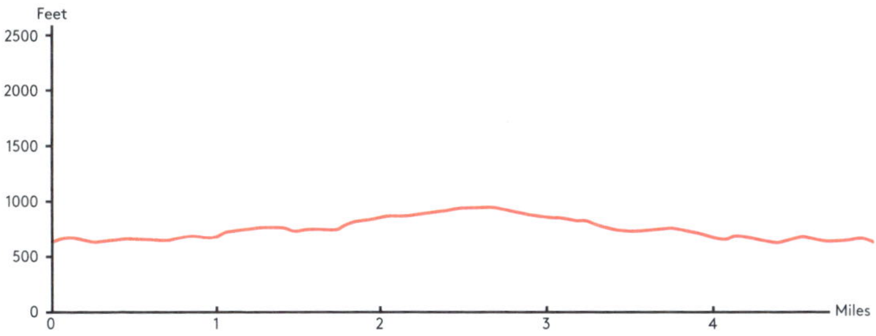

HIKE DESCRIPTION

Let the invigorating sound of rushing water accompany you on your trek to stunning riverside cliffs and the split rock column. Cool down afterward with a pint of Maple Märzen on the patio at Castle Danger Brewery.

Split Rock State Park, situated along the North Shore of Lake Superior, often ranks as one of Minnesota's top state parks, and as soon as you start exploring, it's easy to see why. The park features an iconic lighthouse (one of the most photographed places in the state), jagged cliffs, lush forests, and a picturesque shoreline. At the southern end, the Split Rock River carves a wide, rough path down to Lake Superior. The Superior Hiking Trail (SHT) winds through the park, showcasing river gorge vistas, rocky ridges, and numerous waterfalls.

This route takes you along a captivating stretch of the SHT next to the Split Rock River. Starting from the trailhead, you'll embark on the path marked by the distinctive white SHT spur marker. After a gentle half mile through the birch, fir, and spruce forest, you'll connect with the main SHT trail, identifiable by its blue blaze.

From here, the trail brings you alongside the river and ascends at a steady but moderate rate, climbing about 300 feet over the next two miles. The river and the sound of rushing water accompany you most of the way up to your turnaround point. Keep your eyes peeled for glimpses of rapids, cascades, and waterfalls peeking through the trees between you and the river.

After about a mile and a half, a short spur trail leads to a breathtaking view of the water tumbling south between the striking red cliffs of the gorge. This red rock, or red rhyolite, resulted from an ancient volcanic eruption and was later carved out by a series of glaciers moving across the land. Take a moment to immerse yourself in the beauty of the scene before retracing your steps back to the main trail.

As you reach the two-mile mark, two striking rock towers rise dramatically just off the trail along the clifftop. This formation of a seemingly split column of rock is one of the common explanations behind the naming of the Split Rock area. An alternate idea mentions fishermen who thought two high cliffs east of the river mouth seemed to split as their boats got closer to shore. Behind these rock towers, you'll enjoy a grand view of the gorge cliffs topped with majestic pines along the opposite bank. You'll know you're nearing the end of your uphill climb when you reach the N.W. Split Rock River backcountry campsite on your left. You'll veer right to head toward the river, where a fabulous river panorama awaits. This hike used to be a popular loop trail until spring floods washed away a bridge spanning the river in this location. Now, it transforms into a loop only when the water is low enough to hop across the rocks in the riverbed, typically in the summer and fall months. After appreciating the rugged landscape, make your way back to the trailhead.

TURN-BY-TURN DIRECTIONS

1. From the trailhead map, follow the gravel path marked with a SHT white blaze.
2. At 0.5 miles, reach a junction with a trail map. Turn right onto the trail marked with a SHT blue blaze and signposted as the Split Rock Loop.
3. At 1.6 miles, turn right onto the trail spur marked with a SHT white blaze. In 200 feet, reach an overlook; once you've enjoyed the view, return to the main trail to continue.
4. At 2.0 miles, reach the split rock column on the right.
5. At 2.4 miles, reach the N.W. Split Rock River campsite on the left. Bear right to continue to the river. After admiring the view, return to the trailhead the way you came.

FIND THE TRAILHEAD

From Two Harbors at Highway 61 and 6th Street, head northeast on Highway 61. After 17.2 miles, at the Wayside Rest/Split Rock Trailhead sign, turn left into the parking lot. The trail begins near the stacked rock formation and the trail map.

CASTLE DANGER BREWERY

Castle Danger Brewery, established in 2011, started as a three-barrel brewery in Castle Danger township on Minnesota's North Shore. As the demand for their beer grew, so did the business. In 2014 co-owners Lon and Mandy Larson joined forces with the founders in opening a new taproom and production facility in Two Harbors overlooking beautiful Lake Superior. The Larsons took over full ownership in 2024 to continue the mission of "Crafting a North Shore Experience" for all who enjoy their beer in the taproom and those who carry it with them on adventures throughout the state.

In keeping with their love for the North Shore, Castle Danger Brewery donates a portion of Maple Märzen sales to the Superior Hiking Trail Association, the nonprofit managing the SHT. Maple Märzen is an interesting twist on the traditional Märzen style, incorporating the rich flavors of a locally sourced maple syrup. The resulting brew delivers notes of toasted malt, maple, caramel, and graham cracker.

LAND MANAGER

Split Rock Lighthouse State Park
3755 Split Rock Lighthouse Road
Two Harbors, MN 55616
(218) 595-7625
dnr.state.mn.us/state_parks/park.html?id=spk00266#homepage
files.dnr.state.mn.us/maps/state_parks/spk00266_summer.pdf

BREWERY/RESTAURANT

Castle Danger Brewery
17 7th Street
Two Harbors, MN 55616
(218) 834-5800
castledangerbrewery.com

Distance from trailhead: 17.7 miles

BREWER PARK

A FOREST LOOP WITH DULUTH AND LAKE SUPERIOR VIEWS

STARTING POINT	DESTINATION
HAINES SHT TRAILHEAD	DULUTH HARBOR OVERLOOKS
BREWERY	**HIKE TYPE**
URSA MINOR BREWING	MODERATE
DOG FRIENDLY	**SEASON**
YES (LEASH REQUIRED)	MAY–OCTOBER
FEES	**DURATION**
NONE	1 HOUR 30 MINUTES
MAP REFERENCE	**LENGTH**
DULUTH PARKS & RECREATION	3.1 MILES (LOOP)
HIGHLIGHTS	**ELEVATION GAIN**
DULUTH VIEWS, LAKE VIEWS	242 FEET

6.8% ALCOHOL CONTENT

GALACTIC FACE SLAP IPA

HAZY, STRAW

TROPICAL, FRUITY

CITRUS, TANGERINE, PEACH

BITTERNESS

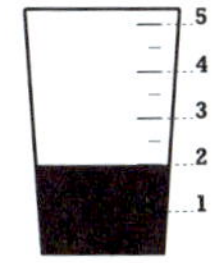

SWEETNESS

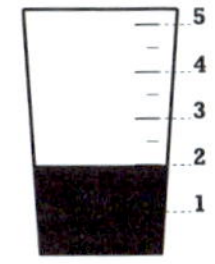

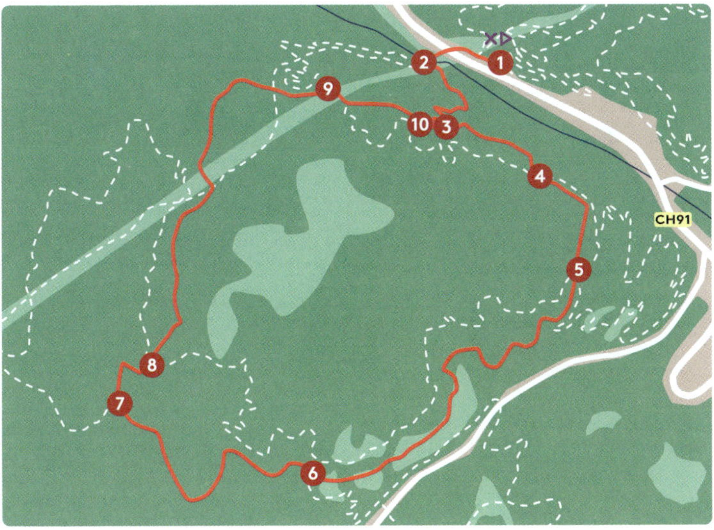

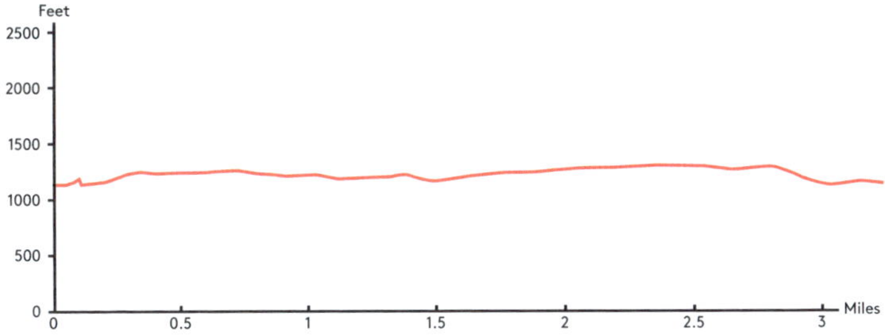

HIKE DESCRIPTION

Loop through Brewer Park for fantastic views of Duluth, Lake Superior, and Saint Louis Bay. Then, head down the hill to Ursa Minor Brewing for a hazy IPA and freshly made pizza.

While Brewer Park sounds like it might be an ode to a beer brewer, the name comes from the person, Frank Brewer, who donated the land to the city of Duluth. Frank was a local businessperson who transferred the property to Duluth in 1962. Brewer Park and its next-door neighbor, Bellevue Park, provide 168 acres of space for outdoor pursuits, including rock climbing, bouldering, and several trail systems. The Superior Hiking Trail (SHT) runs through the parks, as does an extensive mix of mountain bike trails.

Our route runs clockwise through Brewer Park to catch the Duluth and Lake Superior views early in the hike and then dip into the shaded forest for the remainder of the loop. Reverse the route if you'd rather save the overlooks for the latter half of your adventure.

Your hike begins near the Superior Hiking Trail sign on the west side of the trailhead parking lot. On a narrow dirt path, you'll head down the hill parallel to the roadway. As you near the bottom of the hill, you'll catch sight of the SHT tunnel that'll transport you under the roadway to Brewer Park. Once you've gone through the tunnel and over a short wooden bridge, you'll head into the forest and up a short series of switchbacks. From here, you'll turn onto the SHT Loop Trail (white trail markers), which circles through Brewer Park. The trail is rocky and rooted, with a few wooden boardwalks and stone steps. A mountain bike trail weaves its way through the park as well, so be mindful of bikers. The trails cross paths several times, but you'll always continue straight, following the markers for the SHT Loop Trail.

About a half mile in, you'll catch your first view of the Duluth harbor and the John A. Blatnik Bridge. This distinctive through arch bridge links Duluth to Superior, WI, via Interstate 535. Over the next three-quarters of a mile, the trail dips in and out of the forest, offering alternate viewpoints of the harbor and Saint Louis Bay. As the bay comes into view, you'll see the winding curves of the 11,800-foot Richard I. Bong Memorial Bridge (Bong Bridge), which connects Duluth and Superior via US Highway 2.

As you reach the end of the open views, the trail sweeps back into the forest and casually works its way uphill. Just shy of two miles into your stroll, the main SHT breaks off to the left to continue beyond Brewer Park; you'll keep to the right to finish your loop around the park. Enjoy the peaceful forest for the remainder of your journey until you reach the initial stem of the SHT that brings you back down to the tunnel and trailhead.

TURN-BY-TURN DIRECTIONS

1. From the trailhead, follow the signposted SHT down the hill and through the Superior Hiking Trail tunnel.
2. At 0.1 miles, cross the wooden bridge and then turn left to continue on the SHT.
3. At 0.3 miles, at a T-junction, turn left.
4. At 0.5 miles, continue straight through an intersection with the bike trail.
5. At 0.7 miles, continue straight through an intersection with the bike trail.
6. At 1.4 miles, continue straight through an intersection with the bike trail.
7. At 1.8 miles, bear right at the fork to remain on the SHT Loop Trail.
8. At 1.9 miles, continue straight through an intersection with the bike trail.
9. At 2.6 miles, continue straight through an intersection with the bike trail.
10. At 2.7 miles, reach the junction from Step 3 and turn left, closing the loop. From here, retrace your steps back to the trailhead.

FIND THE TRAILHEAD

From downtown Duluth at N 1st Street, head southeast on N Lake Avenue. After 0.1 miles, turn right onto the ramp for I-35 S. Continue on I-35 S for 3 miles, then take Exit 353B for 40th Ave W. After 0.2 miles, merge onto W Michigan Street. After 350 feet, turn right onto 40th Avenue W. After 0.7 miles, continue straight on C.S.A.H. 91/ Haines Road. After 1 mile, turn right into the signed Superior Hiking Trail Parking Lot. The trail begins on the west side of the parking lot.

URSA MINOR BREWING

Ben Hugus, Ursa Minor's co-founder, loves to see hikers stop by the taproom. They'll prop up their backpacks, order a pint of beer, and enjoy an entire pizza. Some of what hikers seek on the trail isn't that different from what Ben aims to provide at Ursa Minor: a welcoming space and a sense of connection. The Ursa Minor tools? Craft beer and woodfired pizza—classic, well-loved items to bring people together and promote conversation and connection.

Ursa Minor Brewing opened in 2018 and now brews more than 100 unique beers a year. However, they don't brew a new beer just to create something new—they brew to continue learning. The taproom houses a pilot brewhouse for experimental brews (the production brewery is in another building). Ursa Minor delivers a high-quality, ever-rotating beer selection along with several flagship brews. Galactic Face Slap, an award-winning hazy IPA, uses the highly sought-after Galaxy hops to deliver a flavorful brew jammed with citrus and tropical fruit. It's juicy, full-bodied, and an easy drinker.

LAND MANAGER

Duluth Parks & Recreation
411 W 1st Street
Duluth, MN 55802
(218) 730-4300
duluthmn.gov/parks/parks-listing/brewer-parkbellevue-park
duluthmn.maps.arcgis.com/apps/View/index.html?appid=858a94c6007f-4bafbe45afa08e47e054

BREWERY/RESTAURANT

Ursa Minor Brewing
2415 W Superior Street, Suite B
Duluth, MN 55806
(218) 481-7886
ursaminorbrewing.com

Distance from trailhead: 2.8 miles

ELY'S PEAK

SUMMIT ELY'S PEAK FOR A PANORAMIC VIEW

STARTING POINT	DESTINATION
MAGNEY-SNIVELY TRAILHEAD	ELY'S PEAK

BREWERY	HIKE TYPE
BENT PADDLE BREWING COMPANY	STRENUOUS

DOG FRIENDLY	SEASON
YES (LEASH REQUIRED)	MAY–OCTOBER

FEES	DURATION
NONE	3 HOURS 30 MINUTES

MAP REFERENCE	LENGTH
POSTED AT TRAILHEAD	6.8 MILES (ROUND TRIP)

HIGHLIGHTS	ELEVATION GAIN
MAPLE FOREST, SUMMIT VIEWS	629 FEET

6.2%
ALCOHOL CONTENT

BENT HOP GOLDEN IPA

DEEP GOLD

HOPPY,
BISCUIT

HOPPY,
CITRUS,
PINE

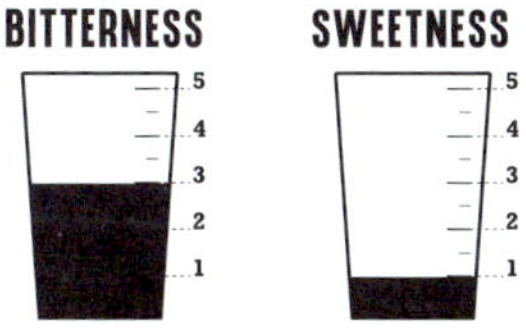

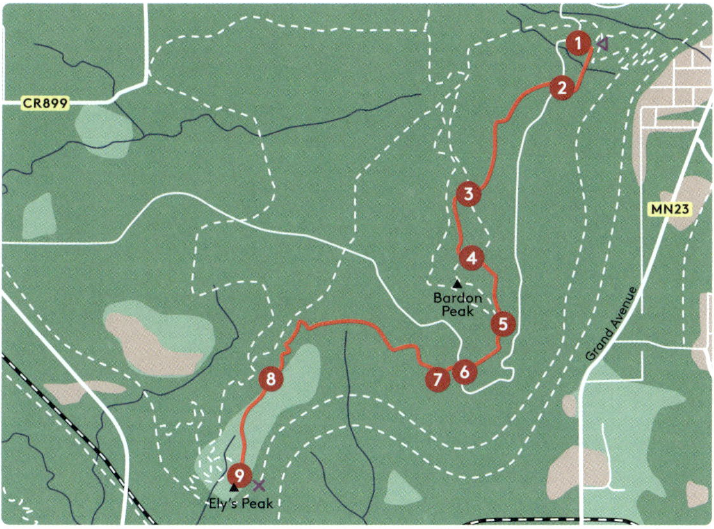

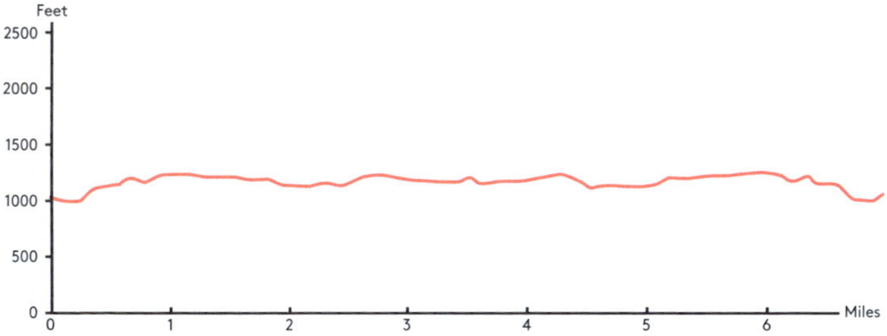

HIKE DESCRIPTION

Explore a section of the Superior Hiking Trail as it winds through a maple forest up to Ely's Peak for expansive views of the St. Louis River and surrounding forests. Round out your adventure with a fresh pint of Bent Hop IPA on Bent Paddle's spacious taproom patio.

The Superior Hiking Trail (SHT) spans more than 300 miles from the Canada-U.S. border to the Minnesota-Wisconsin border through the rugged landscape of Minnesota's North Shore region (Lake Superior shoreline). Inspired by the Appalachian Trail, the SHT began taking shape in the 1980s and is now a popular thru-hiking route. Completing the full route typically takes 2–4 weeks, but the many intersecting trails along the way make it incredibly accessible for section and day hikers. The Superior Hiking Trail Association, a Minnesota-based non-profit, builds and maintains the trail and signage. Blue blazes on trees, rocks, and trail posts mark the main SHT route. White blazes indicate SHT spurs, such as those leading to lookouts, peaks, and trailheads.

This day hike along the SHT takes you through Magney-Snively Park to Ely's Peak. Magney-Snively Park has over 700 acres of forests, wetlands, and large rock outcroppings. The park has a wide network of trails for hikers, mountain bikers, and cross-country skiers, though the SHT itself only allows foot traffic. Ely's Peak, topping out at more than 1,100 feet, is a popular destination for its 360-degree view from the top. There are several routes leading to this summit, but this route provides a longer adventure with more time in the forest and additional outlook opportunities.

Our trail begins on a short spur leading to the main SHT, where you'll spot the first blue blaze. Winding your way through the quiet forest, you'll enjoy ferns, mossy rocks, boulder outcroppings, and several seasonal streams. About a mile and a half in, you'll pass by a few trail spurs on your left leading to overlooks (not included in the mileage or map) as well as a few spectacular views of Duluth right from the trail. While these lookouts offer impressive sights, they're not the only mid-hike attractions; during the spring and summer, you'll encounter splashes of color from wildflowers along open sections of the trail. In the fall, the primarily maple forest shines as the leaves change to bright yellows, oranges, and reds.

About two and a half miles into your hike, you'll climb up out of the forest to trek on top of the precipitous cliffs. Enjoy the views, but don't forget to look down for blue blazes painted on the rocks to ensure you stay on route. The trail takes you across large stretches of flat rock and up and down a few small ledges. Keep an eye out for the white trail marker for the Ely's Peak spur; from the marker, it's just a few hundred feet to your panoramic summit views of the abundant forest and the St. Louis River, which separates Minnesota and Wisconsin. After taking in the views, you'll retrace your steps back to your car.

TURN-BY-TURN DIRECTIONS

1. From the trailhead, head down the signposted SHT spur. In 250 feet, at the T-junction, turn right onto the signposted SHT Main Trail to Bardon's Peak.
2. At 0.3 miles, reach a dirt road and continue straight across the road.
3. At 0.9 miles, continue straight across a wide grassy trail.
4. At 1.2 miles, continue straight across another wide grassy trail.
5. At 1.3 miles, continue straight, ignoring the signposted Bardon's Peak Trail Spur on the left.
6. At 1.8 miles, reach a dirt road and continue straight across the road.
7. At 1.9 miles, continue straight, ignoring an unsigned trail spur on the left. In 450 feet, reach a second unsigned spur trail on the left and continue straight.
8. At 2.8 miles, bear left at the fork on the blue-blazed SHT.
9. At 3.3 miles, turn right onto the signposted SHT spur for Ely's Peak. Continue for 300 feet to Ely's Peak. Return the way you came.

FIND THE TRAILHEAD

From Duluth, at I-35 and Highway 53, take I-35 south. After 5.4 miles, take Exit 249 for Boundary Avenue and then turn left onto W Skyline Parkway. After 0.4 miles, turn left to continue on W Skyline Parkway. After 2 miles, turn left into the Magney-Snively Trailhead parking area.

BENT PADDLE BREWING COMPANY

Co-owners Karen and Bryon Tonnis and Laura and Colin Mullen met at a charity event in 2010 where Laura told Karen that the guys should connect over their brewery interests. After many conversations, a lot of planning and building, and the addition of babies in both families (born within a few days of each other!), Bent Paddle Brewing Company launched in 2013. Just five years after opening, they expanded the brewery and moved the taproom next door into the old Enger & Olson Furniture Warehouse (the original signage is

still visible on the outer brick face). The team worked hard to create a welcoming, community-oriented gathering place—in addition to good beer, of course. It's a family- and pet-friendly space with a heated patio, firepits, and games.

Bent Paddle has won multiple awards for its taproom, business, and beers. The team aims to brew classic beers that "bend the tradition" to become something unique. Bent Hop is one of several award-winning beers, having won a World Beer Cup Bronze Medal in the International India Pale Ale Category. Its malty profile balances well with American and European hops giving hints of citrus and pine.

LAND MANAGER

Duluth Parks & Recreation
411 W 1st Street
Duluth, MN 55802
(218) 730-4300
duluthmn.gov/parks/parks-listing/magney-snively-park
duluthmn.gov/media/8474/duluthrecmap-2019-reduced.pdf

BREWERY/RESTAURANT

Bent Paddle Brewing Company
1832 W Michigan Street
Duluth, MN 55806
(218) 279-2722
bentpaddlebrewing.com

Distance from trailhead: 8 miles

MOOSE LAKE WOODLAND TRAILS

FORESTED LOOP TO AN IDYLLIC STREAM AND RIVER VIEWS

STARTING POINT	DESTINATION
TRAILHEAD PARKING LOT	FOREST CREEK

BREWERY	HIKE TYPE
MOOSE LAKE BREWING COMPANY	MODERATE

DOG FRIENDLY	SEASON
YES (LEASH REQUIRED)	MAY–OCTOBER

FEES	DURATION
NONE	2 HOURS

MAP REFERENCE	LENGTH
POSTED AT TRAILHEAD	4 MILES (LOLLIPOP LOOP)

HIGHLIGHTS	ELEVATION GAIN
MOOSE HORN RIVER, FALL COLORS	141 FEET

7.6% ALCOHOL CONTENT

MORNING HAZE NEW ENGLAND IPA

HAZY ORANGE

CITRUS

CITRUS, JUICY

BITTERNESS **SWEETNESS**

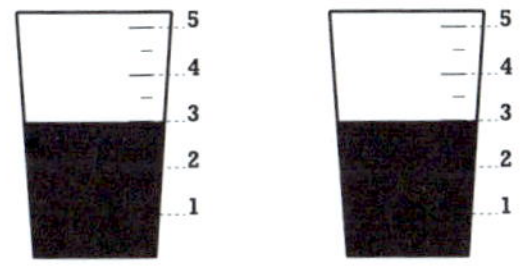

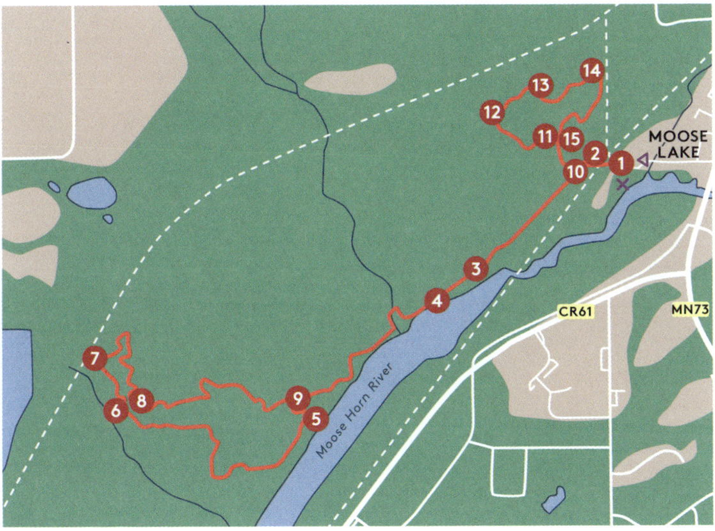

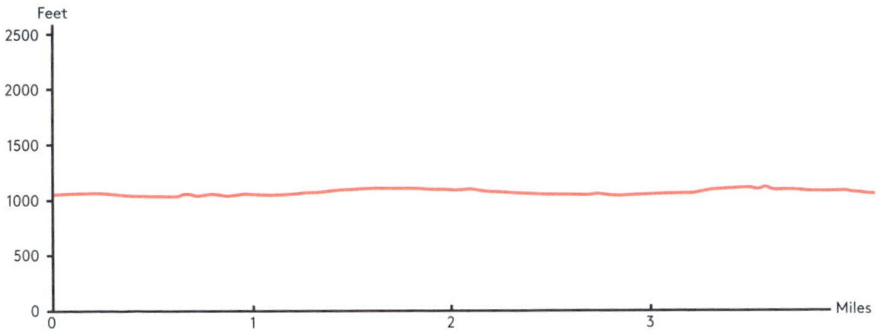

HIKE DESCRIPTION

Step onto sun-dappled trails winding through a tranquil forest to explore picturesque waterways, wildflowers, and seasonal colors. Then head to Moose Lake Brewing Company to relax on the patio with a pint of their Morning Haze New England IPA.

The Moose Lake Woodland Trails weave through the forest on the edge of town sandwiched between the paved Willard Munger State Trail to the southeast and the Soo Line ATV Trail to the northwest. The woodland trails branch off into several loops offering visitors a choose-your-own-adventure type of exploration: Pick a short loop, head to the river and back, or circle through each of the sections for an extended excursion. Our route follows the third option to include a sampling of tracks from each branch of the trail system.

Your journey begins in a corridor cleared of trees where you'll set out on a wide, mowed-grass path under the powerline running east-west. As you head up a small hill, there's a trail map posted where the path splits in three directions. First, you'll hop on a boardwalk for a quick

trip to discover the local "Dinosaur Bones." This collection of old excavating equipment may not be Jurassic-era old, but it is fascinating to explore up close.

Next, you'll return to the intersection to meander along the River Rock Trail. Several boardwalks lift you above the soggy ground as you approach three spur trails leading to the Moose Horn River. Soak up the views along this wide waterway, then ramble on. Just around the next curve, the trees open up around a small, peaceful stream. A few mild cascades dot the stream as it courses over rocks to make its way to the Moose Horn River. You'll cross a boardwalk and bridge to reach the opposite bank and then dive back into the lush forest.

About a mile into your hike, you'll pick up the Moose Wallow Trail for the first half of a loop, which then continues as the Moose Shed Trail. You'll navigate more rocks through this portion, but there are also more wildflowers adding pops of color to the sea of green and gray. In the fall, you'll be immersed in a stunning array of autumn colors amidst stands of aspen and maple trees.

Once you close your loop, you'll return to the powerline and take the Loose Moose Loop (say that three times fast!). This route begins as a wood-chipped path and switches to mowed grass and boardwalks as you wind deeper into the forest. Large angular boulders occasionally jut from the earth, but overall, this is a softer, gentler footpath than the southern trails. Enjoy the calm, quiet atmosphere of this forest as you lace through the aspen and circle back to the main trail, ending your journey at the trailhead.

TURN-BY-TURN DIRECTIONS

1. From the trailhead map, cross the road and head west on the mowed-grass path. In 100 feet, cross the paved pathway and then continue on the grassy path under the power line.
2. At 300 feet, at the trail map and junction, turn right onto the boardwalk. Explore the "Dinosaur Bones," then return to the junction and continue straight on the River Rock Trail.
3. At 0.4 miles, turn left onto the spur trail to reach the river. Enjoy the view, then return to the main trail. In 300 feet, turn left to explore another short spur trail to the river.
4. At 0.5 miles, turn left onto a third spur trail offering river views, then continue on the main trail.
5. At 0.9 miles, bear left at the trail map and fork to begin a loop on the Moose Wallow Trail.
6. At 1.5 miles, continue straight, ignoring the unsigned spur trail on the right.
7. At 1.6 miles, bear right at the trail map and fork to continue on the Moose Shed Trail.
8. At 1.9 miles, continue straight, ignoring the unsigned spur trail on the right.
9. At 2.3 miles, keep left at the fork from Step 4 to close the loop and return to the junction from Step 2.
10. At 3.1 miles, at the junction from Step 2, turn left.
11. At 3.2 miles, bear left at the trail map and fork to begin the Loose Moose Loop.
12. At 3.4 miles, turn right at the T-junction and trail map to continue on the Loose Moose Loop.
13. At 3.5 miles, turn right again at the T-junction and posted trail map to remain on the Loose Moose Loop.
14. At 3.6 miles, continue straight at the trail map to stay on the Loose Moose Loop. In 100 feet, continue straight, ignoring a spur trail and gravel road on the left.
15. At 3.8 miles, return to the intersection from Step 10 to close the loop; keep left to return to the trailhead.

FIND THE TRAILHEAD

From Duluth at I-35 and I-535, head south on I-35 for 39.0 miles. Take Exit 216 for MN-27 to Moose Lake and turn left onto MN-27. After 1.6 miles, continue straight onto MN-73/State Highway 61 and proceed for 0.6 miles. Turn left onto Earl Ellens Drive. After 0.2 miles, at the trail map, turn right into the gravel parking area. The trail begins under the powerline across the paved road.

MOOSE LAKE BREWING COMPANY

Moose Lake Brewing Company's five partners, Shawn Wigg, Travis Anderson, Dusty Wilson, Janet Anderson, and Bev Radel, came together through a mix of friendships and a love of beer. As the idea to open a brewery took hold, a building came up for sale next to Moosehead Lake, and they knew it was the perfect location for their venture—the patio offers a picture-perfect Northwoods lake view. They renovated the interior to include old signs from around the community as an homage to the businesses and families who have played a part in the town's history and growth.

In the winter, the team takes advantage of the frozen lake access by offering several fun events out on the ice. They put on an ice fishing contest to raise money for the Wounded Warrior Project, a charity aimed at helping wounded military members, and the Lions Club, a group that brings people together who want to improve their local community. They also organize a tournament of ice bocce, a hybrid game that combines curling and bocce ball.

Moose Lake Brewing Company's Morning Haze is a hazy New England IPA featuring Citra, Chinook, and Cascade hops. It boasts juicy, citrus flavors with a smooth finish.

LAND MANAGER

City of Moose Lake
412 4th Street
Moose Lake, MN 55767
(218) 485-4010
cityofmooselake.net/
alltrails.com/trail/us/minnesota/moose-lake-woodland-trails-loop

BREWERY/RESTAURANT

Moose Lake Brewing Company
244 Lakeshore Drive
Moose Lake, MN 55767
(218) 485-4585
mooselakebrewing.com

Distance from trailhead: 0.2 miles

SANDSTONE BLUFFS LOOP

HIKE ATOP RIVER CLIFFS TO A SEASONAL WATERFALL

STARTING POINT	**DESTINATION**
INTERSTATE STATE PARK VISITOR CENTER	SANDSTONE BLUFFS
BREWERY	**HIKE TYPE**
UNCOMMON LOON BREWING COMPANY	MODERATE
DOG FRIENDLY	**SEASON**
YES (LEASH REQUIRED)	MAY–OCTOBER
FEES	**DURATION**
YES	1 HOUR 30 MINUTES
MAP REFERENCE	**LENGTH**
POSTED AT TRAILHEAD	3.2 MILES (LOOP)
HIGHLIGHTS	**ELEVATION GAIN**
RIVER GORGE, SANDSTONE BLUFFS, WATERFALL	282 FEET

6.5% ALCOHOL CONTENT

SHAPESHIFTER IPA

HAZY ORANGE

FRAGRANT TROPICAL FRUIT

GRAPEFRUIT, MANGO

BITTERNESS

SWEETNESS

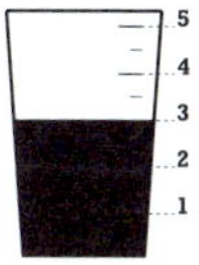

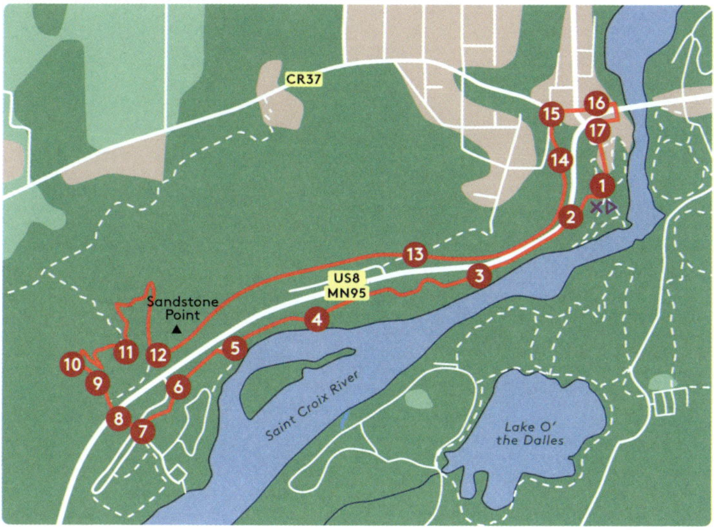

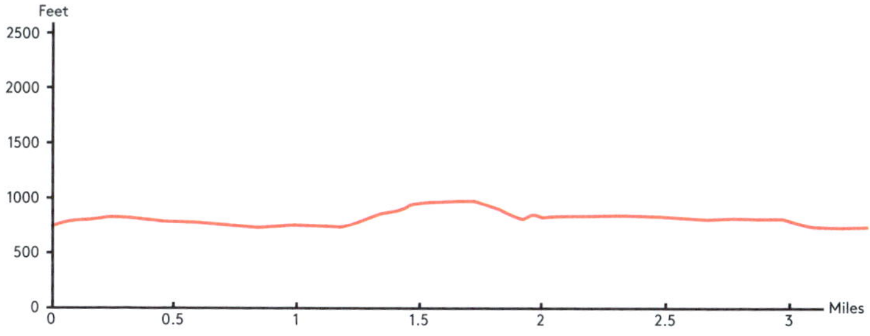

HIKE DESCRIPTION

Hike the Minnesota border along cliffs high above the St. Croix River before heading deeper into the woods to sandstone bluffs and a seasonal waterfall. Afterward, head to Uncommon Loon Brewing to relax with a tropical pint of Shapeshifter IPA.

Interstate State Park was the first multi-state park in the United States, spanning across the St. Croix River to include both Minnesota and Wisconsin. The work to protect the St. Croix Dalles began when the threat of mining reached the area. Minnesota secured its side of the park in 1895, and Wisconsin followed suit in 1900.

About one billion years ago, earthquakes disrupted the region, setting loose lava flows that hardened into basalt rock. After, across millions of years, several ancient seas covered the area, depositing sedimentary rock. Next came the glaciers, carving up the land and then ultimately receding, sending torrents of meltwater downriver—a much larger and more turbulent version of today's St. Croix River.

The melting glaciers released rocky sediments into the river, which, when caught in swirling eddy currents, drilled holes into the river bottom. More than 400 of these glacial potholes are visible across the park, the deepest of which is several feet wide and reaches almost 60 feet into the rock. You can explore these potholes at the front of the park near the trailhead.

As you begin your hike on the River Trail, the path immediately transitions from the pavement of the main park walkway to stone steps leading into the woods. Expect a rocky trail ahead with a mix of stone and wooden steps. The trail runs across the basalt cliff tops high above the river. While most of the trail meanders through the woods, you'll find several fantastic viewpoints along the way. Once you reach the southern visitor center around one mile in, you'll hike through a tunnel to cross under the highway.

Next, you'll begin the hardest climb of the hike up a series of steep wooden stairs. The climb is worth it once you reach the massive sandstone bluffs hidden away in the forest. While rain can make the wooden walkways slick, it can also deliver an occasional waterfall tucked behind the bluffs. After hiking up above the bluffs, you'll work your way down along a quaint forest stream to the Railroad Trail. As you pass by a few more sandstone bluffs, look closely for fossils from the ancient seas. From here, you'll enjoy a wide trail and a casual hike back to Taylors Falls and the park entrance where you started.

TURN-BY-TURN DIRECTIONS

1. From the visitor center parking lot, follow the paved walkway into the park and turn right onto the trail marked with the Walter F. Mondale River Trail map and River Trail signpost.
2. At 0.2 miles, climb the stairs as the trail becomes level with the roadway. Enjoy the river overlook.
3. At 0.3 miles, reach a wooden deck on the left offering a view of the river below.
4. At 0.7 miles, reach a viewpoint for Folsom Island.
5. At 0.9 miles, keep right at the fork to stay on the signposted River Trail.
6. At 1.0 miles, keep left, continuing on the signposted River Trail.
7. At 1.1 miles, turn right onto the paved road. Pass between the visitor center and a garage following the sign for Sandstone Bluffs & Railroad Trails.
8. At 1.2 miles, follow the trail through the tunnel under the highway. Walk up a few steps and then keep left at the fork onto the signposted Sandstone Bluffs Trail.
9. At 1.3 miles, climb an extended series of wooden stairs up to the sandstone bluffs.
10. At 1.4 miles, pass a set of stairs cut into the stone on the right. For now, ignore the stairs and continue on the wooden walkway to the seasonal waterfall, Curtain Falls. Enjoy the view, then return to the stone stairway and climb up to resume the hike.
11. At 1.6 miles, reach an overlook with informational signs about the St. Croix River Valley. Continue on the trail, keeping right at the fork.
12. At 2.0 miles, reach the junction with the Railroad Trail and turn left onto the Railroad Trail, passing more sandstone bluffs.
13. At 2.5 miles, keep left at the fork to stay on the Railroad Trail.
14. At 2.9 miles, the trail ends. Continue down the sidewalk along Government Street into Taylors Falls.
15. At 3.0 miles, reach the intersection with 1st Street. Cross 1st Street and then turn right on 1st Street to cross the St. Croix Scenic Byway.
16. At 3.1 miles, 1st Street ends at a park. Keep left on the sidewalk, following it as it goes downhill, curves right under the Highway 8 overpass, and then up the hill.
17. At 3.2 miles, turn left into the Interstate State Park parking lot to end your hike.

FIND THE TRAILHEAD

From Chisago City, take US Highway 8 east for 13 miles to Taylors Falls. Turn right onto South Street and then immediately right again into the Interstate State Park entrance and parking lot. The trailhead is straight ahead, to the right of the visitor center.

UNCOMMON LOON BREWING COMPANY

Uncommon Loon Brewing began in 2018 when three friends, Brad Klatt, John Cariveau, and Mark Skoglund, came together post-retirement for a second act. They purchased the old fire station in Chisago City and built not just a brewery but a gathering place for the community. Uncommon Loon hosts showings for local artists, serves as the post for the American Legion, features many local musicians, and more.

With a 10-barrel brewing system and 16 taps, Uncommon Loon offers a diverse range of brews. Shapeshifter, one of Uncommon Loon's most popular beers, is a hazy New England IPA with fruity, tropical flavors. They also include a variety of non-alcoholic options, further supporting their goal to be a welcoming place for all, from travelers to families and even your dog.

LAND MANAGER

Interstate State Park
256 Traprock Street
Taylors Falls, MN 55084
(651) 539-4500
dnr.state.mn.us/state_parks/park.html?id=spk00178#homepage
files.dnr.state.mn.us/maps/state_parks/spk00178.pdf

BREWERY/RESTAURANT

Uncommon Loon Brewing Company
10825 Lake Boulevard
Chisago City, MN 55013
(651) 321-4468
uncommonloonbrewing.com

Distance from trailhead: 13.2 miles

THEODORE WIRTH REGIONAL PARK

A WINDING WILDFLOWER WALK AND LAKESIDE LOOP

MINNEAPOLIS, MN

STARTING POINT	DESTINATION
WIRTH BEACH HOUSE	WIRTH LAKE
BREWERY	**HIKE TYPE**
UTEPILS BREWING	EASY
DOG FRIENDLY	**SEASON**
NO	MAY–OCTOBER
FEES	**DURATION**
NO	2 HOURS
MAP REFERENCE	**LENGTH**
POSTED AT TRAILHEAD	3.2 MILES (ROUND TRIP)
HIGHLIGHTS	**ELEVATION GAIN**
WILDFLOWER GARDEN, WIRTH LAKE	142 FEET

5.2%
ALCOHOL CONTENT

EWALD THE GOLDEN BAVARIAN HEFEWEIZEN

HAZY GOLDEN

BANANA, CLOVE

BANANA, CLOVE, TANGY

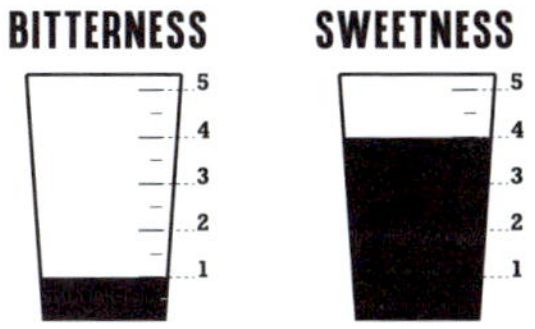

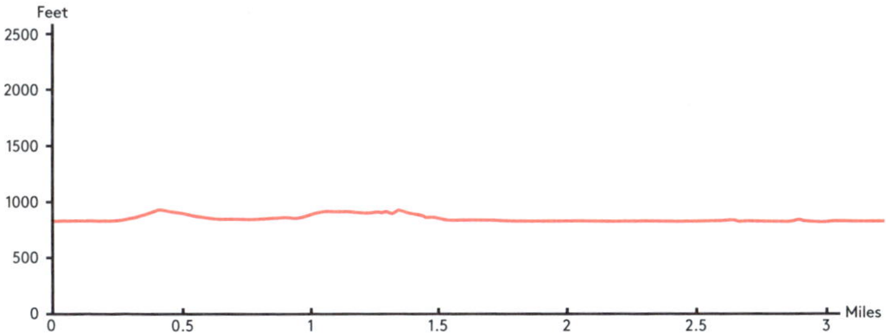

HIKE DESCRIPTION

Ramble forested park trails to diverse blooms in a wildflower garden, then loop Wirth Lake for pristine views across its sparkling waters. Explore more of the neighborhood with a visit to Utepils Brewing for a fresh pour of their Bavarian-style hefeweizen.

Theodore Wirth Regional Park encompasses 740 acres of forests, lakes, and streams just west of downtown Minneapolis. Among the park's many highlights are Wirth Lake, the central lake of the park, and the Eloise Butler Wildflower Garden & Bird Sanctuary, named after a garden volunteer and retired botany teacher. The garden showcases native plants, wildflowers, and landscapes of the region.

You'll set off on your quest for wildflowers and lake views from the Beach House at Wirth Lake. After crossing to the opposite side of Glenwood Avenue, you'll wander along a gravel path as it cuts through

a marsh and sweeps into a forest of large, lofty trees. Within the shade of the forest, the path transitions to pavement for the remainder of your walk to the wildflower garden.

Nearly a half mile into your stroll, you'll pass through the entrance gate onto a soft wood-chip path that meanders around the wildflower garden. The blooming flowers change with the season, but you're sure to see a wide mix of plants regardless of season as the terrain changes from forest to wetland to meadow. Enjoy the serenity of the space and respect the local flora and fauna—take only photos.

After emerging from the garden, you'll follow your tracks back to the Beach House to pick up the paved loop wrapping around Wirth Lake. At the north end of the lake, you'll head directly across the water on a bridge linking the east and west shorelines. Once you've surveyed the lake scenery, you'll amble through the forest and around the southern end of the lake. Just before you reach the Beach House, you'll turn onto a sidewalk leading to a floating boardwalk that arcs in a semicircle over the water. Check the water for crappies, walleyes, and largemouth bass as you make your way around the walkway and then wrap up your trip back at the Beach House.

TURN-BY-TURN DIRECTIONS

1. From the trail map, follow the crosswalk across Glenwood Avenue. Turn right at the signpost to follow the E.B. Garden arrow. In 300 feet, bear left toward the trail map and then immediately right onto the wide dirt path.
2. At 0.2 miles, continue straight through the junction onto the paved path.
3. At 0.3 miles, bear left at the fork, walking on the left side of the road.
4. At 0.4 miles, bear right at the fork to stay on the paved path. In 80 feet, turn left to go down the steps and continue straight through the metal entrance gate.
5. At 0.5 miles, turn left at the garden map and T-junction. In 250 feet, turn left at the T-junction with metal benches.
6. At 0.7 miles, bear right at the fork in the boardwalk.
7. At 0.8 miles, turn left at the unsigned T-junction.
8. At 0.9 miles, bear right as the trail forks around a tree, then immediately turn right at the junction.
9. At 1.0 miles, turn left at the unsigned junction. In 200 feet, bear right at the fork.
10. At 1.1 miles, bear left at the fork. In 130 feet, continue straight through the junction.
11. At 1.2 miles, reach the garden map from Step 5. Turn left to exit the garden and retrace your steps back to the trail map from Step 1.
12. At 1.7 miles, reach the trail map from Step 1 and continue straight toward the Beach House. In 30 feet, turn right onto the paved trail to begin a loop around the lake.
13. At 1.8 miles, bear left at the fork to continue along the lakeside.
14. At 2.0 miles, bear left at the fork toward the lake. In 250 feet, continue onto the bridge to cross the lake.
15. At 2.4 miles, turn left at the T-junction to continue around the lake. In 200 feet, turn left at the junction.
16. At 2.9 miles, bear left at the fork to follow the Beach House arrow. In 300 feet, turn left onto the sidewalk.
17. At 3.0 miles, turn left at the junction to get onto the floating boardwalk.
18. At 3.1 miles, at the end of the boardwalk, bear right to reach the Beach House and close the loop back at the parking lot trail map.

FIND THE TRAILHEAD

From Minneapolis at 1st Street and Hennepin Avenue, head northwest on 1st Street and immediately turn left onto 1st Avenue. After 0.2 miles, turn right onto 3rd Street and continue for 400 feet, then bear left to take the I-394 W ramp. Continue on I-394 W for 1.8 miles, then take Exit 7 for Penn Avenue. After 0.1 miles, turn right onto Penn Avenue and proceed for 0.7 miles. Turn left onto Glenwood Avenue, continue for 0.8 miles, and then turn right into the Beach House parking lot. The route begins at the trail map at the far end of the parking lot.

UTEPILS BREWING

Co-owners Deb and Dan Justesen first encountered the term Utepils during a trip to their cabin up north. While caught in traffic, Deb read an article to Dan about words you can't translate into English. One word in particular caught their attention: utepils, a Norwegian term that describes the feeling of wanting to get outside and enjoy a beer in the sunshine but having to wait until the long, dark, cold winter is over. As beer-loving Minnesotans, that feeling hit home.

When Deb and Dan set out in search of a location for their brewery, they wanted a space that felt more like a European beer garden surrounded by nature than a basic building in the middle of the city. After a long list of not-quite-rights, they found the perfect spot tucked along Bassett Creek by Theodore Wirth Park. The location offered easy access to the things they loved—parks, trails, and downtown sports—plus space in the back for a patio by the creek that quieted the presence of the big city.

Utepils Brewery's Ewald the Golden is a Bavarian-style hefeweizen of half barley and half wheat. This award-winning hazy golden brew delivers notes of bananas and clove with a hint of tanginess and effervescence.

LAND MANAGER

Minneapolis Park and Recreation Board
2117 West River Road
Minneapolis, MN 55411
(612) 230-6400
minneapolisparks.org/parks-destinations/parks-lakes/theodore_wirth_regional_park
loppet.org/wp-content/uploads/2023/11/Megamap-8-Summer-11x17-1.pdf

BREWERY/RESTAURANT

Utepils Brewing
225 Thomas Avenue N #700
Minneapolis, MN 55405
(612) 249-7800
utepilsbrewing.com

Distance from trailhead: 0.7 miles

HYLAND LAKE PARK RESERVE

RETREAT TO FORESTED FOOTHILLS AND A QUIET LAKE

STARTING POINT	**DESTINATION**
HYLAND LAKE PARK RESERVE VISITOR CENTER	HYLAND LAKE
BREWERY	**HIKE TYPE**
WOODEN HILL BREWING COMPANY	MODERATE
DOG FRIENDLY	**SEASON**
YES (LEASH REQUIRED)	MAY–OCTOBER
FEES	**DURATION**
NONE	2 HOURS 30 MINUTES
MAP REFERENCE	**LENGTH**
POSTED AT TRAILHEAD	5.4 MILES (ROUND TRIP)
HIGHLIGHTS	**ELEVATION GAIN**
HYLAND LAKE, WETLANDS	200 FEET

4.7% ALCOHOL CONTENT

KOLD SHOULDER KÖLSCH

LIGHT STRAW

EARTHY, SULFUR

BISCUITY, EARTHY

BITTERNESS | SWEETNESS

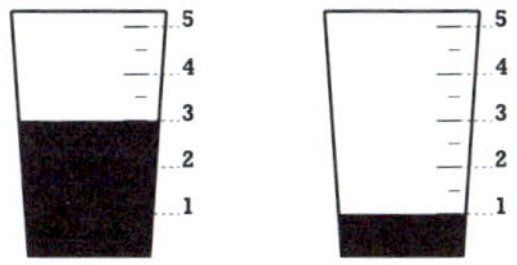

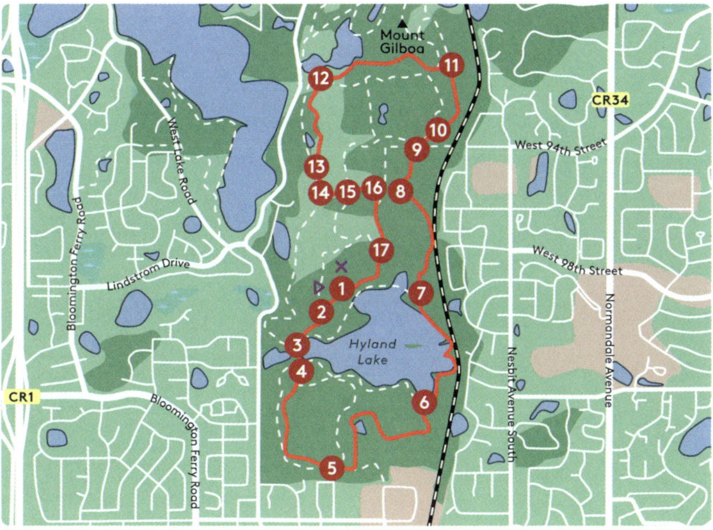

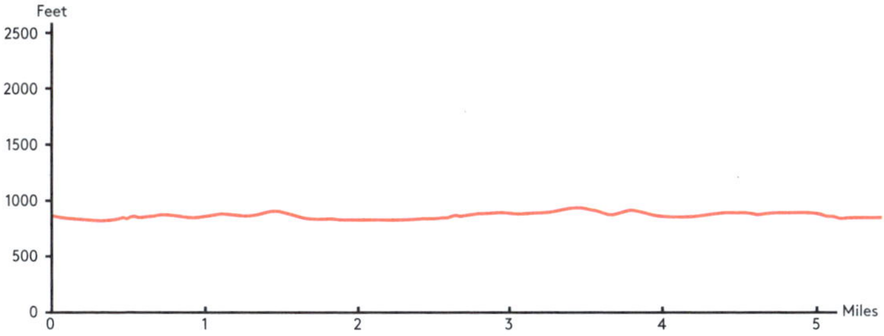

HIKE DESCRIPTION

Escape the concrete jungle of Minneapolis with a peaceful stroll around Hyland Lake and the surrounding area. Refresh posthike with a crisp pint of Kold Shoulder Kölsch at Wooden Hill Brewing Company.

Hyland Lake Park Reserve is a pocket of tranquility in an ever-growing metropolis. With nearly 18 miles of paved and unpaved trails sweeping through the park, there's enough variation for any ability or endurance level. Trail maps and markers are posted at most major intersections to help you stay on track amidst the intertwining pathways.

Your romp through the park begins on the paved trail heading out from the visitor center and traveling in a counter-clockwise direction around Hyland Lake. You'll sweep along the marsh to a viewpoint at the lake's western side. You can catch a splendid sunrise here if you plan an early morning adventure. As you head into the forest, you'll transition to an unpaved path, coursing up and down rolling hills and around a small pond.

The lake views return after you turn onto the Lake Trail, nearly two miles into your jaunt. You'll stroll down a wide, wood-chip path winding around Hyland Lake. Feel free to pause at any of the benches along the shore to soak up the serenity. Near the northern end of the lake, you'll leave the sparkling waters behind to head uphill on the Oak Knob Trail. As the forest opens up around you, the path switches to mowed grass and lopes over foothills just south of the Hyland Hills Ski Area, a popular winter spot for downhill skiing.

Looping around the far end of your circuit, you'll ramble over a few gentle hills and weave around the wetlands. Heading into your final mile, you'll hop onto a paved trail for the remainder of your route. This path cruises past picnic tables and a playground near the shoreline of Hyland Lake, bringing you back to the visitor center to complete the loop.

TURN-BY-TURN DIRECTIONS

1. From the visitor center entrance, head south on the paved trail. In 250 feet, continue straight across the boat ramp entrance road and the overflow parking entrance road.
2. At 0.1 miles, turn left at the T-junction, following the arrow for Sumac Knoll Group Camp.
3. At 0.3 miles, turn left at the T-junction, following the arrow for Sumac Knoll Group Camp. In 300 feet, at the junction, bear left onto the unpaved path at trail marker 3.
4. At 0.4 miles, keep right at the fork at trail marker 4. In 350 feet, continue straight across the gravel road to reach trail marker 5.
5. At 1.0 miles, bear left at trail marker 7 as the dirt path continues alongside a paved path. In 200 feet, continue straight at trail marker 8, ignoring a paved trail spur on the left. In another 200 feet, bear left at trail marker 9 to continue on the unpaved path.
6. At 1.8 miles, turn right at the T-junction onto the signposted Lake Trail.
7. At 2.4 miles, bear right at the fork onto the signposted Oak Knob Trail.
8. At 2.9 miles, bear right at the fork at trail marker 16.
9. At 3.1 miles, continue straight through the junction toward the trail map.
10. At 3.2 miles, at the junction, continue straight to stay on the unpaved path.
11. At 3.5 miles, at trail marker 23, turn left to continue toward trail marker 31.
12. At 4.1 miles, turn left at the junction to cross the paved path and continue toward trail marker 40.
13. At 4.5 miles, continue straight, ignoring the unsigned spur trail on the right.
14. At 4.6 miles, continue straight across the paved path toward trail marker 42.
15. At 4.7 miles, continue straight across another paved path toward trail marker 45.
16. At 4.8 miles, turn right at trail marker 46. In 400 feet, keep left of the bench.
17. At 5.1 miles, bear slightly left onto the paved path. Continue on the paved path to return to the visitor center and close the loop.

FIND THE TRAILHEAD

From Bloomington, take I-35W N at 90th Street and continue for 1.2 miles. Take the exit for I-494 W and continue on I-494 W for 3.1 miles. Take exit 8 for Bush Lake Road and then turn left onto Bush Lake Road. After 0.4 miles, turn right to stay on Bush Lake Road and continue for 2.4 miles. At the sign for Hyland Lake Park Reserve, turn left onto the entrance road. Proceed for 0.2 miles to reach the Hyland Lake Park Reserve Visitor Center. Park in the main lot at the front of the visitor center or in the overflow parking to the right.

WOODEN HILL BREWING COMPANY

With a background in nanoscience technology (biology and chemistry), co-founder James Ewen fell in love with the science of brewing after receiving his first homebrew kit as a gift from his brother and co-founder, Sean Ewen. As James dabbled in recipes and built his craft, he found joy in sharing his beers. James and Sean opened Wooden Hill Brewing Company in 2018, the first brewery and taproom in Edina, MN. Even now, years later, James's favorite part of the business is sharing beer with customers, from regulars ordering their go-to brews to out-of-town visitors sampling a flight.

Kold Shoulder Kölsch started as a homebrew and was the first recipe James thought could become a professional beer. At the time, his cousin was visiting, and her husband was from Germany. So, he thought a kölsch, which originated in Cologne, Germany, would be a fitting option to brew for the occasion. Kold Shoulder is a SMaSH beer—single malt and single hop—made with German pilsner malt, Hallertau hops, and German yeast. It's a light and refreshing award-winning ale.

LAND MANAGER

Three Rivers Park District
3000 Xenium Lane North
Plymouth, MN 55441
(763) 559-9000
threeriversparks.org/location/hyland-lake-park-reserve
threeriversparks.link/HylandLake_ParkReserve_Summer

BREWERY/RESTAURANT

Wooden Hill Brewing Company
7421 Bush Lake Road
Edina, MN 55439
(952) 960-9663
woodenhillbrewing.com

Distance from trailhead: 3.7 miles

PIKE ISLAND

AN ISLAND LOOP ALONG THE MIGHTY MISSISSIPPI

ST. PAUL, MN

STARTING POINT	DESTINATION
THOMAS C. SAVAGE VISITOR CENTER	RIVER CONFLUENCE

BREWERY	HIKE TYPE
URBAN GROWLER BREWING COMPANY	EASY

DOG FRIENDLY	SEASON
YES (LEASH REQUIRED)	MAY–OCTOBER

FEES	DURATION
YES	1 HOUR 45 MINUTES

MAP REFERENCE	LENGTH
POSTED AT TRAILHEAD	3.9 MILES (LOLLIPOP LOOP)

HIGHLIGHTS	ELEVATION GAIN
MINNESOTA AND MISSISSIPPI RIVERS	22 FEET

5.6% ALCOHOL CONTENT

VANILLA LATTE BLONDE ALE

GOLD

LATTE

VANILLA, COFFEE

BITTERNESS

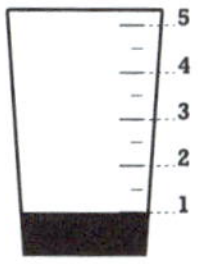

SWEETNESS

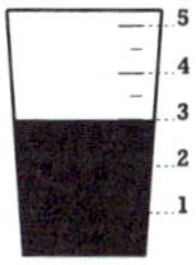

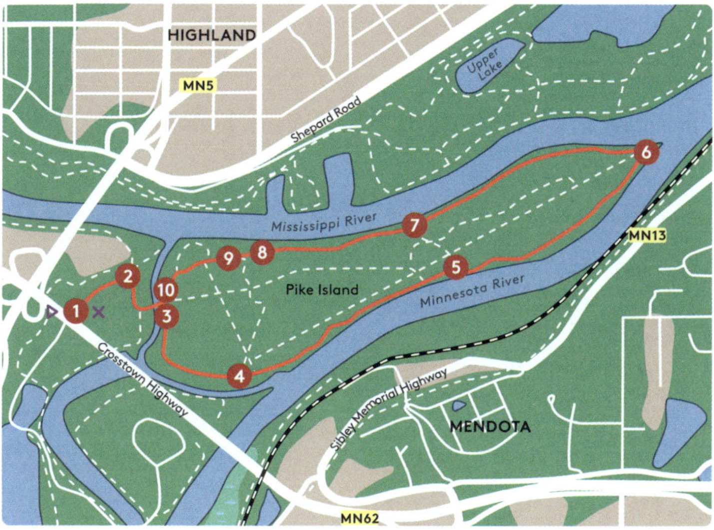

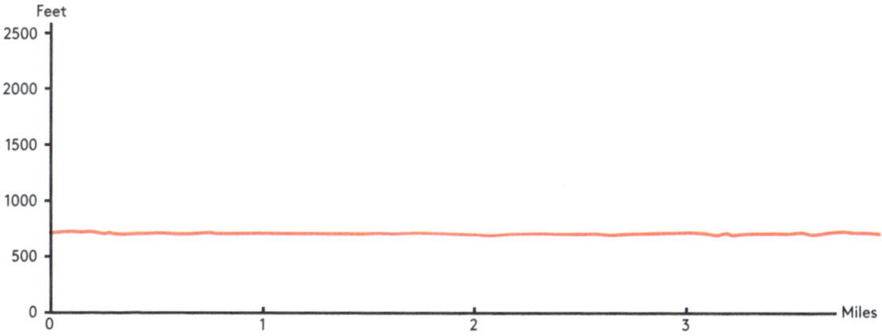

HIKE DESCRIPTION

Traverse a forested island below the historic Fort Snelling to meander along two expansive rivers cutting through the Twin Cities metropolitan area. Salute your adventure with a visit to Urban Growler for a pint of their Vanilla Latte Blonde Ale.

Fort Snelling State Park protects the lands at the confluence of the Minnesota and Mississippi Rivers near the center of the Twin Cities. While the park is named after the historic Fort Snelling situated on the bluffs overlooking the rivers, the confluence is a significant space for the Mdewakanton Dakota people. Some consider it the center of the earth and a sacred place of creation. The visitor center provides exhibits to learn more about the Dakota people, their culture, and their history.

Your journey to explore Pike Island starts on an easy paved trail heading straight into the forest. You'll depart from the pavement at the first junction and continue on a wide, mostly flat gravel path. After crossing the bridge over an arm of the Minnesota River, you'll begin your counter-clockwise loop around the island.

The first half of your journey follows the Minnesota River shoreline. Large, lofty cottonwood, willow, and maple trees cover most of the island and shade the wide, dirt pathway. Two miles in, you'll reach the far end of the island where the Minnesota River feeds into the Mississippi River as it winds its way south. Explore the sand bar at the confluence, or settle into one of the benches to admire the powerful waters flanking the island.

When you're ready, step back on the trail to continue alongside the Mississippi River. Look for wildflowers along the trail and people fishing along the shore. You might even spot turkeys, foxes, or deer who traverse the same bridge you did for their own day trip or to call the island home. You'll reach one more trailside bench as you head into the last mile of your journey. It's the perfect spot to take in one more river view before closing your loop and returning to the trailhead.

TURN-BY-TURN DIRECTIONS

1. From the trailhead, set out on the signposted Hiking Club Trail.
2. At 0.2 miles, at the junction with the trail map, turn right toward the trailside benches. In 50 feet, the path transitions to gravel. In 450 more feet, keep left at the fork.
3. At 0.3 miles, cross the bridge, then immediately bear right onto the signposted Hiking Club Trail.
4. At 0.7 miles, at the trail map, continue straight, ignoring a spur trail on the left.
5. At 1.4 miles, at the T-junction, turn right to continue alongside the river.
6. At 2.0 miles, reach the confluence of the Minnesota and Mississippi Rivers. Explore the view and then continue on the main trail.
7. At 2.7 miles, at the trail map, continue straight, ignoring a spur trail on the left.
8. At 3.2 miles, reach a bench looking over the river. Enjoy the view, then continue on the main trail.
9. At 3.3 miles, continue straight, ignoring an unsigned spur trail on the left. Continue on the main trail for the next 0.3 miles, ignoring three more spur trails—two on the right and one on the left.
10. At 3.6 miles, reach the bridge from Step 3, closing the loop around the island. Cross the bridge and retrace your steps back to the trailhead.

FIND THE TRAILHEAD

From St. Paul at MN-5/Fort Road and Kellogg Boulevard, head west on MN-5/Fort Road for 0.4 miles. Turn left onto Wabash Street and proceed for 0.3 miles. Turn left to merge onto I-35E S. After 3.5 miles, take Exit 103B for MN-5/West 7th Street and proceed for 0.2 miles. Turn right onto MN-5/West 7th Street. In 4.0 miles, bear right to take the Post Road exit and then turn left onto Post Road. After 400 feet, continue straight onto Snelling Lake Road. Proceed for 2.1 miles where the road ends at the Thomas C. Savage Visitor Center parking lot. The trail begins at the trailhead map between the visitor center and parking lot.

URBAN GROWLER BREWING COMPANY

When co-owners Deb Loch and Jill Pavlak met on a dating site, one of the many things they connected over was an interest in entrepreneurial opportunities. As their romantic connection grew, so did the list of business ideas they talked through. Then, while sipping one of their homebrews, the idea of opening a brewery and restaurant took hold. Deb completed her master's in brewing and started working in the industry while Jill took a job with a restaurant and quickly rose through the ranks to management. They drafted a business plan that won the first runner-up position in a national business plan competition and set out to find a location and secure financing. This is when they hit a snag: Conventional financial institutions wouldn't offer them loans because they didn't trust that two women could succeed with a brewery.

Disheartened but not defeated, Deb and Jill dug in and got creative. They began fundraising and connecting with local investors—regular people from their community—to build the funds they needed to kickstart their venture. It took considerable effort, but they successfully raised $500,000 in under 12 months. Urban Growler Brewing Company opened in 2014, and they've worked hard to craft great beer, delicious food, and a welcoming and inclusive community.

Urban Growler brews their Vanilla Latte Blonde Ale with a special espresso roast from a local coffee shop. They add a dab of lactose for a smooth, creamy flavor with a hint of sweetness like a vanilla latte from your favorite coffee shop.

LAND MANAGER

Fort Snelling State Park
101 Snelling Lake Road
St. Paul, MN 55111
(612) 0279-3550
dnr.state.mn.us/state_parks/park.html?id=spk00154#homepage
files.dnr.state.mn.us/maps/state_parks/spk00154_summer.pdf

BREWERY/RESTAURANT

Urban Growler Brewing Company
2325 Endicott Street
St Paul, MN 55114
(651) 340-5793
urbangrowlerbrewing.com

Distance from trailhead: 9.8 miles

MILL TOWNS STATE TRAIL

A RIVERSIDE STROLL TO A MAGNIFICENT DAM WATERFALL

STARTING POINT	DESTINATION
TWO RIVERS PARK	LAKE BYLLESBY DAM

BREWERY	HIKE TYPE
TILION BREWING COMPANY	MODERATE

DOG FRIENDLY	SEASON
YES (LEASH REQUIRED)	MAY-OCTOBER

FEES	DURATION
NONE	2 HOURS 15 MINUTES

MAP REFERENCE	LENGTH
MILL TOWNS STATE TRAIL	4.6 MILES (ROUND TRIP)

HIGHLIGHTS	ELEVATION GAIN
CANNON RIVER, WATERFALL	104 FEET

7.9%
ALCOHOL CONTENT

PEANUT BUTTER COCOA STOUT WITH DOUBLE MARSHMALLOW

CHOCOLATE BROWN

HOT CHOCOLATE, PEANUT BUTTER

PEANUT BUTTER, CHOCOLATE

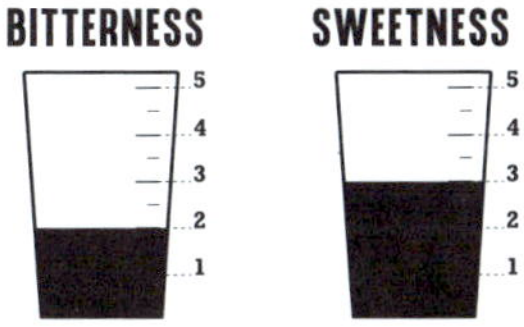

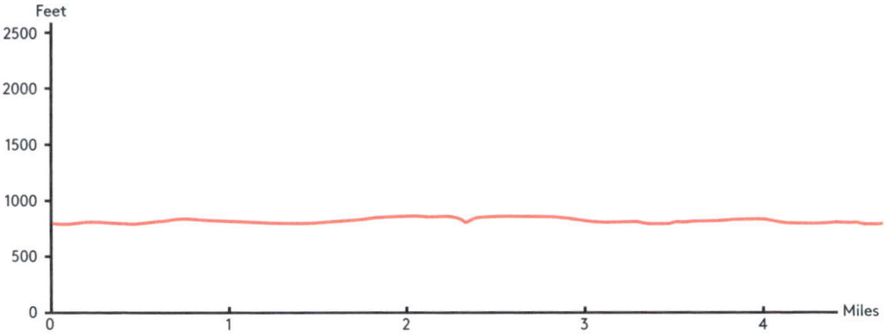

HIKE DESCRIPTION

Venture out to Lake Byllesby Dam on a winding pathway that weaves through parks and forests along the Cannon River. Afterward, make a pitstop at Tilion Brewing Company for a creamy pint of Peanut Butter Cocoa Stout with Double Marshmallow.

The Mill Towns State Trail pays homage to the region's milling history that began in the late 19th century. Flour mills popped up along the Cannon River to take advantage of the power the river could offer. The moving water would spin waterwheels or turbines that in turn spun gears to rotate the millstones that ground grain into flour. A string of these mills stretched down the river from Faribault to Cannon Falls. Sections of this multi-use paved pathway are still in progress, but ultimately, it'll cover 25 miles, passing through the towns of Faribault, Dundas, Northfield, Waterford, Randolph, and Cannon Falls. The western end of the trail connects with the Sakatah Singing Hills State Trail in Faribault and the eastern end links with the Cannon Valley Trail in Cannon Falls.

Your expedition begins at the Cannon Falls Veterans Memorial in Two Rivers Park at the junction of the Cannon River and Little Cannon River. You'll set out toward the Cannon River on a wide paved path. The landscape slopes gently downhill toward the confluence of the rivers, where you'll find a bench to pause and admire the view. When you're ready, you'll continue on, walking with the river on your right and passing under the 5th Street overpass to emerge in Riverside Park. You'll ramble on into a dense mix of trees, with the river to your right and a cliff wall rising to your left.

As you emerge from the trees, you'll see a yellow Mill Towns State Trail sign ahead. You'll leave the river behind and follow the arrow down a short hill into Hannah's Bend Park, a quiet green space tucked into a

bend in the river. Follow the turn-by-turn directions to stick to the trail, or pause here to sit riverside on a beautiful afternoon. Meandering on, you'll pass by the Cannon Valley fairgrounds and a trail parking lot as you sweep around a wetland area and roam along an agricultural field.

About a mile in, you'll briefly dive into another woodland area and emerge alongside the river again. Here, you'll follow the pathway under the Highway 52 overpass and then back into the trees. The landscape continues to fluctuate with a mix of forested patches, farm fields, and prairie until you reach the Lake Byllesby Reservoir and Dam.

The Lake Byllesby Dam is a 60-foot-high hydroelectric dam with a fantastic waterfall flowing over its rim. You'll stroll down a small hill to the bridge extending over the Cannon River, which is also the turnaround point for your adventure. From the bridge, you can see a wonderful view downriver with large trees bordering each side of the water. On the opposite side of the bridge, you'll get a sweeping view of the falls cascading over the dam. Be sure to check out the informational signs along the bridge railings for historical details about the dam and the energy it produces. After exploring the beauty along the bridge, follow your path back to Two Rivers Park to end your quest.

TURN-BY-TURN DIRECTIONS

1. From the parking lot, turn left onto the paved trail as it wraps behind the Veterans Memorial, down the hill, and under the overpass.
2. At 0.3 miles, bear right at the fork to continue on the signposted Mill Towns State Trail. In 150 feet, bear left at the fork to follow the trail marker with the yellow arrow.
3. At 0.5 miles, continue straight, ignoring two unsigned spur trails on the right. In 250 feet, bear left to continue up a small incline and reach the road. Continue straight across the road.
4. At 0.6 miles, continue straight, ignoring a spur trail and parking lot on the left.
5. At 1.1 miles, at the overpass, continue straight to pass under the roadway.
6. At 2.2 miles, continue straight, ignoring an unsigned spur trail on the left.
7. At 2.3 miles, reach the bridge crossing over the Cannon River. Explore the views and informational signs along the bridge, then retrace your path back to Two Rivers Park.

FIND THE TRAILHEAD

From Cannon Falls at 4th Street and Main Street/Colvill Memorial Highway, head north on 4th Street. After 0.3 miles, turn right into the parking lot for the Cannon Falls Veterans Memorial and Two Rivers Park. The trail begins at the far end of the parking lot.

TILION BREWING COMPANY

When co-founders Chris Larson, Ryan Seabright, and Scott Larson started searching for a location for Tilion Brewing Company, Cannon Falls was nowhere on their list of options. They were exploring spots around St. Paul, though without much luck. Then the economic director of Cannon Falls called them up: "Have you ever thought of a smaller market? We're looking to have a brewery in Cannon Falls."

At first, the thought of opening a brewery in a smaller town didn't make sense—why limit their opportunities? But they still went down to Cannon Falls to explore the idea. As they toured a building that interested them, members of the community started showing up, from the mayor and other business owners to people from the city council and chamber of commerce. Chris, Ryan, and Scott knew they would be one of many breweries in St. Paul, but here, they'd be a part of the community. The show of support from the local organizations made the difference, and Tilion Brewing Company opened in Cannon Falls in 2018.

Tilion Brewing Company's Peanut Butter Cocoa Stout with Double Marshmallow delivers flavors reminiscent of a peanut butter hot chocolate with a handful of marshmallows sprinkled on top. It's a smooth, easy-drinking stout with a touch of sweetness that won't overwhelm your tastebuds.

LAND MANAGER

Minnesota Department of Natural Resources
500 Lafayette Road
St. Paul, MN 55155-4040
(888) 646-6367
dnr.state.mn.us/state_trails/mill_towns
files.dnr.state.mn.us/maps/state_trails/mill_towns.pdf

BREWERY/RESTAURANT

Tilion Brewing Company
432 Mill Street W
Cannon Falls, MN 55009
(507) 263-4497
tilionbrewing.com

Distance from trailhead: 0.3 miles

ROOT RIVER STATE TRAIL

EXPLORE THE RIVER ON AN ABANDONED RAILROAD ROUTE

STARTING POINT	DESTINATION
BASS POND	ROOT RIVER BRIDGES

BREWERY	HIKE TYPE
SYLVAN BREWING	MODERATE

DOG FRIENDLY	SEASON
YES (LEASH REQUIRED)	MAY–OCTOBER

FEES	DURATION
NONE	3 HOURS 30 MINUTES

MAP REFERENCE	LENGTH
POSTED AT TRAILHEAD	8.3 MILES (ROUND TRIP)

HIGHLIGHTS	ELEVATION GAIN
RIVER OVERLOOKS, LIMESTONE BLUFFS	55 FEET

7.4%
ALCOHOL CONTENT

GNARLY OLD ALE

WINE RED

RAISINS

DATES, RAISINS

BITTERNESS

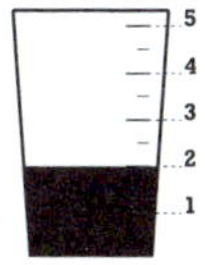

SWEETNESS

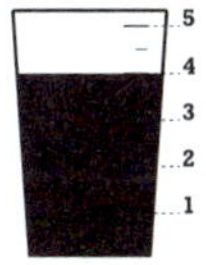

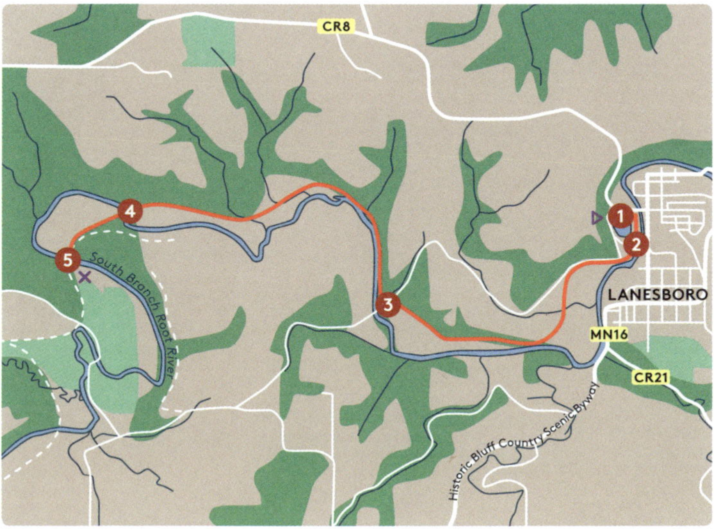

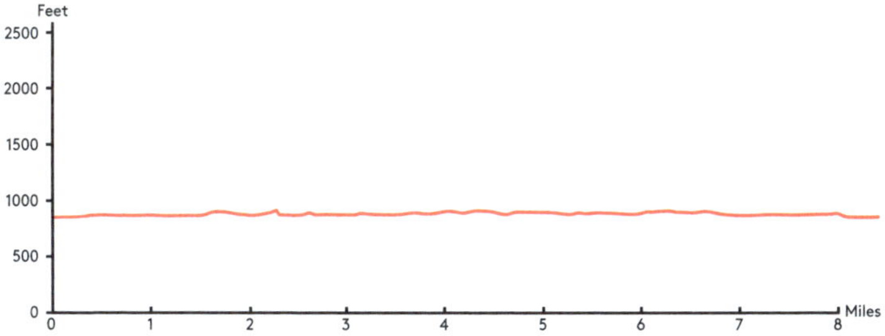

HIKE DESCRIPTION

Venture out to Minnesota's driftless region for a peaceful stroll along the accessible Root River State Trail. After exploring the lush countryside, settle into a seat at Sylvan Brewing for a smooth sip of their Gnarly Old Ale.

The driftless region is an area located around the Mississippi River in southeastern Minnesota, southwestern Wisconsin, and northern Iowa that was not covered by glaciers during the last ice age. While this landscape lacks the deposits, scrapes, and depressions from the most recent ice sheets, the meltwater still etched through the land on its way to the Mississippi River, leaving behind high, flat-topped bluffs. Our route passes through this region on the Root River State Trail, a 42-mile paved trail constructed on an abandoned railroad lane. The multi-use pathway follows the Root River from Fountain to Houston, passing through several more towns along the way and connecting with other state trails.

Your Root River exploration begins in Lanesboro at Bass Pond. You can step onto the dock to check out the lakeside scenery, then take the paved path along the shoreline to connect with the Root River State Trail. As you leave town behind, you'll pass Mill Pond and the waterfall flowing over the Lanesboro Stone Dam. The 220-foot dam, built in 1868, is one of six gravity dams left in the United States. After enjoying the beautiful display, you'll cross through a section of trail bordered on both sides by moss-covered limestone walls.

The landscape opens up as you wander past a series of farm fields sandwiched between you and the river. Sprawling box elder and oak trees flank the trail for most of your journey, along with a scattering

of wildflowers. After crossing a gravel road two miles in, you'll see more of the river as the path swings closer to its bank. While sightings are somewhat rare, you might catch a glimpse of a timber rattlesnake soaking up the warmth of the pavement or curled up on a log or rock along the river.

Over the next mile and a half, you'll pass by two grassy pullouts, each with a picnic table. Take a break to enjoy a snack or admire the view overlooking the Root River. Your next stop is a trailside shelter next to the first of two bridges on this route. The second bridge will be your turnaround point. It's a truss bridge with metal beams forming the support above the walkway. This is a great spot to pose for a fun snapshot of your adventure. Scope out the waterway and look for ducks and geese floating by, then follow your path back to the parking lot at Bass Pond to finish your journey.

TURN-BY-TURN DIRECTIONS

1. From the parking lot, head east on the paved path alongside Bass Pond.
2. At 0.2 miles, at the T-junction, turn right onto the Root River State Trail.
3. At 1.9 miles, continue straight across the gravel road.
4. At 3.7 miles, reach a trailside shelter on the left. Continue straight to cross the bridge over the river.
5. At 4.1 miles, reach a second bridge. Explore the bridge and river views, then retrace your steps back to the parking lot.

FIND THE TRAILHEAD

From Rochester, head south on Highway 52 for 32.0 miles. Turn left onto County Highway 8/County Road 8 and proceed for 8.8 miles. At the Root River State Trail Parking Area sign, turn right onto Mill Pond Road and then turn right again into the parking lot. A trail map is posted at the information kiosk near the parking lot entrance. The trail begins from the paved walkway next to the pond.

SYLVAN BREWING

Owners Karen and Andy Heimdahl opened Sylvan Brewing out of a love for beer and a desire to create a gathering space in their community of Lanesboro. Between Andy's homebrewing experience and their growing collection of growlers from breweries they visited on vacation, the idea of starting their own place hit home. They spent hours crafting business plans at a local coffee shop and checked out plenty of less-than-optimal buildings. They were out on a walk when they realized they wouldn't get many more of these relaxing moments once they opened the brewery. So, they decided to hit pause to reaffirm that starting their own business was right for them.

Not long after, while Andy was visiting a nearby brewery, another customer mentioned to him that they'd heard a new brewery was going to open in Lanesboro. That was exciting news for the community, but Karen and Andy were heartbroken to realize someone else would be making their dreams a reality. That is, until they discovered that the customer had unknowingly been talking about them! This renewed their drive, and when the coffee shop happened to close, they took the leap to purchase and remodel the building.

Sylvan Brewing opened in 2020 with a three-and-a-half barrel brewing system. Gnarly Old Ale brings a sweetness that falls between a standard brown ale and a barley wine—just the right amount to enhance its warm notes of raisins and dates. It's the perfect nightcap of sorts when celebrating an adventure or relaxing by the campfire.

LAND MANAGER

Minnesota Department of Natural Resources
500 Lafayette Road
St. Paul, MN 55155-4040
(888) 646-6367
dnr.state.mn.us/state_trails/root_river
files.dnr.state.mn.us/maps/state_trails/rootriver_harmonypreston.pdf

BREWERY/RESTAURANT

Sylvan Brewing
100 Beacon Street W
Lanesboro, MN 55949
(507) 467-4677
sylvanbeer.com

Distance from trailhead: 0.3 miles

WISCONSIN

CHIPPEWA MORAINE CIRCLE

HIKE ROLLING, FORESTED HILLS TO GLACIAL LAKES

STARTING POINT
INTERPRETIVE CENTER

DESTINATION
SOUTH SHATTUCK LAKE

BREWERY
BLOOMER BREWING COMPANY

HIKE TYPE
MODERATE

DOG FRIENDLY
YES (LEASH REQUIRED)

SEASON
MAY–OCTOBER

FEES
NONE

DURATION
2 HOURS

MAP REFERENCE
POSTED AT TRAILHEAD

LENGTH
4.7 MILES (LOOP)

HIGHLIGHTS
LAKE VIEWS, GLACIAL FEATURES

ELEVATION GAIN
228 FEET

5.2% ALCOHOL CONTENT

OKTOBERFEST LAGER

COPPER

MALTY

MALTY, SWEET

BITTERNESS

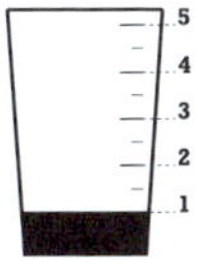

SWEETNESS

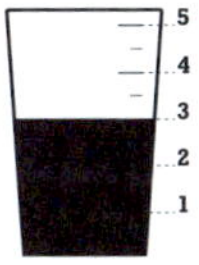

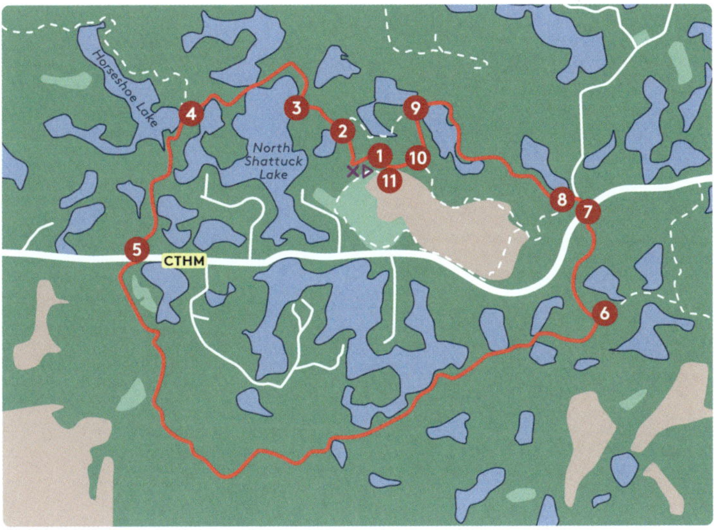

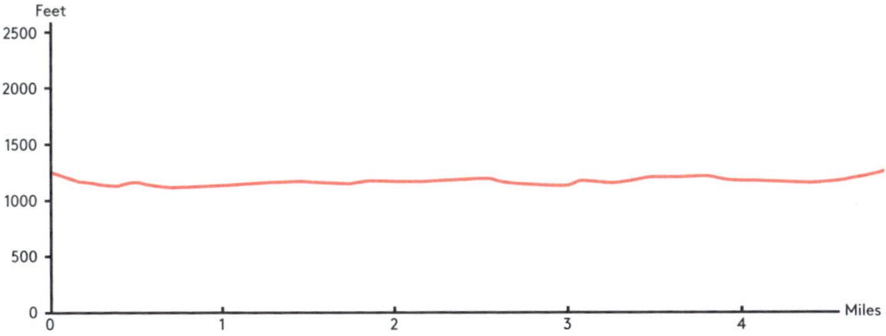

HIKE DESCRIPTION

Embark on a loop across a diverse glacial landscape where you'll see kettle lakes, rolling hills, and a winding esker. Posthike, drive down to Bloomer Brewing for a flight or pint to toast your adventure.

The Chippewa Moraine State Natural Area is a beautiful place to explore a landscape formed by glaciers during the last Ice Age. A moraine is an accumulation of debris (rocks, sand, gravel) left behind from a melting glacier. The Chippewa Moraine formed when a glacier traveled from Canada to just south of today's David R. Obey Ice Age Interpretive Center. Here, the ice had reached far enough south that, between the warmer, southern latitude and the general warming of the Earth's climate, it began melting, leaving behind a 10-mile-wide moraine. The interpretive center offers exhibits and information about the area's geological history and the impact of glaciers if you want to learn more or pick up an interpretive trail map before you head out on your hike.

Our route follows the Chippewa Moraine Circle Trail in a counterclockwise direction, beginning from the interpretive center. The center sits atop a flat, high plain—a buildup of sediments that remained after the glacier melted. From here, you'll walk into the thick forest and descend to several lakes, the biggest of which is North Shattuck Lake. This northern segment of the Circle Trail is also part of the Ice Age Trail (IAT), an extensive route exploring even more of the glacial features across Wisconsin. On the far side of North Shattuck, the IAT veers right, and you'll continue on your loop.

Once you've crossed the highway for the first time, you'll make your way up a gentle incline. This portion of trail runs along the top of an esker, a winding ridge of sand and gravel deposited by a meltwater stream running under a glacier. There's a bench about a mile ahead if you want to take a break to enjoy the tranquil forest or take in the fall colors. As you continue on, the trail passes along the southern end of South Shattuck Lake and then into a section of kettle lakes and rolling hills. Kettle lakes formed when large chunks of ice fell off the glacier and became surrounded by sediment from meltwater streams. As the ice melted away, it left a depression, or kettle. A water-filled kettle is called a kettle lake; the Chippewa Moraine has more than 100 of these lakes dimpling the region.

About three miles in, you'll emerge from the forest to a recently logged section of trail where it's a bit easier to see this rolling terrain amidst fewer trees. You'll cross the highway a second time and then rejoin the IAT as you round back up to the northern half of the circuit. You'll meander through the forest and past a few more small lakes before climbing back up to the trailhead at the top of the high plain.

TURN-BY-TURN DIRECTIONS

1. From the trailhead map, follow the path into the woods. In 50 feet, reach a T-junction. Turn left onto the signposted Circle Trail/IAT.
2. At 0.2 miles, bear left at the fork to continue on the signposted Circle Trail/IAT.
3. At 0.4 miles, reach a T-junction. Turn right to continue on the signposted Circle Trail/IAT.
4. At 0.9 miles, reach a fork and a trail map. Bear left, diverging from the IAT and continuing on the signposted Circle Trail.
5. At 1.3 miles, reach a parking area. Continue straight, keeping right of the "Parking" sign. In 50 feet, continue down the short embankment and cross the paved road.
6. At 3.4 miles, reach a junction with a bench and a trail map. Turn left to continue on the signposted Circle Trail and rejoin the IAT.
7. At 3.8 miles, cross a paved road. In 180 feet, reach a junction and turn left to continue on the signposted Circle Trail/IAT.
8. At 3.9 miles, continue straight on the signposted Circle Trail/IAT, ignoring a trail spur on the left.
9. At 4.5 miles, reach a fork and keep left to continue on the signposted Circle Trail/IAT.
10. At 4.6 miles, reach a T-junction. Turn right to continue on the signposted Circle Trail/IAT.
11. At 4.7 miles, reach the T-junction from Step 1. Turn left to return to the trailhead.

FIND THE TRAILHEAD

From Bloomer at Main Street and 17th Avenue, head north on Main Street/WI-40. After 1.4 miles, continue straight onto County Hwy F. After 7.4 miles, turn right onto County Hwy M. After 3.4 miles, turn left at the sign for Chippewa Moraine Ice Age Unit. After 0.3 miles, the road ends at the David R. Obey Ice Age Interpretive Center and trailhead parking lot. The trail begins at the map near the woods to the right of the interpretive center.

BLOOMER BREWING COMPANY

Ryan Stolt started brewing with a home kit, as many brewery owners do. However, it was his dad, Dan Stolt, who first took the leap into making beer as a business after learning about brewing from Ryan. Dan opened Bloomer Brewing in 2013, and Ryan took over in 2018 to work alongside his dad.

One of Ryan's favorite parts about having the brewery, aside from it being a family-run business, is getting to know the range of folks who stop by, from their tried-and-true regulars to anyone visiting the area or passing through. The brewery even serves as a host for an RV camping program, so travelers can book a site and stay at the brewery.

Bloomer's Oktoberfest, a tribute to the traditional fall brew, is a smooth, malty lager with a touch of sweetness.

LAND MANAGER

Wisconsin Department of Natural Resources
101 S. Webster Street PO Box 7921
Madison, WI 53707
(715) 967-2800
dnr.wisconsin.gov/topic/parks/chipmoraine
dnr.wisconsin.gov/topic/parks/chipmoraine/maps

BREWERY/RESTAURANT

Bloomer Brewing Company
1103 9th Avenue
Bloomer, WI 54724
(715) 933-4995
bloomerbrewingco.com

Distance from trailhead: 12.7 miles

SANDROCK CLIFFS

A RIVERSIDE JOURNEY TO GLACIER-CARVED CLIFFS

STARTING POINT	DESTINATION
SANDROCK CLIFFS TRAILHEAD	SANDSTONE CLIFFS
BREWERY	**HIKE TYPE**
BRICKFIELD BREWING	EASY
DOG FRIENDLY	**SEASON**
YES (LEASH REQUIRED)	APRIL–OCTOBER
FEES	**DURATION**
NONE	1 HOUR
MAP REFERENCE	**LENGTH**
POSTED AT TRAILHEAD	2.8 MILES (LOOP)
HIGHLIGHTS	**ELEVATION GAIN**
ST. CROIX RIVER, SANDSTONE CLIFFS	85 FEET

5.8%
ALCOHOL CONTENT

FEELIN' YOUR OATS IPA

GOLDEN

TROPICAL, PINE

PASSIONFRUIT, PEACH

BITTERNESS

SWEETNESS

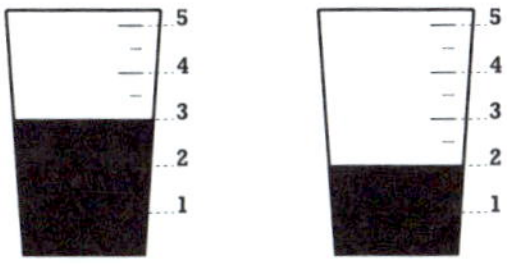

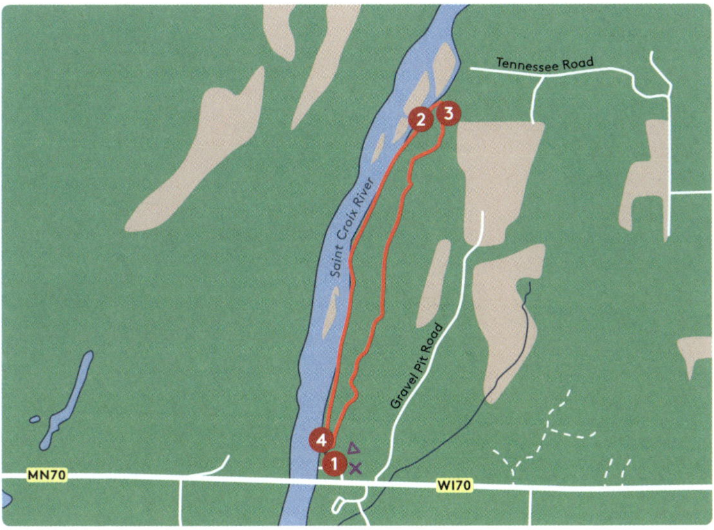

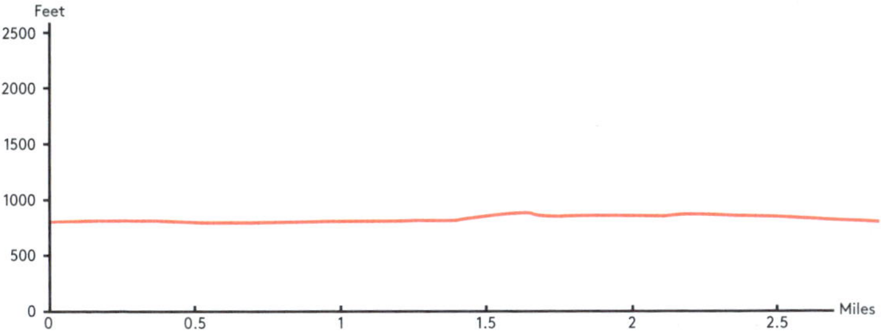

HIKE DESCRIPTION

Wander beneath towering pines along the scenic St. Croix River. Marvel at the immense sandstone walls bordering the waterway, then head to Brickfield Brewing for a fruity pour of Feelin' Your Oats IPA.

The St. Croix National Scenic Riverway protects 252 miles of waterway from the headwaters of the Namekagon and St. Croix Rivers to their confluence, and then further south to Prescott, Wisconsin. This riverway was one of the first eight protected under the 1968 Wild and Scenic Rivers Act, which preserves especially remarkable rivers as free-flowing, without human interference. The river's protection extends to sprawling forests and wetlands along both banks. While the river attracts boaters and anglers, the forested corridors draw campers and hikers.

You'll begin your adventure on a wide, dirt trail carpeted in pine needles. For most of the route, the path remains flat and clear of tripping hazards—a perfect setting for peaceful solitude. Sunbeams filter through the trees as you pass through groves of white pine, with trillium blooming in spring and pops of colorful foliage in the fall. To your right, a dense forest borders the trail, while to your left, the St. Croix River shimmers just beyond a more open stretch of trees.

A little over a mile into your journey, you'll reach a large "Warning: Cliff Area" sign at the top of a series of sandstone cliffs. Stately white pines dot the clifftop where you can take in views of the St. Croix River. Along the eastern riverbank, several islands break up the current, formed over time as the river carved channels through the softer terrain.

Millions of years ago, a sea covered this area. As the water warmed and evaporated, it left behind layers of sand deposits that compressed into rock. Much later—about 11,000 years ago—rushing meltwater from glaciers sluiced through the St. Croix Valley, eroding the landscape and leaving behind the grand cliffs beneath your feet.

When you're ready to move on, you'll continue past a small campground and a couple of short trail loops. You'll journey up a small hill and hike along the top of a ridge. Along the ridgeline, you'll leave behind the spacious pines for a thick, mixed forest and a soft, grassy footpath. This section of the adventure sets you up to notice the smaller details of the forest. Look for wildlife, delicate mushrooms, and a tree with a beach ball–sized burl. Burls are rounded growths on tree trunks resulting from injury or infection, such as insect activity, a fungal infection, or even a virus. On large trees, these bulging growths can reach several feet wide. While burls might look rough on the outside, the inner wood grain is often in a beautiful swirled or scalloped pattern.

For the last half mile of your woodsy wandering, you'll gradually descend from the ridge. Enjoy the final stretch of nature's beauty before reaching the trailhead, where glimpses of the magnificent St. Croix reappear just beyond the pines.

TURN-BY-TURN DIRECTIONS

1. From the trailhead map, follow the dirt path into the forest. In 120 feet, keep left at the fork.
2. At 1.3 miles, keep left at the fork. In 400 feet, reach a "Warning: Cliff Area" sign. Explore along the clifftop, then keep right on the path, ignoring an unmarked trail spur on the left.
3. At 1.4 miles, keep right, ignoring a trail spur on the left.
4. At 2.8 miles, reach the fork from Step 1. Keep left to return to the trailhead.

FIND THE TRAILHEAD

From Grantsburg at Pine Street and Wisconsin Avenue, head south on Pine Street. After 0.2 miles, turn right onto WI-70 and proceed for 4.6 miles. At the sign for Highway 70 Landing, turn right. After 400 feet, turn right again to continue into the paved parking lot. There's a bathroom near the parking lot entrance, and the trail begins next to the map at the opposite end.

BRICKFIELD BREWING

When owners Nicki and Ben Peterson first scoped out the building that would become Brickfield Brewing, they were searching for a space to renovate for Nicki's marketing business. She launched the Grantsburg Revitalization Operation to help reinvigorate the town, so updating a downtown Grantsburg building for her business made sense. However, this building had more character and history than they expected, and it deserved to be more than just an office space. That's when they got the idea to open a brewery. They loved visiting breweries and exploring towns off the main track, so why not create that same opportunity in their own town?

Nicki and Ben opened Brickfield Brewing in 2018, and since then, 15 new businesses have started in downtown Grantsburg. Nicki loves that they've not only created a delicious product and a family-friendly space, but also helped invigorate the economy in their local community.

Brickfield Brewing uses a 15-barrel system, plus a 1-barrel system for experimental recipes and taproom-only specials. Feelin' Your Oats IPA, a West Coast–style IPA, delivers a refreshing tropical taste with notes of tangerine, peach, and passionfruit.

LAND MANAGER

St. Croix National Scenic Riverway
401 N. Hamilton Street
Saint Croix Falls, WI 54024
(715) 483-2274
nps.gov/sacn
nps.gov/sacn/planyourvisit/hiking.htm

BREWERY/RESTAURANT

Brickfield Brewing
130 W Olson Drive
Grantsburg, WI 54840
(715) 463-1900
brickfieldbrewing.com

Distance from trailhead: 4.8 miles

MAKWA ZIIBIINS MIIKANA

HIKE THIS WOODSY TRAIL TO A LAKE SUPERIOR BEACH

STARTING POINT	DESTINATION
BEAR CREEK PARK	WISCONSIN POINT
BREWERY	**HIKE TYPE**
EARTH RIDER BREWERY	MODERATE
DOG FRIENDLY	**SEASON**
YES (LEASH REQUIRED)	YEAR-ROUND
FEES	**DURATION**
NONE	2 HOURS 45 MINUTES
MAP REFERENCE	**LENGTH**
MAKWA ZIIBIINS MIIKANA	6.4 MILES (ROUND TRIP)
HIGHLIGHTS	**ELEVATION GAIN**
RIVER VIEWS, LAKE SUPERIOR	110 FEET

5.0% ALCOHOL CONTENT

TAP SHACK CARIBBEAN-STYLE LAGER

LIGHT GOLDEN SUN

FRESH, LIME

LIME ZEST

BITTERNESS

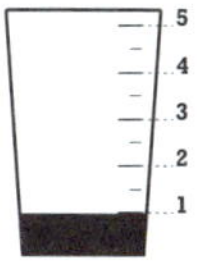

SWEETNESS

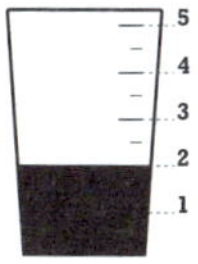

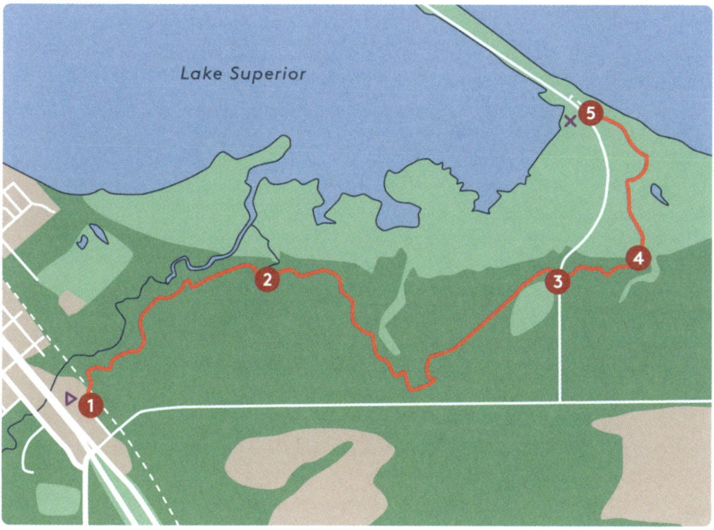

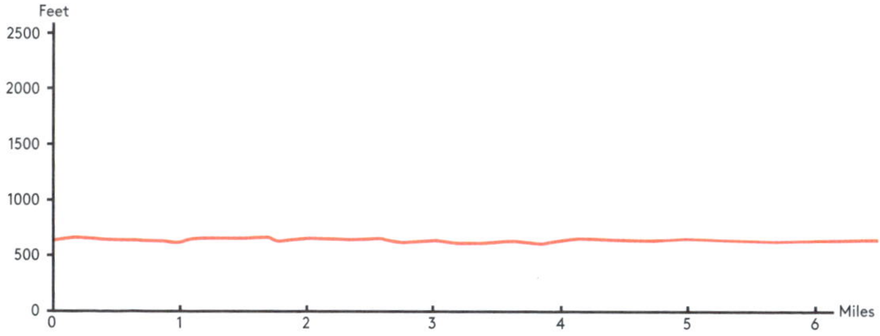

HIKE DESCRIPTION

Meander through the forest and over rivers and marshland to one of Lake Superior's beaches on Wisconsin Point. After enjoying the beach, Earth Rider's Caribbean-style lager, Tap Shack, is the perfect way to round out your adventure.

Lake Superior is the biggest of the five Great Lakes (Superior, Michigan, Huron, Erie, and Ontario) and one of the world's largest freshwater lakes. It holds about 10% of the planet's freshwater. The Ojibwe people refer to the lake as gichigami (great sea).

Your destination, Wisconsin Point, sits at the western end of Lake Superior. Together, Wisconsin Point and Minnesota Point make up one of the largest freshwater sandbars. The points protect the Superior and Duluth harbors and create the Allouez and Superior Bays, respectively. While the turnaround for our route is at the base of Wisconsin Point, you can explore further if you have time; there's over two miles of beach including a stand of old-growth pine trees, a sacred Chippewa burial ground, and the Superior entry lighthouse.

Your hike begins at Bear Creek Park and winds through the woods near Bear Creek and Allouez Bay. Throughout spring and summer, wildflowers and wild raspberries border the trail. You'll cross more than 40 sequentially numbered boardwalks and bridges, from the park to the beach.

About two and a half miles into your hike, you'll reach a floating boardwalk. This boardwalk traverses over a marsh, bringing you from the woods to a grassy field. Poles secure the boardwalk in the marsh, but the walkway can rise and fall with the water level. It may move like gentle waves as you walk across, so take your time if too much movement makes you uneasy.

Back on solid ground, you'll meander up a hill through the field toward a gazebo at the top. Enjoy the view from the gazebo, then continue down to the beach. Sit back and take it all in or explore along the beach for interesting pieces of driftwood and rocks—agates are a popular find along Lake Superior thanks to former volcanic and glacial activity in the area. Once you've soaked up all that this beach has to offer, follow the same path back to the park.

TURN-BY-TURN DIRECTIONS

1. From the parking lot, follow the signposted Makwa Ziibiins Miikana (Bear Creek Trail). In 200 feet, continue straight across a paved trail.
2. At 0.9 miles, cross the #13 bridge over a small river.
3. At 2.2 miles, continue straight across Wisconsin Point Road.
4. At 2.6 miles, reach the floating boardwalk and cross the marsh.
5. At 3.2 miles, reach bathrooms and parking along Wisconsin Point Road. Bear right to continue to the beach along Lake Superior. Return the way you came.

FIND THE TRAILHEAD

From central Superior at Tower Avenue, head east on US-2/Belknap Street. After 1.7 miles, turn right onto US-52 S/E 2nd Street. After 4.8 miles, turn left onto Moccasin Mike Road. After 400 feet, turn left onto E Itasca Street. After another 400 feet, the road ends at the Bear Creek Park parking lot. The trail begins at the end of the parking lot.

EARTH RIDER BREWERY

Earth Rider Brewery is a blend of histories that came together through the vision of founder Tim Nelson. Tim started working in the beer industry in his twenties, co-founded a brewery, and then branched out on his own to start Earth Rider in 2017. The Earth Rider brewing facilities live in a building that started as a bakery in the 1880s and then transitioned to a beer wholesaler post-prohibition. Right next door sits Earth Rider's Cedar Lounge taproom, which used to be a tied-house tavern in the early 1900s. Being a tied house meant the tavern had to buy beer from a specific producer, whereas free houses could purchase their products from anyone. Northern Brewing Company controlled the beer at Cedar Lounge until they ceased operations in 1967. Fifty years later, Earth Rider opened and became the first beer producer in Superior since that time.

Earth Rider Brewery works hard to contribute to the local community and stands out as a source of live music. They host bands each week and bring in bigger acts to their outdoor area. They even rent out the living space above the taproom for anyone who wants more than a one-day adventure in the Superior area.

Earth Rider's award-winning beer ranges from their Duluth Coffee Pale Ale to their North Tower Stout. The featured brew, Tap Shack Caribbean-style Lager, is a bright, crisp drink with a touch of lime zest. Tap Shack is one of four flagship beers that also include North Tower, Superior Pale Ale, and Caribou Lake India Pale Ale.

LAND MANAGER

City of Superior
1316 N. 14th Street
Superior, WI 54880
(715) 395-7200
superiorwi.gov
superiorwi.gov/DocumentCenter/View/14434/Makwa-Ziibiins-Miika-na-Map-2023?bidId=

BREWERY/RESTAURANT

Earth Rider Brewery – Cedar Lounge Taproom
1715 N 3rd Street
Superior, WI 54880
(715) 394-7391
earthrider.beer

Distance from trailhead: 7 miles

LAKESHORE TRAIL

A MEDLEY OF SEA CAVES, CLIFFS, AND CREVASSES

STARTING POINT	DESTINATION
LAKESHORE TRAILHEAD	LUNCH BEACH

BREWERY	HIKE TYPE
ADVENTURE CLUB BREWING	STRENUOUS

DOG FRIENDLY	SEASON
YES (LEASH REQUIRED)	MAY–OCTOBER

FEES	DURATION
YES	4 HOURS 45 MINUTES

MAP REFERENCE	LENGTH
POSTED AT TRAILHEAD	9.5 MILES (ROUND TRIP)

HIGHLIGHTS	ELEVATION GAIN
SEA CAVES, MEYERS BEACH	112 FEET

5.7%
ALCOHOL CONTENT

APOSTLE BEAR BROWN PORTER

DARK BROWN

MALT

SMOOTH, ROASTY

BITTERNESS

SWEETNESS

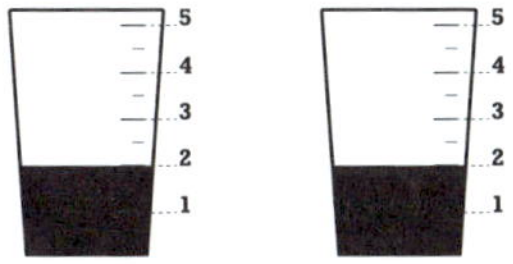

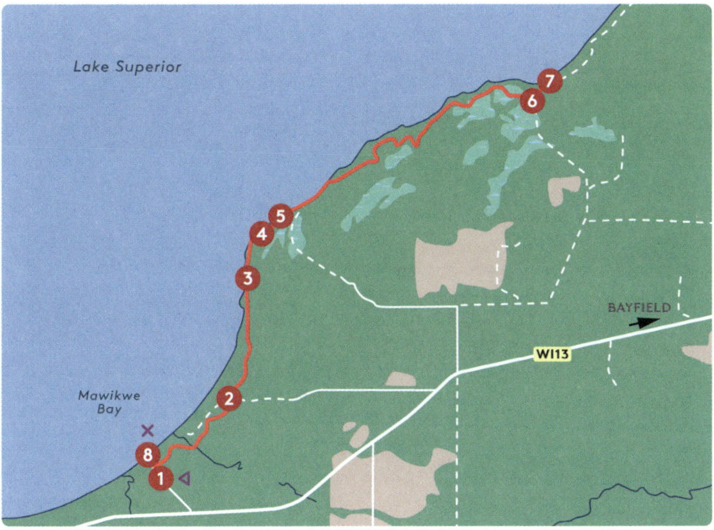

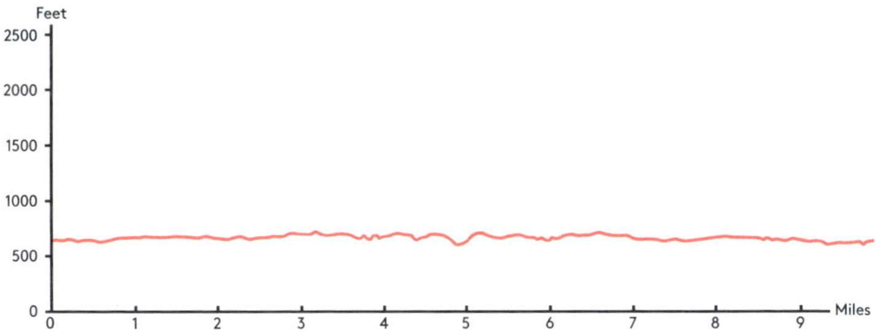

HIKE DESCRIPTION

Navigate Bayfield Peninsula's lush forests as you trek along lakeshore cliffs in search of sea caves, sandy beaches, and a crevasse. Celebrate your discoveries with a flight or cold pint of craft beer at Adventure Club Brewing.

The Apostle Islands might sound like the name of a tropical getaway, but this chain of sandstone formations sits just off the northern tip of Wisconsin's Bayfield Peninsula in the chilly waters of Lake Superior. The Apostle Islands National Lakeshore, part of the Ojibwe people's ancestral homeland, protects 21 islands and 12 miles of Lake Superior's shoreline. The islands and lakeshore are well-known for the sea caves, arches, and pillars formed in the red sandstone cliffs.

Your expedition begins at the Meyers Beach ranger station on the western end of the Apostle Islands National Lakeshore. You'll dive into the thick forest on a two-plank wooden walkway that lifts you above the forest floor's damp, fragile ecosystem for the first three-quarters of a mile. At its end, you'll step off at a trail junction where campers can access two of the three hike-in campsites. From here, you'll continue on a primarily dirt path, trekking up and down ravines and crossing bridges over lively streams.

The fluorescent-orange emergency life ring (in case someone falls in the lake) will likely be the first thing you spot as you approach the crevasse nearly two miles into your jaunt. You'll step into a grove of lofty pines where the forest understory opens to reveal the cliff edge overlooking Lake Superior to your left. Ahead of you, just beyond the buoy, the crevasse cuts deep into the earth. As waves wore away the sandstone and undercut the cliff, some of the rocks gave way within, leaving a narrow, jagged cut. If you're brave enough to peer into the opening from a safe distance, you can see the waves crashing into the rock far below your feet.

You'll continue along the rooted path until you reach an overlook along the clifftop where the trees open up to a view of the Bowl, a massive cutout in the shoreline. Look up the shoreline to spot sea caves etched into the cliff face just above the water's edge. If the water is active, you'll hear the thundering booms of the waves crashing into the hollowed-out spaces. You can take advantage of the bench here or at the opposite end of the Bowl to relax, enjoy a snack, and take in the roar of the waves echoing off the walls of the surrounding cliffs.

From the Bowl, you'll briefly continue along the cliff top before diving deeper into the trees. You'll traverse several ravines and a few seasonal streams until you reach the dead end of a forest road at four and a half miles. You'll follow the signs featuring a hiker to stay on track, and then, at the fork with a campsite sign, you'll head toward the lake to make your way down to Lunch Beach. Explore the washed-up driftwood and have a bite to eat, as the name suggests, then work your way back to the trailhead. Ditch your backpack at your vehicle if you need a break, then head down the staircase next to the ranger station to reach Meyers Beach. Dip your toes in the water, soak up some sun, and admire the beauty of Lake Superior to wind down your adventure.

TURN-BY-TURN DIRECTIONS

1. From the trailhead map, follow the signposted Lakeshore Trail into the forest.
2. At 0.8 miles, continue straight through a junction to stay on the signposted Lakeshore Trail
3. At 1.7 miles, reach the crevasse. Explore the cliff top, then continue on the main trail.
4. At 2.1 miles, reach a bench with a view overlooking the Bowl. Admire the cliff and sea-cave views, then continue on the trail.
5. At 2.2 miles, reach another bench on the other side of the Bowl. Take in the view, then continue on the trail.
6. At 4.5 miles, turn left at a T-junction to follow the hiker sign.
7. At 4.6 miles, at the fork with the campsite trail marker, bear left onto the trail heading toward Lake Superior. In 200 feet, you'll reach Lunch Beach. Take your time here, then retrace your steps back to the trailhead.
8. At 9.3 miles, reach the trailhead and bear right toward the ranger station. In 250 feet, head down the stairs to access Meyers Beach. Enjoy Lake Superior, then return to the trailhead and parking lot to complete your trip.

FIND THE TRAILHEAD

From Bayfield at the intersection of Rittenhouse Avenue and 3rd Street, head west on Rittenhouse Avenue for 0.2 miles. Turn left onto 1st Street and continue straight on State Highway 13. After 16.9 miles, at the "Apostle Islands Nat'l Lakeshore/Meyers Beach" sign, turn right onto Meyers Road. The road dead-ends in 0.3 miles at the Meyers Beach parking area. The trail begins at the trail map on the right side of the parking lot.

ADVENTURE CLUB BREWING

When brewmaster Matthew Gerdts first heard about the idea for a Bayfield brewery from his aunt and uncle, he thought they just wanted help with the design and build. They were moving their business, Howl Bike Shop (now Howl Adventure Center), and wanted to include a brewery in the same building. As Matthew realized they meant for him to run the brewery, he hesitated—he already had a great job at a brewery in another city.

Still, his aunt and uncle encouraged him to return to Bayfield for a visit (he'd once lived with them). They took him out sailing and mountain biking to remind him of all that the area has to offer. Matthew loved the adventure opportunities, but it was the location for the bike shop and brewery that sealed the deal. Set just on the edge of town, the building overlooks a small field and is perfectly positioned to connect with the local trails.

Adventure Club Brewing opened in 2019 and operates on a two-barrel system. Apostle Bear is a dark and toasty brown porter with a hint of caramel. This surprisingly refreshing brew goes down easy with a creamy mouthfeel.

LAND MANAGER

Apostle Islands National Lakeshore
415 Washington Ave
Bayfield, WI 54814
(715) 779-3397
nps.gov/apis
nps.gov/apis/planyourvisit/maps.htm

BREWERY/RESTAURANT

Adventure Club Brewing
35265 S County Hwy J
Bayfield, WI 54814
adventureclubbrewing.com

Distance from trailhead: 15.5 miles

NORTH LAKELAND

ROAM GENTLE TERRAIN ALONG LUSH LAKES AND WETLANDS

STARTING POINT	DESTINATION
DISCOVERY CENTER TRAILHEAD	BOG BOARDWALK
BREWERY	**HIKE TYPE**
SOME NERVE BREWING COMPANY	MODERATE
DOG FRIENDLY	**SEASON**
YES (LEASH REQUIRED)	MAY–OCTOBER
FEES	**DURATION**
NONE	2 HOURS
MAP REFERENCE	**LENGTH**
POSTED AT TRAILHEAD	3.9 MILES (LOOP)
HIGHLIGHTS	**ELEVATION GAIN**
STATEHOUSE LAKE, BOG BOARDWALK	46 FEET

5.4%
ALCOHOL CONTENT

MR. FRIENDLY OATMEAL CREAM ALE

LIGHT ORANGE

ORANGE, VANILLA

DREAMSICLE

BITTERNESS

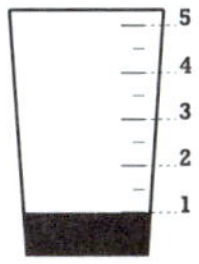

SWEETNESS

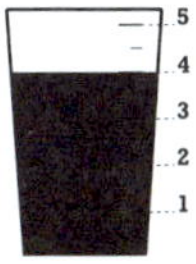

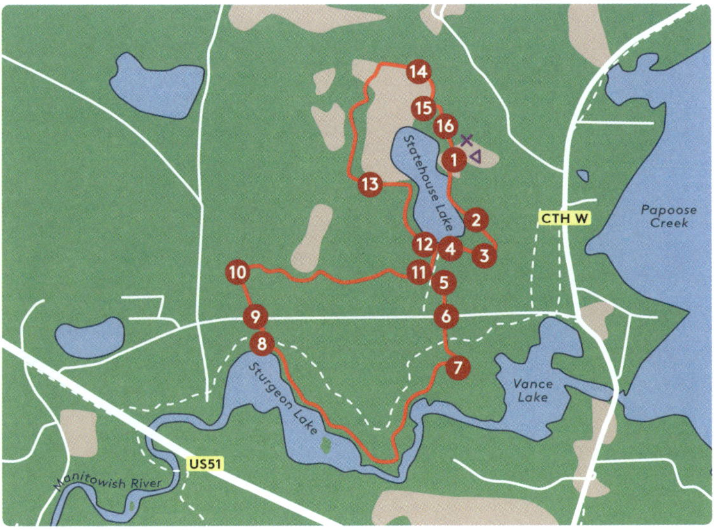

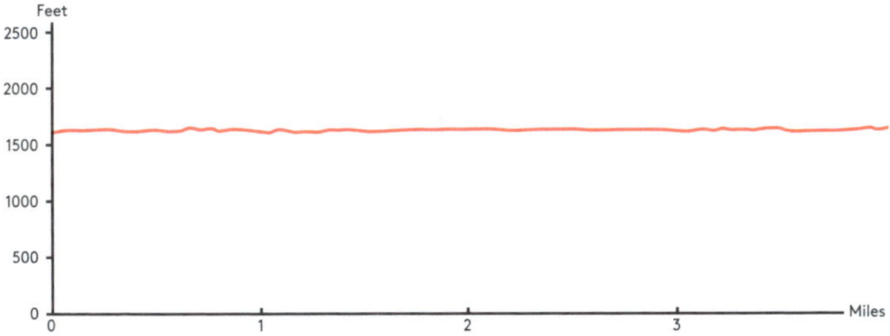

HIKE DESCRIPTION

Explore a variety of habitats as you wander under stately pines, along sparkling lakes, and into a secluded bog. Toast your adventure at Some Nerve Brewing Company with a fresh pour of their oatmeal cream ale, Mr. Friendly.

In 1995, a group of community leaders came together to revitalize a youth conservation corps property at Statehouse Lake in Manitowish Waters. They transformed the space and created the North Lakeland Discovery Center, a non-profit organization focused on building connections between people and nature to support the conservation of Wisconsin's Northwoods. The center provides environmental education programs, conducts research projects, and offers outdoor activities such as hiking or snowshoeing on the 12-mile trail system.

Your expedition begins with a short stroll through the forest to Statehouse Lake. You'll emerge from the trees near the boathouse and dock with a stunning view across the water. Pines line the lakeshore, lily pads

dot the shallows, and the deep blue water reflects a pristine image on a calm day. Soak up this scene as you wander along a short stretch of shoreline before diving back into the woods on a wide dirt path.

While you're ultimately making a loop around the Statehouse Lake, your journey includes a side trip to the Big River Trail. You'll follow the dark-blue trail markers on a lollipop loop lacing through thick patches of ferns, over boggy ground covered in moss, and under stands of tall, majestic pines. The far side of the circuit winds along the Manitowish River and Sturgeon Lake, a sprawling body of water bulging out from the river. This waterway, as the lake's name may imply, is home to lake sturgeon, a massive fish often growing 4–6 feet in length and living for 50–100 years. If you're lucky, you might spot one of these giants leaping out of the water. Scientists believe the leaps to be a way to communicate with other sturgeon and take in air to regulate their buoyancy.

Back at Statehouse Lake, you'll continue on the Bog Boardwalk Trail, which has light-blue trail markers. This path swings wide around the northern half of the lake, where you'll be immersed in the neighboring bog and marsh ecosystems. You'll stay high and dry on the wooden boardwalk while meandering over waterlogged terrain thick with reeds, shrubs, and tamarack trees. From here, the last half mile of your exploration brings you back under the cover of pines for a shaded and peaceful close to your tour around Statehouse Lake.

TURN-BY-TURN DIRECTIONS

1. From the trailhead kiosk, follow the trail heading southwest from the office down a gentle hill toward Statehouse Lake.
2. At 0.2 miles, bear right at the fork and trail map to follow the dark-blue marker for the Big River Trail. In 150 feet, keep left to remain on the Big River Trail.
3. At 0.3 miles, at the map, keep left again to stay on the dark-blue Big River Trail.
4. At 0.5 miles, turn left at the junction and map on the Big River Trail.
5. At 0.6 miles, turn left at the map to begin a loop on the Big River Trail.
6. At 0.7 miles, continue straight across the paved road. In 300 feet, cross the paved pathway.
7. At 0.9 miles, bear right at the fork, following a dark-blue arrow.
8. At 1.8 miles, continue straight across the paved pathway. In 180 feet, reach a small paved parking lot and reconnect with the trail diagonally across the lot at the map kiosk.
9. At 1.9 miles, continue straight across the paved road.
10. At 2.0 miles, turn right at the map to continue on the Big River Trail.
11. At 2.6 miles, reach the map from Step 5, closing the loop. Turn left to return to the junction and map from Step 4.
12. At 2.7 miles, reach the map from Step 4. Turn left, leaving the Big River Trail and following the light-blue Bog Boardwalk Trail.
13. At 3.0 miles, keep right at the map to continue on the Bog Boardwalk Trail.
14. At 3.6 miles, continue straight at the map to remain on the Bog Boardwalk Trail.
15. At 3.7 miles, bear left to keep following the light-blue markers for the Bog Boardwalk Trail.
16. At 3.8 miles, continue straight across a gravel road. In 250 feet, reach the discovery center and continue straight to return to the trailhead and parking lot.

FIND THE TRAILHEAD

From Woodruff at US-51/Elm Street and WI-47/1st Avenue, head north on US-51/Elm Street for 21.3 miles. Turn right onto County Highway W and proceed for 1.2 miles. At the North Lakeland Discovery Center sign, turn right onto Discovery Lane. After 0.2 miles, the road ends at the circular driveway and parking lot for the North Lakeland Discovery Center. The trail begins from the trailhead kiosk at the main office building.

SOME NERVE BREWING COMPANY

Owners Jessica and Bill Reuf were exploring a bookstore when they came across *Wisconsin's Best Beer Guide* with the slogan: "Buy this book for free beer!" Of course, as beer lovers, they purchased the book and started visiting breweries. After a few tours, Jessica was inspired to start homebrewing, and soon they were brewing their own beer every weekend. Jessica and Bill had previously considered moving from New Glarus to northern Wisconsin to open a bar. However, as their passion for brewing grew, that idea transitioned to opening a brewery. When an opportunity arose for Bill to sell his business, they made the leap.

Some Nerve Brewing Company opened in 2018. Just as Jessica and Bill were inspired by the brewers who shared their beer-making process with them, they love talking with customers about beer and what it takes to brew. The couple thrives on the creativity that springs from brewing and sharing that craft at the brewery.

Some Nerve Brewing Company's Mr. Friendly is an oatmeal, orange, and vanilla cream ale. It's a sweet treat that brings tropical vibes to Wisconsin's Northwoods.

LAND MANAGER

North Lakeland Discovery Center
14006 Discovery Lane
Manitowish Waters, WI 54545
(715) 543-2085
https://www.discoverycenter.net/
irp.cdn-website.com/da9800db/files/uploaded/NLDC.trail.map.2024.pdf

BREWERY/RESTAURANT

Some Nerve Brewing Company
5586 US-51
Manitowish Waters, WI 54545
(608) 576-6040
somenervebrewingcompany.com

Distance from trailhead: 4.0 miles

CATHERINE WOLTER WILDERNESS AREA

EXPLORE THE UNDEVELOPED LAKES OF A QUIET PRESERVE

PRESQUE ISLE, WI

STARTING POINT	DESTINATION
CATHERINE WOLTER TRAILHEAD	CANTEEN LAKE
BREWERY	**HIKE TYPE**
FIVE SONS BREWING	MODERATE
DOG FRIENDLY	**SEASON**
YES (LEASH REQUIRED)	JUNE–OCTOBER
FEES	**DURATION**
NONE	2 HOURS
MAP REFERENCE	**LENGTH**
POSTED AT TRAILHEAD	5.3 MILES (LOOP)
HIGHLIGHTS	**ELEVATION GAIN**
WILDERNESS LAKES, FALL COLORS	100 FEET

5.4%
ALCOHOL CONTENT

QUAIL'S IRISH RED

RED

MALTY

MALT FORWARD, SWEET

BITTERNESS **SWEETNESS**

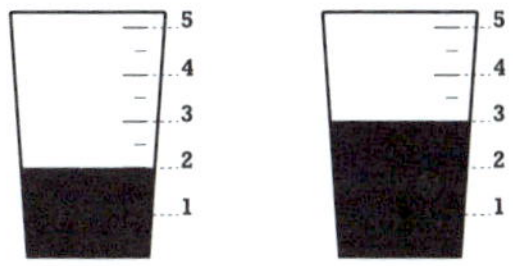

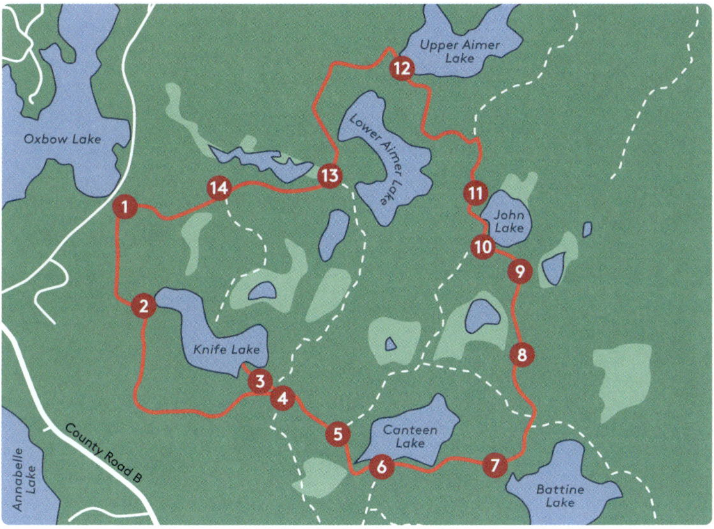

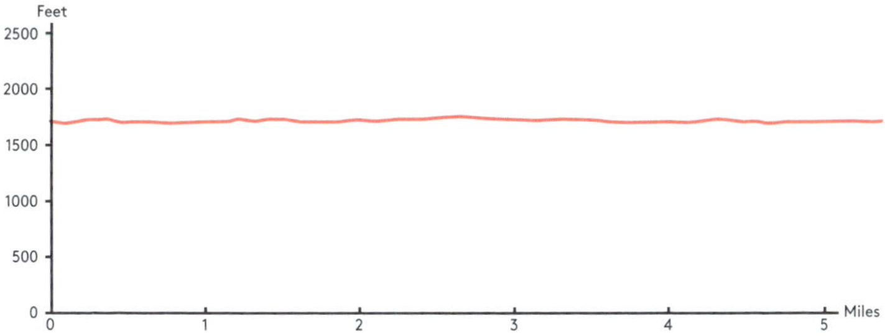

HIKE DESCRIPTION

Stroll through a peaceful nature preserve to enjoy a large assortment of pristine lake views. Post-adventure, cruise up to Marenisco for a fresh pint of beer at Five Sons Brewing.

The Catherine Wolter Wilderness Area originated in 2000 when The Nature Conservancy purchased a section of land from Mrs. Catherine Wolter. Today, the preserve protects more than 2,600 acres. Fifteen lakes and ponds dot the property, almost half of which you'll get to see during this hike. The Conservancy's goal in preserving these forests and wetlands is to protect water quality, stop the spread of invasive species, and save the land from development.

This wilderness area is a part of the Border Lakes Area, 24,000 acres of protected space along the Wisconsin-Michigan border. Border Lakes connects Wisconsin's Northern Highland–American Legion State Forest and Michigan's Ottawa National Forest, creating an extensive travel corridor for Northwoods animals such as moose, wolves, bears, and lynx.

Two partially overlapping loop trails circle through the Catherine Wolter Wilderness Area: the Yellow Loop and the Green Loop. Both trails start on the same path, but the Green Loop continues farther out before reconnecting with the Yellow Loop as you close the circle. Our route follows the Green Loop, which is just over five miles if you stop to check out each of the lakes you'll pass. Most trail junctions have a map and trail markers (yellow and green arrows) to aid navigation as you encounter secondary trails throughout the forest. Your trail through the preserve is a wide, mowed grass path that's easy to follow. It's a dog-friendly route if you want to bring your pup—just be sure to leash them from April 1 to August 1 to protect ground-nesting birds.

From the trailhead, you'll reach a spur for the first lake, Knife Lake, in less than a half mile. This lake is L-shaped; here, you're at the top, and you'll get to see it from the lower portion at the next spur. Between these first two spurs is a short section of trail that gets soggy after a significantly rainy spring due to lake overflow. Consider wearing water-resistant footwear and be prepared to step across a few strategically placed logs and rocks.

After the second spur for Knife Lake, the yellow and green routes split from each other. While the yellow route bears left for a shorter loop back to the trailhead, you'll continue on the Green Loop to go further into the wilderness area. From here, you'll wander over a few gentle hills and pass six additional lakes: Canteen, Battine, Bug, John, Upper Aimer, and Lower Aimer. Canteen Lake is the only one with a sign, but the maps posted along the trail include lake names, so it's easy to track which lake you're approaching. These peaceful lakes are ideal for spotting wildlife, and the mixed forest provides an especially vibrant backdrop around the lakes when the leaves turn in the fall.

Near the shorelines, you'll see an array of beaver or muskrat houses. Also, look (and listen) for loons. Common loons are aquatic birds well-known for their haunting calls: the wail, tremolo, yodel, and hoot. The wail and tremolo in particular are often described as both eerie and enchanting.

TURN-BY-TURN DIRECTIONS

1. From the trailhead map, begin on the unmarked Green/Yellow Loop Trail to the right.
2. At 0.4 miles, turn left onto the spur to reach Knife Lake, then return to the Green/Yellow Loop Trail.
3. At 1.2 miles, turn left to follow the second spur to Knife Lake, then return to the Green/Yellow Loop Trail.
4. At 1.4 miles, reach a junction and continue straight onto the Green Loop Trail, marked with a green arrow.
5. At 1.6 miles, continue straight, ignoring a trail spur on the left.
6. At 1.8 miles, reach a junction. Turn left onto a short spur to Canteen Lake. Then return to the junction and turn left to continue on the Green Loop Trail, marked with a green arrow.
7. At 2.2 miles, turn right onto a spur leading down to Battine Lake. Enjoy the view, then return to the main trail.
8. At 2.7 miles, continue straight, ignoring a trail spur on the right.
9. At 3.0 miles, continue straight, ignoring another trail spur on the right.
10. At 3.1 miles, bear right at the fork to remain on the Green Loop Trail.
11. At 3.3 miles, bear left at the fork, following the green arrow.
12. At 3.9 miles, turn right onto the spur for a view of Lower Aimer Lake. Then, return to the Green Loop Trail and continue.
13. At 4.5 miles, keep right at the fork.
14. At 5.0 miles, continue straight, ignoring a spur on the left. Proceed ahead to the trailhead, closing the loop.

FIND THE TRAILHEAD

From Marenisco, MI, at M-64/Fair Avenue and Main Street, head south on M-64. After 8.6 miles, the road becomes County Highway B as you cross into Wisconsin. Continue for 4.1 miles, then turn left onto E Bay Road. After 0.5 miles, turn right into the driveway for the Catherine Wolter Wilderness Area. The trailhead and a small parking area will be 200 feet down the driveway. The trail begins to the right of the parking area.

FIVE SONS BREWING

Bruce Mahler opened Five Sons Brewing after serving as a police officer for 42 years, a portion of which he spent as the police chief in his hometown of Marenisco, MI. He and his wife, Kim, had always enjoyed craft beer, but they took that interest up a notch with an introductory brewing class at Gogebic Community College run by Cold Iron Brewing in Ironwood, MI (see page 284). Not long after, Bruce started brewing at home with a 15-gallon brewing system. With each new batch, more and more friends started showing up at his garage, and with retirement from the police force on the horizon, opening a brewery seemed like a solid next step. Once Kim retired and closed her medical practice, they transformed the old medical building into the home of Five Sons Brewing.

Bruce likes crafting beers with Austrian and German influences as a nod to his family heritage. He generally keeps a variety of browns, reds, and stouts on tap, as well as a few seasonals to mix up the rotation. Quail's Irish Red delivers a malt-forward taste with a light, sweet finish.

LAND MANAGER

The Nature Conservancy
Wisconsin Chapter
633 West Main Street
Madison, WI 53703
(608) 251-8140
nature.org/en-us/get-involved/how-to-help/places-we-protect/catherine-wolter-wilderness-area
nature.org/content/dam/tnc/nature/en/graphics/maps/web_map_wolter_no_aerial.pdf

BREWERY/RESTAURANT

Five Sons Brewing
236 Main Street
Marenisco, MI 49947
(906) 787-2000
fivesonsbrewingmi.com

Distance from trailhead: 13.6 miles

RAVEN RED LOOP

A HILLY LOOP TO SCENIC LAKESHORES AND HEMLOCK GROVES

STARTING POINT	DESTINATION
RAVEN TRAILHEAD	CLEAR LAKE
BREWERY	**HIKE TYPE**
ROCKY REEF BREWING COMPANY	MODERATE
DOG FRIENDLY	**SEASON**
NO	MAY-OCTOBER
FEES	**DURATION**
YES	2 HOURS
MAP REFERENCE	**LENGTH**
POSTED AT TRAILHEAD	4.2 MILES (LOOP)
HIGHLIGHTS	**ELEVATION GAIN**
MAPLE GROVES, FALL COLORS	155 FEET

7.2%
ALCOHOL CONTENT

MUSKY BITE IPA

GOLDEN

CITRUS,
STONE FRUIT

CITRUS,
STONE FRUIT,
FLORAL

BITTERNESS

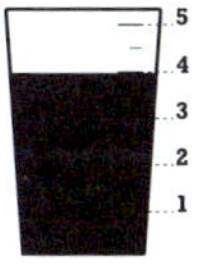

SWEETNESS

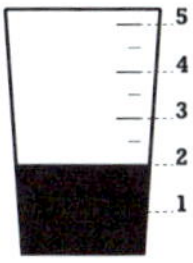

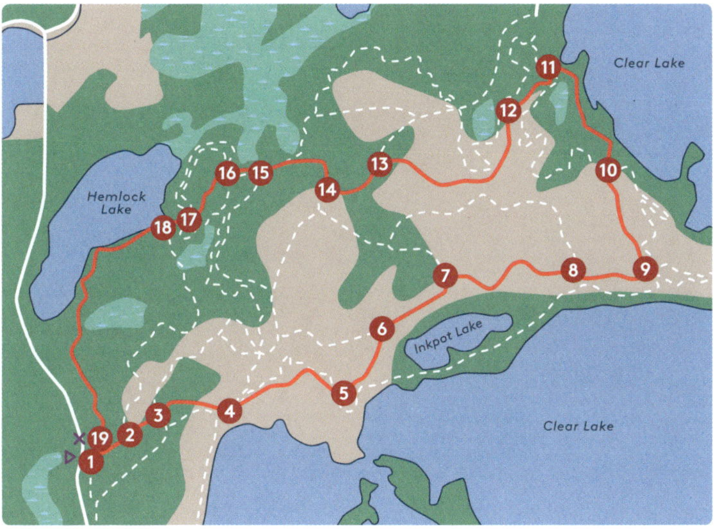

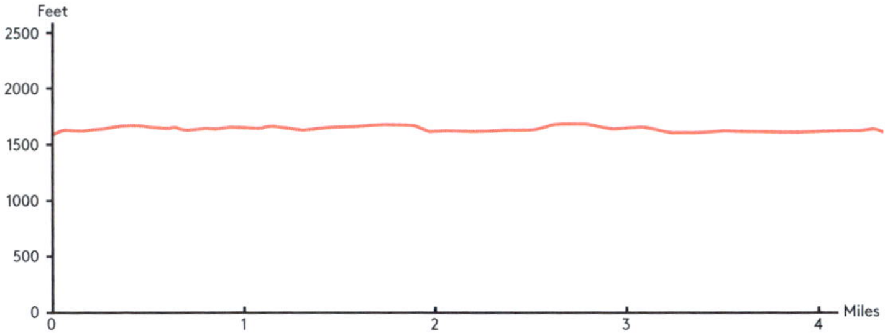

HIKE DESCRIPTION

Hike over rolling hills and past quiet bogs through a mix of maples, pines, and hemlocks to perfectly framed lakeshore views. When your legs are ready for a break, head to Rocky Reef Brewing for a refreshing pint of Musky Bite.

The Northern Highland–American Legion State Forest (NHAL) covers 236,000 acres in the Wisconsin Northwoods. Tucked between two of the 900+ lakes scattered across the NHAL sits the Raven Trail System, with more than 14 miles of trails for hikers, bikers, skiers, and snowshoers. Well-signed routes and color-coded markers for each of the different loops make this an easy network to navigate. Dogs can hike all the trails except the Nature Trail. Our route, the Red Loop, includes the outer half of the Nature Trail, so if you want to hike with your canine companion, be sure to alter your course.

Your journey around the Red Loop begins next to the main trailhead kiosk at the top of the parking lot (bathrooms are at the opposite end). About 100 feet in, you'll come to a signpost with markers for the red, blue, green, and yellow trails. Take note of the red square and watch for it along the way to help ensure you stay on the intended route. The first mile and a half of your hike meanders through the forest under a lush canopy of maples.

While you're hiking among these big trees, keep an eye down low for ghost plants, or ghost pipes. These plants might look like fungi at first because they don't have any green leaves, but they're a translucent, white wildflower. The ghost plant isn't green because it doesn't have chlorophyll, which is what makes plants green and is essential for photosynthesis. Rather than using photosynthesis, ghost plants are heterotrophic, meaning they pull their nutrition from other organisms. Heterotrophic plants are either parasites, nabbing nutrients directly from a green plant, or fungus-feeding, pulling in food via a fungus attached to the root system of another plant. Ghost plants are the latter, using the fungus as a go-between to obtain nutrients.

As you near the two-mile mark, you'll descend a steep hill into a section of towering pines. The path continues down to the Clear Lake shoreline. Pause at the bench along the edge of the lake to take in the scenery and then continue through the pines. You'll climb a sharp incline as you approach two and a half miles and then slowly wind back down until you reach the Nature Trail along Hemlock Lake a mile later. As the lake's name implies, you'll stroll through a grove of large hemlock trees for the last section of your adventure. Enjoy the lake views and shaded, peaceful vibe of the grove as you finish your loop back to the trailhead.

TURN-BY-TURN DIRECTIONS

1. From the trailhead kiosk, begin hiking on the trail to the left. In 100 feet, continue straight, ignoring a trail spur on the left, and follow the red square trail markers for the Red Loop.
2. At 0.1 miles, keep right at the fork, following the "Hiking Trail" sign.
3. At 0.2 miles, continue straight across a paved trail.
4. At 0.4 miles, reach signposted Intersection 1 and a trail map. Continue straight.
5. At 0.7 miles, reach signposted Intersection 2 and a trail map. Continue straight up the hill.
6. At 0.9 miles, turn right at a T-junction.
7. At 1.1 miles, bear right at the fork.
8. At 1.4 miles, at a T-junction, turn right.
9. At 1.6 miles, continue straight, ignoring the trail spur on the right.
10. At 2.0 miles, reach signposted Intersection 3 and a trail map. Continue straight. In 200 feet, reach a bench with a scenic view of the lakeshore.
11. At 2.2 miles, reach signposted Intersection 4 and a trail map. Continue straight.
12. At 2.4 miles, turn left at a T-junction.
13. At 2.8 miles, turn left onto the paved trail.
14. At 3.0 miles, reach a junction where a small wooden building sits 50 feet past the intersection. Turn right onto the dirt trail.
15. At 3.2 miles, reach signposted Intersection 6 and a trail map. Bear right at the fork.
16. At 3.3 miles, continue straight, ignoring a trail spur on the right.
17. At 3.4 miles, continue straight, ignoring another trail spur on the right.
18. At 3.5 miles, keep right on the signposted Nature Trail.
19. At 4.2 miles, turn right to close the loop and return to the trailhead.

FIND THE TRAILHEAD

From Woodruff, at 1st Avenue and U.S. Highway 51, drive east on 1st Avenue. After 3.6 miles, turn left onto Woodruff Road. After 0.7 miles, turn right into the Raven Trailhead parking area. The trail begins near the northeast corner of the parking area.

ROCKY REEF BREWING COMPANY

When Christie and Tyler Smith moved to Newport Beach, CA, for work, the area's craft beer scene took them by surprise. They fell in love and soon purchased their own home brewing kit. As they reached another crossroads with work, they realized it was time to blend their love for entrepreneurship with their love for beer. Christie and Tyler moved home to Chicago and leaned into their family's support as they built up savings and mapped out their plans. Their vacations to the Northwoods shined a little brighter as they noticed a gap in local breweries. The perfect building came up for sale in Woodruff, and Rocky Reef Brewing opened in 2015.

With a lot of research and hard work aimed at expanding without going into debt, the brewery slowly grew from a half-barrel system brewing all day to now a 15-barrel brewhouse with multiple fermenters. Musky Bite, a classic West Coast IPA, was one of their first beers. It delivers a fresh dose of citrus with a backing of stone fruit for a rejuvenating post-hike drink.

LAND MANAGER

Northern Highland–American Legion State Forest
4125 Forestry Headquarters Road
Boulder Junction, WI 54512
(715) 356-3668
dnr.wisconsin.gov/topic/StateForests/nhal
widnr.widen.net/view/pdf/kmdqoeea85/FR712_RavenTrail2021.pdf

BREWERY/RESTAURANT

Rocky Reef Brewing Company
1101 1st Ave.
Woodruff, WI 54568
(715) 439-4055
rockyreefbrewing.com

Distance from trailhead: 4.2 miles

ANVIL NATIONAL RECREATION TRAIL

TREK OVER CHALLENGING HILLS THROUGH A MAGNIFICENT, HARDWOOD FOREST

STARTING POINT	DESTINATION
ANVIL TRAILHEAD	DEVIL'S RUN
BREWERY	**HIKE TYPE**
TRIBUTE BREWING COMPANY	MODERATE
DOG FRIENDLY	**SEASON**
YES (LEASH REQUIRED)	MAY-OCTOBER
FEES	**DURATION**
YES	2 HOURS 30 MINUTES
MAP REFERENCE	**LENGTH**
POSTED AT TRAILHEAD	6.1 MILES (LOOP)
HIGHLIGHTS	**ELEVATION GAIN**
STRENUOUS HILLS, OLD-GROWTH FOREST	256 FEET

5.0%
ALCOHOL CONTENT

BLUEBERRY TRAIN WHEAT ALE

HAZY STRAW

BLUEBERRY MUFFIN

BLUEBERRY

BITTERNESS

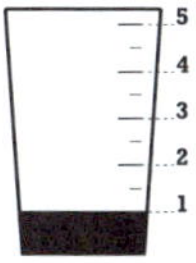

SWEETNESS

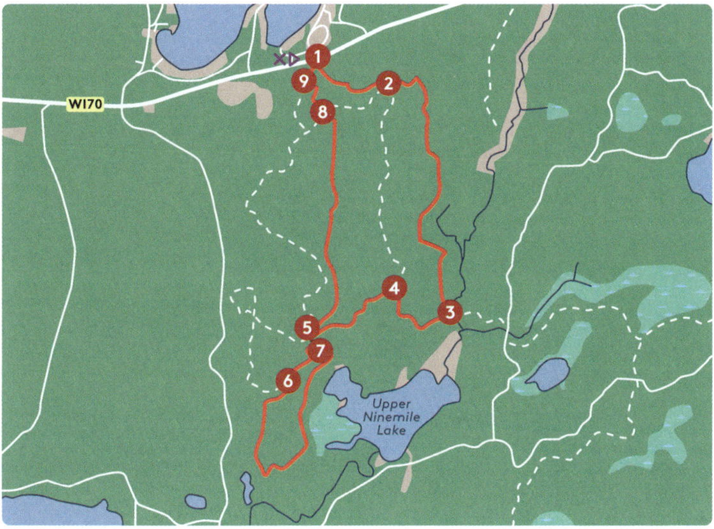

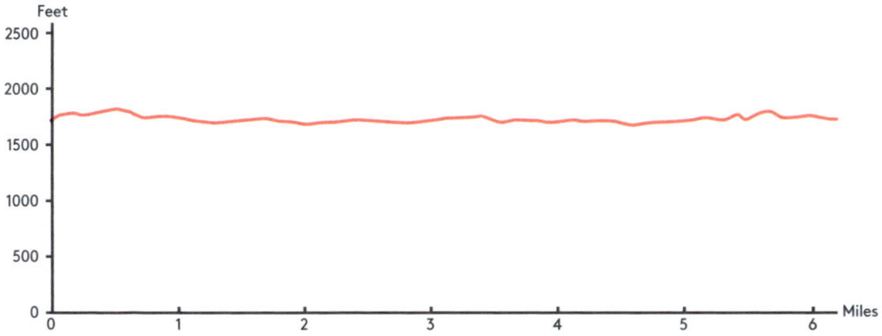

HIKE DESCRIPTION

Lace up your shoes for an engaging romp through a hardwood forest over a series of challenging but fun hills. Continue on to Tribute Brewing to recover with a fresh pint of Blueberry Train Wheat Ale and airfield views from the patio.

The Anvil National Recreation Trail is a federally recognized trail situated in a Wisconsin State Natural Area (SNA). The National Recreation Trail Program, created by the National Trail System Act of 1968, highlights top-tier trails throughout the United States. These trails are complete with no gaps, open to public use, expertly designed, and well-maintained. SNAs protect native landscapes with exceptional natural communities, geological features, or archeological finds. The Anvil Lake SNA preserves a hardwood forest with natural springs, conifer-dominated peat, and mature hemlock stands. Some of the pines and hemlocks here originated in the late 1880s.

You'll set out on the Ninemile Trail, a wide and flat path weaving around giant pines and hemlocks. What this hike lacks in vistas, it makes up for with engaging hills in a majestic, old-growth forest. Ferns, grasses, and various mushrooms dot the forest floor. Ancient moss-covered stumps and snags (dead trees still standing but likely missing their top half) provide homes for critters and birds. You'll wind over one significant hill followed by several moderate ones before the trail levels out and the forest transitions to one dominated by sugar maples.

Nearly three miles into your adventure, you'll reach a clearing with a bathroom, picnic tables, and a small cabin (a warming shack for winter visitors). Multiple trails connect here, but they're well-signed, and

a map is posted near the cabin if you need to reorient yourself. You'll hop on the Military Trail to reach the Lake Loop, which swings by the western side of Upper Ninemile Lake, though not close enough to see it from the trail. The loop swoops through a dense section of forest with hazelnut thickets and an occasional raspberry bush. When you return to the junction with the bathroom, you'll transition to the Devil's Run Trail. Here, along the most strenuous section of the route, the forest transitions back to the bigger, older trees with an open understory. You'll hustle up and over several steep hills, working your way back to the trailhead.

TURN-BY-TURN DIRECTIONS

1. From the trailhead, head out on the Ninemile Trail to the left of the map kiosk.
2. At 0.4 miles, reach a trail junction. Keep left on the signposted Ninemile Trail.
3. At 1.9 miles, bear right at the fork to stay on the signposted Ninemile Trail.
4. At 2.3 miles, turn left at a T-junction.
5. At 2.8 miles, reach a bathroom and a small cabin at a trail junction. Turn left onto the signposted Military Trail. In 150 feet, keep right at the fork to stay on the Military Trail.
6. At 3.1 miles, turn left onto the signposted Lake Loop Trail.
7. At 4.6 miles, reach the fork from Step 5 and keep right. In 150 feet, reach the junction with the bathroom from Step 5. Continue straight onto the signposted Devil's Run Trail.
8. At 5.8 miles, reach a junction and then continue straight on the signposted Devil's Run Trail.
9. At 6.0 miles, continue straight, ignoring a trail spur on the left, and then continue ahead to return to the trailhead.

FIND THE TRAILHEAD

From Eagle River at US-45 S/Pine Street and Railroad Street, head east on US-45 S/Pine Street. After 1.2 miles, continue straight onto WI-70 E. After 8.6 miles, turn right into the trailhead parking lot, signposted for the Anvil Trailhead Chequamegon-Nicolet National Forest. The trail begins to the left of the map kiosk.

TRIBUTE BREWING COMPANY

One of Bill Summers's first experiences with craft beer was in the late 90s at a brewery in Sioux Falls, SD. The variety of options intrigued him, and he started trying everything. When he moved to Eagle River, the lack of craft beer options in the area didn't deter his interest. In 2005, Bill and six friends started a beer festival (Great Northern Beer Festival, now managed by the Eagle River Chamber of Commerce as the Up North Beer Fest). In 2007, a home-brewing club formed from friendships developed at the festival's home-brewing booth. A few years later, Bill approached Marc O'Brien, the best brewer in the club, according to Bill, about opening a brewery. Not too long after, Marc reached out to Bill about checking out some brewing equipment at a brewery that was expanding and selling their old equipment. They purchased some equipment and placed it in storage until they found the right space, which wound up being an industrial building next to the airport. The blank interior made it easier to build out the brewhouse, and the location offered the perfect space for a patio with views of the occasional plane traffic and radiant sunsets across the airfield.

Bill and Marc opened Tribute Brewing in 2012 with 12 taps of guest beers. As they finalized each of their own recipes, they slowly swapped out the taps until they had a full row of Tribute beers. The flagship beers range from a dark chocolate porter to an amber lager. Blueberry Train is a tribute to the train that used to haul blueberries from Conover, WI, down to Chicago, IL, for processing in the early 1900s. It's a wheat-based beer that tastes like a fresh blueberry muffin without getting too sweet.

LAND MANAGER

U.S. Forest Service
1247 East Wall Street
Eagle River, WI 54521
(715) 479-2827
fs.usda.gov/recarea/cnnf/recarea/?recid=27859
fs.usda.gov/Internet/FSE_DOCUMENTS/stelprdb5448064.pdf

BREWERY/RESTAURANT

Tribute Brewing Company
1106 N Bluebird Road
Eagle River, WI 54521
(715) 480-2337
tributebrewing.com

Distance from trailhead: 11.3 miles

GRANDFATHER FALLS

A SERIES OF CASCADING WATERFALLS AND A FOREST CREEK

STARTING POINT

GRANDFATHER FALLS DAM

DESTINATION

WISCONSIN RIVER

BREWERY

SAWMILL BREWING COMPANY

HIKE TYPE

MODERATE

DOG FRIENDLY

YES (LEASH REQUIRED)

SEASON

MAY–OCTOBER

FEES

NONE

DURATION

2 HOURS 30 MINUTES

MAP REFERENCE

POSTED AT TRAILHEAD

LENGTH

5.1 MILES (ROUND TRIP)

HIGHLIGHTS

RIVER, CASCADES, DAM

ELEVATION GAIN

241 FEET

6.8%
ALCOHOL CONTENT

BOOM DECKER BECKER IPA

DARK GOLD

CITRUS, HOPPY

CITRUS, HOPPY, SMOOTH

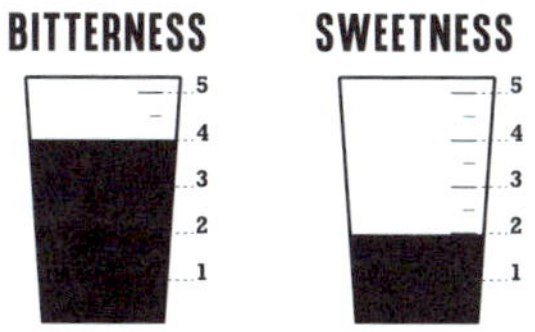

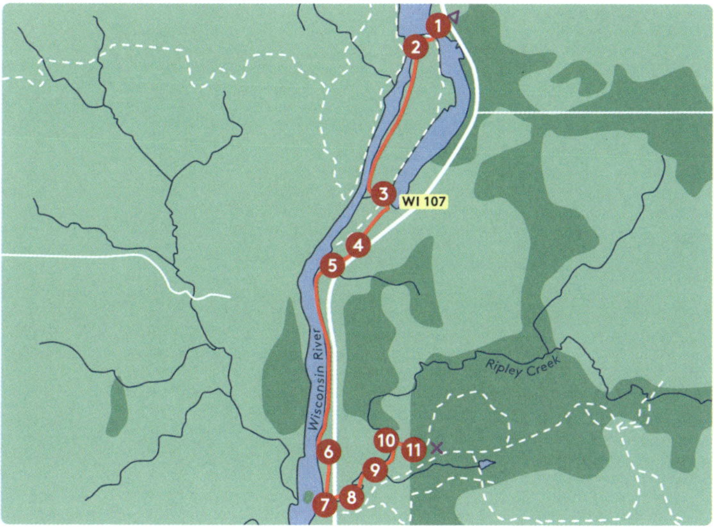

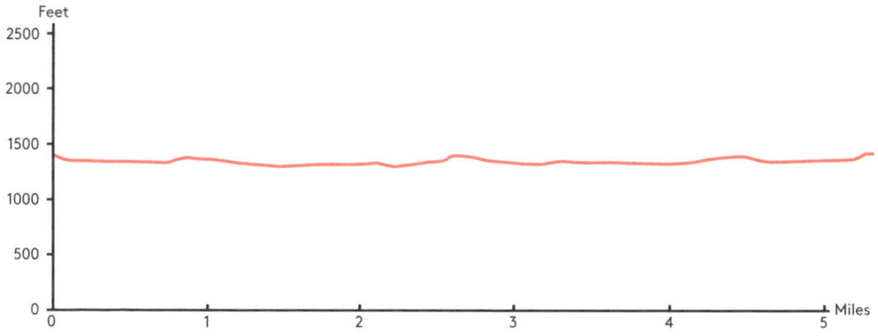

HIKE DESCRIPTION

Traverse a rocky trail along the Wisconsin River and Grandfather Falls cascades to a creek that meanders through a haunted forest. Dive deeper into the spooky legend with a pint of Boom Decker Becker IPA at Sawmill Brewing.

In the 1800s, before railroads were available to haul logs and lumber, men floated the logs downriver to the sawmills and market cities. Along the Wisconsin River, however, Grandfather Falls, a series of cascades dropping 89 feet over a mile through Merrill, Wisconsin, became a pain point, as they couldn't safely navigate the logs over the falls. In 1876, Simon Sherman built three dams in an attempt to raise water levels over the falls, but it didn't help. So, in 1880, Peter Champagne built a dam at the falls to power a sawmill—if they couldn't bring the logs to the sawmill, they'd bring the sawmill to the logs. By the turn of the 20th century, there were 16 active sawmills in Merrill.

Your hike begins at the trailhead near the Grandfather Falls Dam. Following the dirt road, you'll cross a bridge over the flowage (the body of water built up by the dam) and then head downhill toward the base of the dam. Getting on the Ice Age Trail (IAT), you'll follow the bank of the Wisconsin River, picking your way around and over the jumble of large, mossy rocks. As you near one mile, you'll leave the river and woods to emerge near the power station intake building. Here, you'll notice two large, yellow pipes (penstocks) making their way down the hill. They direct the water from the flowage to the hydroelectric power plant. In

the 1930s, when Wisconsin Public Works converted the dam into the power system it is today, the pipes were redwood planks tightly bound together with steel bands. In 2017, the wood pipes received an upgrade to steel. As you hike alongside the pipes, you'll see a section of the wooden version on display. Over the next mile, you'll follow the trail around the power station and back into the woods.

The IAT Grandfather Falls Segment ends at New Wood County Park (about two miles into your hike), but a spur continues east through the Merrill School Forest. Following the spur trail, you'll cross the highway and then enter the forest on the other side. According to local legend, a lumberjack ghoul, Boom Decker Becker, haunts the Merrill School Forest. At the annual class campout in this forest, teachers recount the story around the campfire in hopes of keeping students in their bunkhouses throughout the night. The tale morphs a bit with each class, but Boom Decker Becker has endured the test of time.

Haunted or not, the forest is lush and peaceful where the trail winds along Ripley Creek. You'll pass by several wooden bridges on your left that cross over the creek, but our route stays to the right. About two and a half miles into your hike, you'll climb a steep hill and emerge from the woods into a grassy clearing under the powerlines. The IAT spur continues farther into the Merrill School Forest, but this is the turnaround for our route. Admire the wildflowers in the clearing, then work your way back to the trailhead at Grandfather Falls Dam.

TURN-BY-TURN DIRECTIONS

1. From the trailhead, follow the dirt road through the gate, across the bridge, and down the hill toward the dam's base.
2. At 0.1 miles, the road ends at the woods where you'll transition onto the signposted Ice Age Trail (IAT) Grandfather Falls Segment.
3. At 0.8 miles, reach a T-junction. Turn right to cross the wooden bridge, then immediately after crossing the bridge, turn left onto the dirt road. Follow the road over two large yellow pipes and then turn right to follow the trail with the pipes on the right.
4. At 1.0 miles, reach a dirt parking lot. Continue straight across to the IAT marker.
5. At 1.1 miles, reach a power station and keep to the left. Hike through the woods for 100 feet, then cut straight across another dirt lot.
6. At 1.9 miles, reach a small campground. Bear right to continue along the road through the campground and rejoin the trail on the opposite end.
7. At 2.1 miles, reach a T-junction at a creek. Turn left, keeping the creek to the right. In 150 feet, cross the paved road.
8. At 2.2 miles, bear left at the fork.
9. At 2.4 miles, continue straight, ignoring a wooden bridge on the left.
10. At 2.5 miles, continue straight, ignoring another wooden bridge on the left.
11. At 2.6 miles, reach a powerline at a break in the forest. Turn around and return the way you came.

FIND THE TRAILHEAD

From Merrill, at Main Street and Center Street, drive north on Center Street. In 300 feet, at the traffic circle, exit onto E 1st Street. After 0.3 miles, 1st Street bears slightly right and becomes E 2nd Street. After 0.5 miles, 2nd Street turns left and becomes N Polk Street. After 350 feet, turn right onto 1st Street. After 0.2 miles, turn right onto Grand Avenue/WI-107 N. After 12.3 miles, turn left into the trailhead parking lot signposted as Ice Age Trail Grandfather Falls Segment.

SAWMILL BREWING COMPANY

Zach Kubichek, Sawmill Brewing's manager and part-owner, has grown into the beer business right along with the brewery itself. He and his wife started as investors until Zach decided to go hands-on and became a part-time bartender at the brewery. He'd gone to school for radiation therapy, so this was a new world. But he put in the work and learned more about managing staff and a brewery until he was able to make it his full focus.

Sawmill Brewing lives in a 1940s DNR ranger station, an impressive structure from the moment you see it. The big granite blocks and heavy wood beams make it feel as much a part of nature as the giant white pines surrounding it. Sawmill Brewing's flagships include a blonde ale, an IPA, an Irish red ale, and an oatmeal stout. The IPA, Boom Decker Becker, has a classic hoppy flavor with a smooth, bitter finish.

LAND MANAGER

Wisconsin Public Service
PO BOX 19002
Green Bay, WI 54307
(800) 450-7260
wisconsinpublicservice.com
iceagetrail.org/wp-content/uploads/Merrill_Itinerary_2023_withMaps.pdf

BREWERY/RESTAURANT

Sawmill Brewing Company
1110 E 10th Street
Merrill, WI 54452
(715) 722-0230
sawmillbrewing.net

Distance from trailhead: 13.7 miles

SCHLITZ AUDUBON LOOP

WANDER THE TRAILS WHERE SCHLITZ BREWING DRAFT HORSES USED TO LIVE

STARTING POINT	DESTINATION
VISITOR CENTER	OBSERVATION TOWER
BREWERY	**HIKE TYPE**
BLACK HUSKY BREWING	EASY
DOG FRIENDLY	**SEASON**
NO	YEAR-ROUND
FEES	**DURATION**
YES	1 HOUR 20 MINUTES
MAP REFERENCE	**LENGTH**
SCHLITZ AUDUBON CENTER	2.3 MILES (LOOP)
HIGHLIGHTS	**ELEVATION GAIN**
LAKE MICHIGAN, WETLAND PONDS, OBSERVATION TOWER	92 FEET

8.6% ALCOHOL CONTENT

SPROOSE DOUBLE IPA

GOLD

GRAPEFRUIT, PINE

MALT, GINGER

BITTERNESS 3

SWEETNESS 4

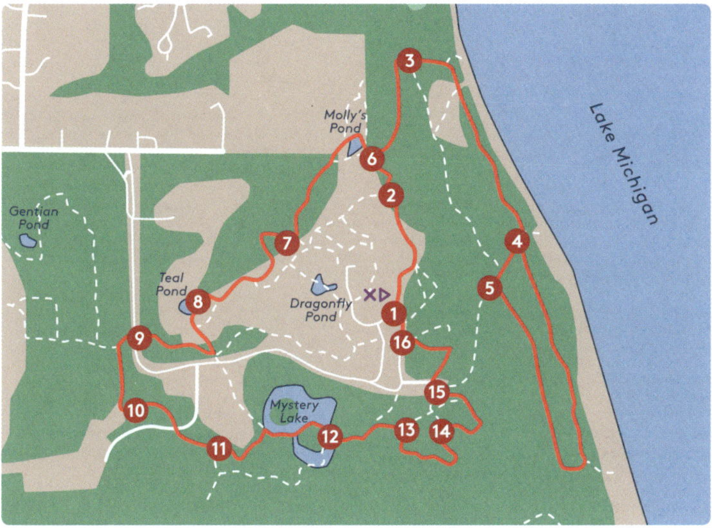

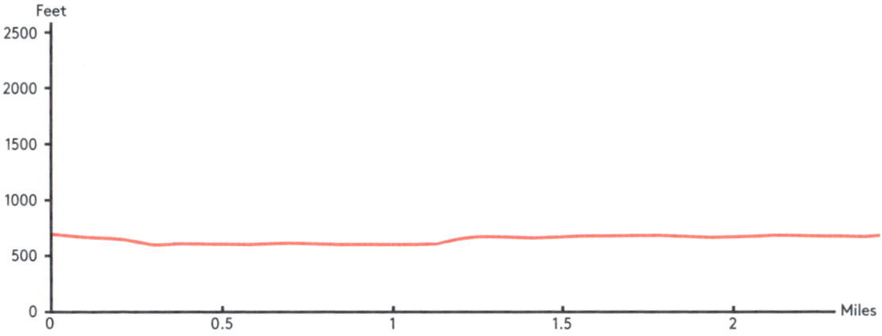

HIKE DESCRIPTION

Explore the Schlitz Audubon trails, ponds, and observation tower for a dose of nature in the big city. Posthike, head down to Black Husky Brewing for a pint of Sproose IPA.

In the late 1880s, the Uihlein-Schlitz family began purchasing small farms to combine into one large property. They named the land "Nine Mile Farm" because it was nine miles from the Schlitz Brewery. The farm housed the draft horses used to pull the wagons delivering beer. Once automobiles became more popular and took over deliveries, the farm transitioned into a recreational space. In 1971, the Schlitz Foundation donated the land to the National Audubon Society, and the nature center officially opened in 1973.

Your adventure through the Schlitz Audubon Nature Center follows the Central Wetlands Loop in combination with several spurs to notable features. A short detour on Elizabeth's Trail Spur is your first side trip. You'll descend to Milner Deck for a grand view of Lake Michigan along with beach access to check out the lake up close. Back on the main trail, you'll continue along the Central Wetlands Loop to Molly's Pond and Teal Pond. Two wetland plants you'll see bordering both ponds include the broad-leaf arrowhead (white flowers) and pickerelweed (purple flowers).

Shortly after Teal Pond, you'll venture off the Central Wetlands Loop onto the Gateway Trail. This path leads you to the Turtle Trail and a long boardwalk across Turtle Pond. Several dead trees border the edge

of the pond, and some have fallen into the water, making for perfect turtle hangout spots. The Turtle Trail takes you back to the Central Wetlands Loop, where you'll hop on another boardwalk, this time wrapping around part of Mystery Lake. This is a great space to check for more wetland wildlife such as herons, muskrats, and frogs. From here, you'll take one last detour from the main loop onto the Green Tree Accessible Trail for access to the observation tower. At the top of the tower, you'll enjoy a bird's-eye view of the surrounding forest and Lake Michigan.

TURN-BY-TURN DIRECTIONS

1. From the parking lot, follow the sidewalk up to the visitor center. Take the gravel path setting out from the right side of the visitor center.
2. At 0.1 miles, continue straight, ignoring a trail spur on the left. In 200 feet, turn right onto a dirt path signposted for Elizabeth's Trail/ Milner Deck; this begins a 1.1-mile-long side trip.
3. At 0.2 miles, pass a trail spur and a bench on the right. In 300 feet, reach the signposted Milner Deck. Take the steps down to explore the beach, then return to Elizabeth's Trail.
4. At 0.5 miles, reach an unmarked fork and bear left to begin a short loop.
5. At 0.9 miles, reach a T-junction with a paved trail and then turn right. After 150 feet, the pavement turns to dirt. In another 50 feet, reach the fork from Step 4. Bear left, closing the loop and retracing your steps back to the start of Elizabeth's Trail (Step 2).
6. At 1.2 miles, reach the junction from Step 2; turn right onto the signposted Central Wetlands Loop.
7. At 1.4 miles, keep right onto the trail signposted for Teal Pond, ignoring a trail spur on the left.
8. At 1.5 miles, reach Teal Pond. In 200 feet, reach a junction with a map and then turn right onto the Gateway Trail.
9. At 1.6 miles, cross a road. In 100 feet, turn left onto the signposted Turtle Trail.
10. At 1.7 miles, reach a bench at a fork in the trail; bear left to stay on the signposted Turtle Trail. In 250 feet, cross a road and continue on the main trail.
11. At 1.8 miles, at a junction, keep left onto the signposted Mystery Lake/Central Wetlands Loop. In 250 feet, reach a T-junction at a boardwalk and then turn right onto the signposted Central Wetlands Loop.
12. At 1.9 miles, continue straight, ignoring a trail spur on the right.
13. At 2.0 miles, turn right onto the paved path signposted as the Green Tree Accessible Trail.
14. At 2.1 miles, ignore a trail spur on the left. In 300 feet, reach the observation tower. Climb the tower. When you've had your fill of the view, climb back down and then continue on the trail.
15. At 2.2 miles, at a T-junction, turn right. In 200 feet, turn left at the pavilion.
16. At 2.3 miles, reach the parking lot.

FIND THE TRAILHEAD

From Milwaukee at I-794 W/I-94W and I-43 N, head north on I-43 N. After 8 miles, take the exit for Good Hope Road and continue for 0.3 miles. Bear right at the fork in the ramp, then turn right onto Good Hope Road. Immediately bear left into the left turn lanes and turn left onto N Port Washington Road. After 0.5 miles, turn right onto N Calumet Road. After 0.8 miles, turn left onto N Lake Drive and proceed for 1.5 miles. Turn right to stay on N Lake Drive, then immediately turn right again onto N Brown Deer Road. After 0.3 miles, turn right onto E Bay Street and continue for 0.4 miles, following the signs for the Schlitz Audubon Nature Center. The road ends at the parking lot for the nature center.

BLACK HUSKY BREWING

Tim and Toni Eichinger started Black Husky Brewing as a production-only brewery in Pembine, WI, where they raised sled dogs. After attending their first brewery event in 2010, interest in their beer ignited. Tim delivered their beer himself to the bars and restaurants putting it on tap, so his time spent traveling only increased as their business grew. As their process became less sustainable for a two-person team, moving to Milwaukee allowed them to be closer to family and expand their business to include a taproom, which they opened in 2016.

One of the first things you'll notice walking into the taproom is the large log bar, which Tim built from trees he cut down himself up north. Sproose is a double IPA made with spruce harvested in northern Wisconsin. With the mix of hops, malt, and spruce, you'll catch notes of ginger and rosemary with a slightly sweet finish.

LAND MANAGER

Schlitz Audubon Nature Center
1111 E Brown Deer Rd
Milwaukee, WI 53217
(414) 352-2880
schlitzaudubon.org
schlitzaudubon.org/wp-content/uploads/2021/01/Schlitz-Audubon-Trail-Map-December-2020-scaled.jpg

BREWERY/RESTAURANT

Black Husky Brewing
909 E Locust St
Milwaukee, WI 53212
(414) 763-4141
blackhuskybrewing.com

Distance from trailhead: 10 miles

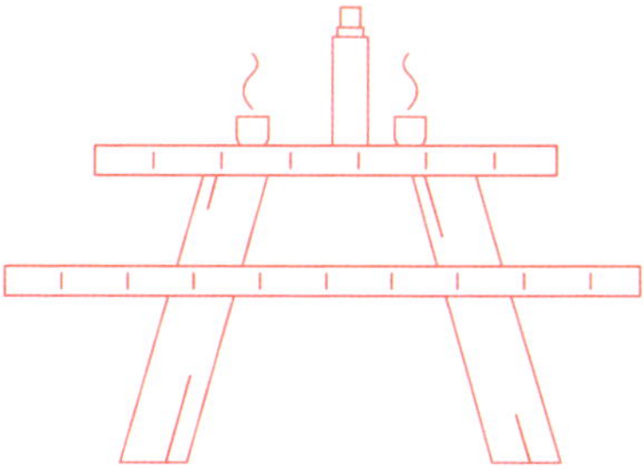

MEQUON NATURE PRESERVE

EXPLORE AN ABUNDANCE OF WILDFLOWERS AND WETLANDS

STARTING POINT	DESTINATION
PIEPERPOWER EDUCATION CENTER	OBSERVATION TOWER
BREWERY	**HIKE TYPE**
THE FERMENTORIUM BREWERY	EASY
DOG FRIENDLY	**SEASON**
YES (LEASH REQUIRED)	APRIL–NOVEMBER
FEES	**DURATION**
NONE	1 HOUR 30 MINUTES
MAP REFERENCE	**LENGTH**
POSTED AT TRAILHEAD	2.8 MILES (LOOP)
HIGHLIGHTS	**ELEVATION GAIN**
OBSERVATION TOWER, WILDFLOWERS	90 FEET

4.8%
ALCOHOL CONTENT

CRISPY AND THE BOIS LAGER

PALE YELLOW

CORN,
LIGHT HOPS

CLEAN,
BALANCED

BITTERNESS | SWEETNESS

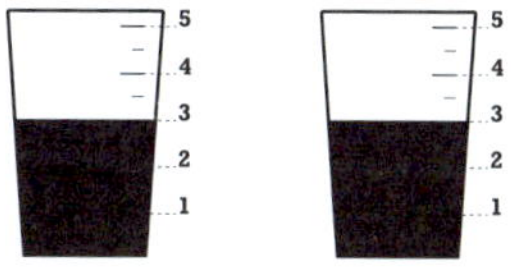

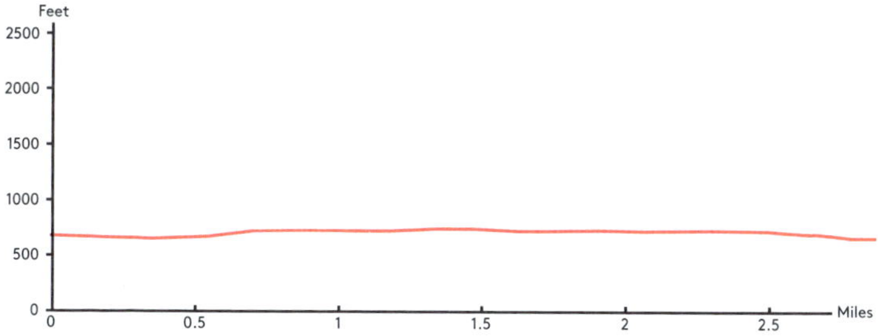

HIKE DESCRIPTION

Meander prairie trails and wetland boardwalks as you learn about the intricacies of this diverse ecosystem. Continue to explore at The Fermentorium Brewery, starting with a pint of Crispy and the Bois.

Discover the beauty of Mequon Nature Preserve, a charming 510-acre sanctuary born from one person's passion for land conservation. The preserve aims to restore the natural ecosystem featuring beech and maple forests, wetlands, and prairie, reminiscent of a time before European settlers disrupted the land. Along with conservation is a goal to educate others on the complex but fragile balance between the land, water, and wildlife. One example of this is the educational signposts dotting the trails; they offer tidbits of knowledge to help you better understand the ecosystem and the work in progress to support it.

Start at the PieperPower Education Center to get your bearings from the trail map. There are a few maps along the trails, as well as signposts with directional arrows for the major features labeled on the

maps, such as Harvey's Woods and Paul's Pond. From the trailhead, you'll head out on the gravel path to a boardwalk leading through the Streich Family Wetlands. Here, you'll get an up-close view of the bright-purple blooms and arrowhead-shaped leaves of pickerelweed, an aquatic plant growing along the edge of the water. As the trail swings into the prairie, you'll be immersed in a sea of grasses and wildflowers: purple prairie clover, wild bergamot (bee balm), purple and prairie coneflowers, wild carrot, and more. Just over a half mile in, you'll cross a narrow gravel road under the power line. From here, your trail transitions to a mowed-grass and two-track dirt path.

The prairie continues as you climb a gentle hill on the way to Paul's Pond, the largest body of water on the preserve. At the pond, look for frogs, cranes, and other wetland wildlife before making your way to Harvey's Woods. You'll follow the wood-chip path on a quiet, secluded journey through the maple, beech, and oak forest. From the far side of the woods, you'll reconnect with the prairie as you loop around to the 40-foot-tall observation tower. Climb to the top observation deck for a bird's-eye view of the preserve and peer through the telescopes to investigate the details. Back on the ground, you'll navigate through the prairie back to the education center, enjoying one last wetland vista at Christine's Pond along the way.

TURN-BY-TURN DIRECTIONS

1. From the trail map at the PieperPower Education Center entrance, bear right to follow the dirt path beginning at the edge of the parking lot. In 200 feet, continue straight, ignoring a trail spur on the left. In another 50 feet, turn right onto a trail spur toward the Streich Family Wetlands.
2. At 0.4 miles, reach an unmarked junction and turn right.
3. At 0.6 miles, reach a T-junction and turn right onto a single-lane gravel road. In 60 feet, turn left onto the two-track dirt path.
4. At 0.8 miles, bear right at the fork, following the arrow for Paul's Pond.
5. At 0.9 miles, reach another fork and bear right toward Paul's Pond.
6. At 1.1 miles, at a T-junction, turn left, following the arrow for Paul's Pond. In 200 feet, cross the bridge over Paul's Pond.
7. At 1.2 miles, turn right at a T-junction onto the gravel path toward Harvey's Woods.
8. At 1.3 miles, turn left onto a wood-chip-covered trail spur leading into the woods. In 200 feet, keep left at a fork in the trail. In another 200 feet, turn left onto the gravel path.
9. At 1.5 miles, bear left onto a mowed-grass trail following the arrow for the observation tower.
10. At 2.0 miles, continue straight, ignoring a trail spur on the right.
11. At 2.1 miles, reach the observation tower at a junction with a gravel trail. Climb to the top to take in the view, then descend back to the trail. Bear right onto the gravel trail. In 50 feet, turn right onto a mowed-grass trail.
12. At 2.3 miles, turn left onto a trail spur signposted as Christine's Pond. Enjoy the view, then return to the main trail.
13. At 2.4 miles, reach the fork from Step 5. Bear right to follow the trail back to the gravel road from Step 3.
14. At 2.6 miles, reach a T-junction at the gravel road. Turn right onto the road and then continue straight, ignoring spurs on the right and left, until you reach the parking lot back at the education center.

FIND THE TRAILHEAD

From Milwaukee, head north on I-43 N for approximately 8 miles to Exit 80 for Good Hope Road. From the exit ramp, turn left onto Good Hope Road. After 1.1 miles, turn right onto N Green Bay Avenue/I-43 ALT. After 2.1 miles, at the traffic circle, bear right to continue on N Green Bay Avenue/I-43 ALT. After 1.0 miles, turn left onto W County Line Road and proceed for 2.3 miles. Just past the Mequon Nature Preserve Entrance sign, turn right into the preserve parking lot. The trail begins to the right of the PieperPower Education Center front entrance.

THE FERMENTORIUM BREWERY

Kristopher Volkman worked in software development when he first launched The Fermentorium Brewery. For Kristopher, brewing beer not only delivered the obvious result (beer!), but also worked the artistic and scientific side of his brain more than his 9-to-5 did.

Now, working full-time at The Fermentorium, brewing beer feeds Kristopher's love of learning—how different ingredients work together, how the hops express different flavors, how fermenting yeasts at different temperatures produce different characteristics. He likes tweaking recipes and trying new techniques, hops, and ingredients. At The Fermentorium, they pride themselves on being experimental. Their flagships include a juicy IPA, a double IPA, a Mexican lager with lime and sea salt, and a crispy lager. Crispy and the Bois is a clean and crushable American lager brewed with a bit of corn.

LAND MANAGER

Mequon Nature Preserve
8200 W County Line Road
Mequon, WI 53097
(262) 242-8055
mequonnaturepreserve.org
mequonnaturepreserve.org/wp-content/uploads/2022/01/new-map.pdf

BREWERY/RESTAURANT

The Fermentorium Brewery
7481 WI-60 Trunk
Cedarburg, WI 53012
(262) 421-8593
thefermentorium.com

Distance from trailhead: 9.5 miles

KOHLER DUNES CORDWALK

STROLL THE CORDWALK ACROSS WHITE SAND DUNES AT LAKE MICHIGAN

STARTING POINT	DESTINATION
PARKING LOT 5	KOHLER DUNES
BREWERY	**HIKE TYPE**
3 SHEEPS BREWING	EASY
DOG FRIENDLY	**SEASON**
YES (LEASH REQUIRED)	YEAR-ROUND
FEES	**DURATION**
YES	1 HOUR 30 MINUTES
MAP REFERENCE	**LENGTH**
POSTED AT TRAILHEAD	3 MILES (ROUND TRIP)
HIGHLIGHTS	**ELEVATION GAIN**
DUNES, LAKE MICHIGAN	29 FEET

5.0% ALCOHOL CONTENT

WISCONSINITIS CREAM ALE

STRAW

CEREAL, FRUITY, LIGHT HOPS

MALTY, HOPPY, FRUITY

BITTERNESS

SWEETNESS

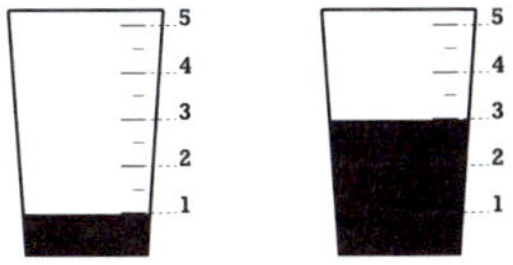

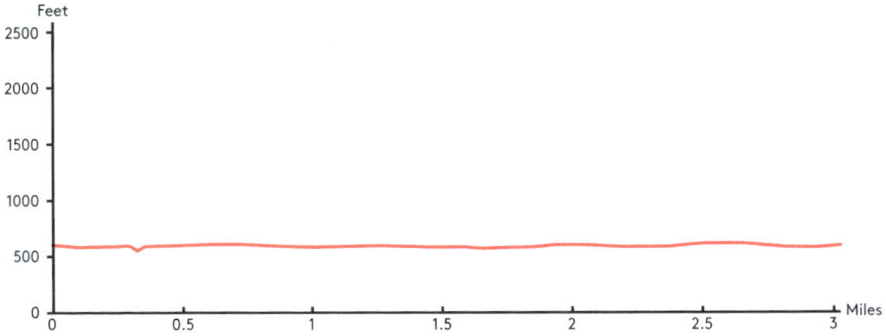

HIKE DESCRIPTION

Discover the unique ecosystem of the Kohler Dunes with a hike along a sandy "cordwalk" trail. Then, cruise up to 3 Sheeps Brewing for a cold pint of Wisconsinitis Cream Ale.

Nestled along the shores of Lake Michigan, Kohler-Andrae State Park is a gem for nature lovers and outdoor enthusiasts with its mix of forests, wetlands, dunes, and sandy beaches. At its center sits Kohler Park Dunes State Natural Area, about a one-mile stretch of protected beach, dunes, and interdunal wetlands. Only ten regions of interdunal wetlands exist across Wisconsin, and this is one of the biggest. Using a "cordwalk" for the trail across the dunes aids in the preservation of this special ecosystem by providing a stable and dedicated walkway for visitors. A "cordwalk" is similar to a boardwalk except the walkway is strung together on long cables rather than nailed onto other boards. The flexible nature of the cordwalk allows it to adjust more easily with the movement of the sand over time.

Your hike begins along the woods at the trail's south end. A short walk through the trees transports you to an entirely different environment of rolling hills covered in long grasses, shrubs, and just an occasional cluster of trees. Here, vegetation has taken over the dunes, creating a more stable environment. Closer to the lake, the bare dunes continuously grow and shift as winds from the lake rearrange the sand. As a result of this, you'll likely traverse several sections of cordwalk partially submerged in sand, which is worth considering as you select your footwear for this adventure. Several benches dot the trail if you need a break to empty sand from your shoes or just want to take in the scenic views.

The cordwalk meanders through the dunes parallel to Lake Michigan's shoreline. Along the way, you'll pass several spurs leading down to the lake; explore the Lake Michigan beach at your leisure. About a half mile in, you'll turn down the Wetland Overlook Spur Trail. Pause at the overlook bench to look for ducks, herons, and other wetland wildlife. Sunrise and sunset are especially good times to hike if you're hoping to spot animals along the route. Back on the main trail, you'll continue past the Creeping Juniper Nature Trail and the Sanderling Nature Center to hike the farthest section of dunes. Neither the Nature Trail nor the Nature Center allows dogs, but they're worth considering for additional adventures if you're hiking without a pup. As you're approaching the far end of your journey, you'll pass a trail spur leading down to the lake just before you reach a grove of trees. This general area near the start of the spur offers a beautiful overlook from the tops of the dunes down to the lake and is popular with photographers at sunset. You'll continue through the trees to access bathrooms and a picnic area at Parking Lot 2 before returning to the trail spur and heading down to a dog-friendly beach on Lake Michigan. When you've had your fill of the beach, you can retrace your steps back to the trailhead at Parking Lot 5.

TURN-BY-TURN DIRECTIONS

1. From the trailhead at Parking Lot 5, follow the only obvious trail into the trees. Over the next 400 feet, pass two trail spurs—one on the right and one on the left; ignore both.
2. At 0.3 miles, turn right onto a trail spur. Explore the beach, then return to the main trail.
3. At 0.6 miles, turn left onto a trail spur signposted as Wetland Overlook. Explore the overlook, then return to the main trail.
4. At 0.9 miles, continue straight, ignoring a trail spur on the left.
5. At 1.0 miles, reach Parking Lot 3. Keep right along the parking lot to rejoin the trail at the Kohler Dunes sign.
6. At 1.1 miles, bear right at the fork. In 450 feet, the forked trails reconnect.
7. At 1.4 miles, continue straight, ignoring a trail spur on the right. In 200 feet, reach Parking Lot 2 for a bathroom and snack break, then return to the spur and turn left onto the spur.
8. At 1.6 miles, reach Lake Michigan. Explore the beach, then return to the main trail and turn left.
9. At 1.7 miles, reach the fork from Step 6; bear right, taking the alternate trail than you did on the way out. In 450 feet, the forked trails reconnect. Continue on the main trail, retracing your steps back to the trailhead.

FIND THE TRAILHEAD

From Sheboygan, at 14th Street/Highway 28 and Erie Avenue/Highway 23, head south on 14th Street/Highway 28 for 1.4 miles. At the intersection with Union Avenue, turn left. After 0.4 miles, turn right onto 12th Street. After 4.1 miles, turn left onto Beach Park Lane. After 1.3 miles, turn left onto Old Park Road. In 300 feet, Parking Lot #5 will be on the left. The trail begins behind the parking spaces next to the Kohler Dunes State Natural Area sign.

3 SHEEPS BREWING

Grant Pauly, 3 Sheeps Brewing's founder, loves creating new beers. The process of crafting a fresh recipe and perfecting it along the way is one of his favorite parts about owning a brewery. He enjoys not just the culinary side of making beer—the journey from how it looks to how it smells to how it tastes—but also the science of making it taste the same every time someone orders a pint. His goal and the vision of the brewery is to make the types of beers Wisconsinites want to drink, beer that becomes synonymous with the "Wisconsin Experience."

Grant recognizes the support the Sheboygan community provides, from the help they received getting started, to the regulars who show up for them even during the slow seasons. Now that the brewery has grown, they give back to community organizations whenever they can. For example, each month, a dollar from every Wisconsinitis pint goes toward a charity. Additionally, one day a month the selected charity comes in to share more about their cause, and a dollar from every pint sold goes toward their cause. Wisconsinitis, one of the brewery's flagship beers, is a light and refreshing cream ale with a hint of sweetness on the backend.

LAND MANAGER

Kohler-Andrae State Park
1020 Beach Park Lane
Sheboygan, WI 53081
(920) 451-4080
dnr.wisconsin.gov/topic/parks/kohlerandrae
dnr.wisconsin.gov/topic/parks/kohlerandrae/maps

BREWERY/RESTAURANT

3 Sheeps Brewing Company
1837 North Avenue
Sheboygan, WI 53083
(920) 395-3583
3sheepsbrewing.com

Distance from trailhead: 9.1 miles

POINT BEACH LOOP

ANCIENT BEACH RIDGELINES ALONG LAKE MICHIGAN

STARTING POINT	DESTINATION
FOREST RANGER OFFICE	POINT BEACH STATE FOREST
BREWERY	**HIKE TYPE**
PETSKULL BREWING	MODERATE
DOG FRIENDLY	**SEASON**
YES (LEASH REQUIRED)	MAY–OCTOBER
FEES	**DURATION**
YES	2 HOUR 30 MINUTES
MAP REFERENCE	**LENGTH**
POSTED AT TRAILHEAD	5.1 MILES (ROUND TRIP)
HIGHLIGHTS	**ELEVATION GAIN**
LAKE MICHIGAN BEACH, WETLANDS	29 FEET

5.75% ALCOHOL CONTENT

SCHNITZKY GERMAN HEFEWEIZEN

CLOUDY GOLD

BANANA

CLOVE, BANANA

BITTERNESS

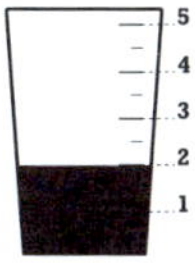

SWEETNESS

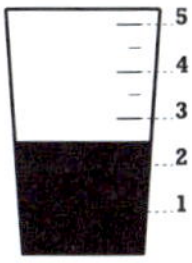

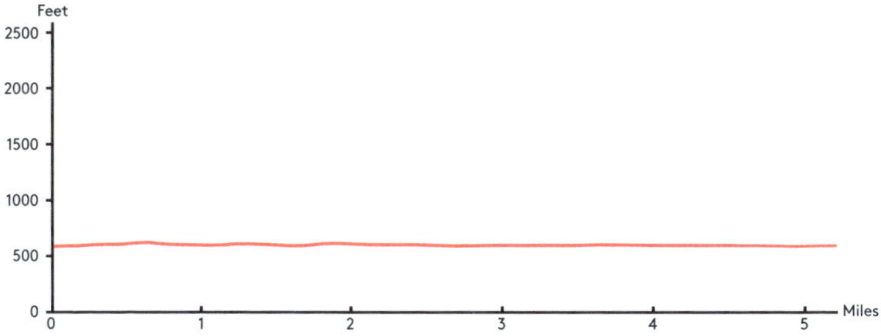

HIKE DESCRIPTION

Wander the Lake Michigan shoreline—both new and old—as you trek from the pristine sands along the water's edge to the forested ridges of beaches past. After emerging from the woods, discover PetSkull Brewing Company's lineup of delicious beers, starting with their German hefeweizen, Schnitzky.

Point Beach State Forest stretches along six miles of Lake Michigan's shores. While this mighty lake is vast and impressive, so too is the forest dappling its former beachfront terrain. Most of our route through the state forest follows the Red, Blue, and Green Loops of the Ridges Trail. The referred-to ridges are ancient Lake Michigan beaches where waves pushed up the sand. The ridges kept forming as the post-glacial water levels dropped. While the forest has since grown over the shorelines of long ago, they're still detectable, particularly in the lower areas between ridges where water collects and forms varying wetlands.

To kickstart your journey, you'll set out across a stretch of vegetated dunes to Lake Michigan and the dog-friendly beach. Once you reach the sand, look north to see the Rawley Point Lighthouse, a steel tower built in 1894 to replace the original brick structure from 1853. Managed by the Coast Guard, the lighthouse is still operational. Once you've snapped a few pictures and marveled at Lake Michigan, you'll continue down the beach for about a half mile until you reach the Ice Age Trail (IAT) and the kayak campsites. From here, you'll head into the forest, past the campsites, and onto a wide, grassy trail bordered by ferns and wildflowers. The mixed forest here is thick with undergrowth, saving for the occasional stretches of water-logged terrain in the low areas.

As you continue down the IAT, you'll make your way onto the Green Loop Trail to swing by Molash Creek. There's a bench to sit along this quiet waterway and watch for herons, ducks, and other wetland wildlife. When you get to the far end of the loop, the IAT heads south, while you'll keep to the Green Loop. Around the final half of your quest, as you connect to the Blue and Red Loops, the forest slowly transitions to one dominated by tall, elegant evergreens. Here, more of the low-lying wetlands parallel the trail, and you'll see standing water, thick spreads of marsh grasses, and swathes of cattails. You'll pick up the IAT once more along the Red Loop to wind down your adventure with a peaceful stroll along a moss-lined path back to the paved entrance road. From here, it's just a short walk back to the forest ranger office where you began.

TURN-BY-TURN DIRECTIONS

1. From the trail map at the forest ranger office, head into the grassy picnic area, following the "Dog Trail to Beach" sign.
2. At 0.2 miles, bear right to follow the "Dog Beach South of Lighthouse" sign to continue along the beach.
3. At 0.8 miles, turn right onto the signposted IAT, leaving the beach to enter the forest. In 200 feet, turn left to follow the yellow-blazed trail.
4. At 1.2 miles, keep right at the fork to follow the yellow-blazed trail.
5. At 1.3 miles, keep right at the fork, ignoring the unmarked trail spur.
6. At 1.4 miles, keep left at the fork to continue on the IAT and Green Loop Trail.
7. At 1.9 miles, continue straight across a gravel road.
8. At 2.7 miles, turn right at the T-junction to continue on the signposted Green Loop Trail, leaving the IAT behind.
9. At 3.4 miles, continue straight across a gravel road.
10. At 3.7 miles, bear left at the fork onto the signposted Blue Loop Trail.
11. At 4.3 miles, turn right onto the signposted Red Loop Trail. In 60 feet, bear left to stay on the signposted Red Loop Trail.
12. At 4.5 miles, bear left at the fork onto the signposted IAT.
13. At 5.0 miles, turn right onto the paved road to return to the forest ranger office.

FIND THE TRAILHEAD

From the intersection of 22nd Street and Washington Street in Two Rivers, head east on 22nd Street. Proceed for 0.8 miles and continue straight when the road transitions to County Road O/Sandy Bay Road. After 4.5 miles, turn right onto Park Road. After 0.1 miles, reach the forest ranger office and park in the lot behind the building. The trail begins at the trail map at the office.

PETSKULL BREWING COMPANY

Paul Hoffman, owner of PetSkull Brewing Company, loved visiting breweries while traveling with his family. He always felt there was something about the ambiance and beers of a microbrewery that you can't get anywhere else. Post-vacation, he'd return home to Manitowoc, sad that they didn't have anything like that locally. That is, until he took it upon himself to make the change. Paul opened PetSkull Brewing Company in 2017 while still working full-time as an IT instructor at a local tech college—he loved his job, but he was also passionate about bringing craft beer to Manitowoc.

Nine months in, and the brewery was already bursting at the seams. Some local developers saw this and suggested a more spacious building they had available—a former 1908 tannery that had since become a scrap metal yard and later a vacant space, right off a peninsula on the Manitowoc River. However, it took a few years and a couple of follow-ups from the developers before Paul was ready to get the property and take on the brewery full-time. He made the move in 2021 from a system welded together by students at the tech college to a shiny new brewing system that lets him keep 20 beers on tap.

Schnitzky, a German-style hefeweizen, features notes of clove and banana. Anytime a glass of this beer is poured, the bartender yells, "Schnitzky!"—a call immediately echoed by the entire room. The tradition started at a brew fest before PetSkull Brewing Company had officially opened, and it's continued ever since.

LAND MANAGER

Point Beach State Forest
9400 County Highway O
Two Rivers, WI 54241
(920) 794-7480
dnr.wisconsin.gov/topic/parks/pointbeach
dnr.wisconsin.gov/topic/parks/pointbeach/maps

BREWERY/RESTAURANT

PetSkull Brewing Company
1015 Buffalo Street
Manitowoc, WI 54220
(920) 717-0237
petskullbrewing.com

Distance from trailhead: 12.4 miles

BAIRD CREEK WEST LOOP

WIND AROUND A LIVELY CREEK OVER HILLS AND WETLANDS

STARTING POINT	DESTINATION
BAIRD CREEK ROAD TRAILHEAD	BAIRD CREEK
BREWERY	**HIKE TYPE**
COPPER STATE BREWING CO.	MODERATE
DOG FRIENDLY	**SEASON**
YES (LEASH REQUIRED)	MAY–OCTOBER
FEES	**DURATION**
NONE	2 HOURS
MAP REFERENCE	**LENGTH**
POSTED AT TRAILHEAD	3.8 MILES (ROUND TRIP)
HIGHLIGHTS	**ELEVATION GAIN**
BAIRD CREEK, WILDFLOWERS	79 FEET

3.5% ALCOHOL CONTENT

WE DRINK AT DAWN! BEERMOSA RADLER

ORANGE

CITRUS, PINEAPPLE

TANGY, JUICY

BITTERNESS SWEETNESS

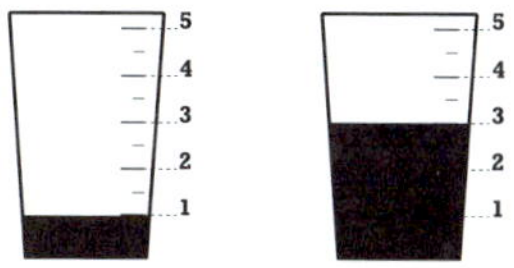

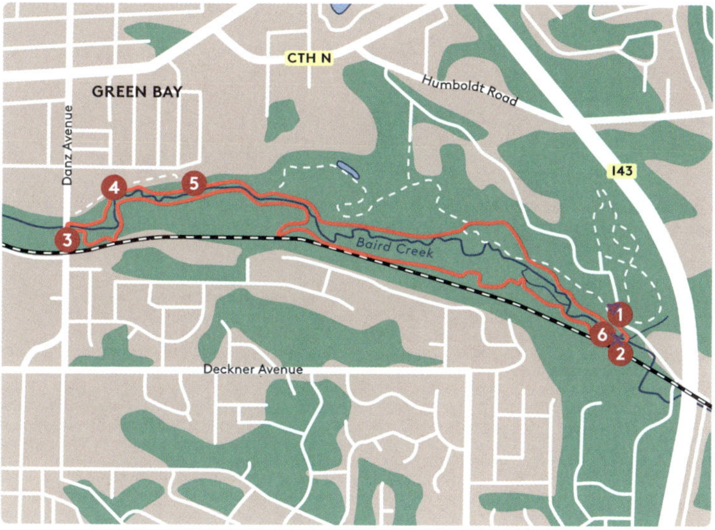

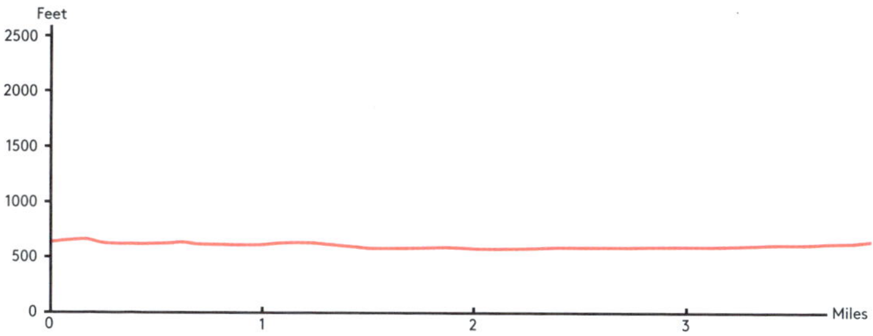

HIKE DESCRIPTION

Dive into an urban oasis on the forested trails along Baird Creek. You'll wander over hills and meander through a vibrant wetland with a colorful array of wildflowers. Afterward, make your way to Copper State Brewing Co. for a tasty pour of their fruity sour, We Drink At Dawn!

Baird Creek winds through the northeastern corner of Green Bay, eventually connecting to the East River and then the Fox River, which runs through the city's center. The Baird Creek Preservation Foundation works to protect the Baird Creek Greenway through prairie and wetland restoration, removing invasive species, building supportive habitats for pollinators, and more. It also aims to improve the physical and mental well-being of community members and visitors with

the miles of trails coursing along Baird Creek and the surrounding forests, prairies, and wetlands. The Baird Creek trails include 14 miles of both single-track dirt trails and paved pathways for biking and foot travel. Our route loops around the creek on the western half of the trail system.

Your loop starts with a bridge crossing to reach Baird Creek's southern bank, where you'll amble along a single-track dirt trail. On this side of the waterway, you're immersed in a thick forest with bursts of purple bee balm dotting the sunny patches along the trail. You'll climb a few steep hills with an occasional overlook of the bubbling waterway below. While cresting the last of these hills, you'll briefly emerge from the woods alongside a railroad track before diving back in and descending toward the creek.

Halfway through your loop, you'll step out of the forest once more, this time onto the sidewalk along Danz Avenue. You'll follow the sidewalk just far enough to cross over the creek, then leave the city sounds behind as you return to the quiet sanctuary of the woods.

About half a mile later, you'll transition to a paved pathway for the final third of your journey. This wide, smooth walkway beckons you to slow your pace. Heaps of bee balm, black-eyed Susans, and purple coneflowers line the path. In the spring, you might spot skunk cabbage along the wetland areas. Pause to enjoy the benches, read the informational plaques, and admire the metal sculptures along the way. Near the journey's end, you'll see a series of shallow cascades in the creek. A short dirt path leads to the water's edge, where you can admire the waterway up close and snap a few last pictures before completing your loop at the trailhead.

TURN-BY-TURN DIRECTIONS

1. From the trailhead map, take the paved path into the woods. In 80 feet, bear right at the fork onto the gravel path. In another 150 feet, turn right to cross the bridge over Baird Creek. On the other side of the bridge, turn right and then immediately left to head up the hill.
2. At 0.1 miles, reach an unmarked T-junction and turn right.
3. At 2.1 miles, turn right onto the sidewalk and then cross the bridge over Baird Creek. In 100 feet, turn right on the dirt path heading back into the woods.
4. At 2.3 miles, continue straight, ignoring an unmarked trail spur on the left.
5. At 2.5 miles, turn right onto the paved path. Continue straight on the pavement, ignoring any dirt trail spurs for the next 1.2 miles.
6. At 3.7 miles, turn right onto a dirt trail spur for 30 feet to reach Baird Creek. Enjoy the view, then return to the paved trail and continue for 150 feet to reach the trailhead.

FIND THE TRAILHEAD

From Green Bay at Monroe Avenue and I-29/Walnut Street, head north on Monroe Avenue for 2.8 miles. Turn right onto University Avenue and proceed for 0.4 miles. Turn right onto County Road N/Humbolt Road. Continue for 0.1 miles, then turn right onto Baird Creek Road. After 0.9 miles, at the Baird Creek Nature & Ski Trail sign, turn right into the paved parking lot. The trail begins at the trail map by the parking lot entrance.

COPPER STATE BREWING CO.

Co-owners Missy and Jon Martens had zero brewing experience when they jumped at the chance to open a brewery in Green Bay, WI. They were living in Minnesota, Missy as a former schoolteacher homeschooling their kids and John as a mechanical engineer, when they learned that Hinterland Brewery in Green Bay was moving and their old location was up for sale. Hinterland Brewery had to keep brewing in their current location until the new site was ready, but they offered John an apprenticeship during that time. So, instead of starting with a homebrew kit as most brewers do, he learned the ropes on a 30-barrel brewing system—the exact one he'd soon be using to brew their own beer.

Copper State Brewing came to life in 2017, not just as a brewery, but also as a full restaurant and coffee shop. Jon is head of brewing operations, and he's tweaked the system along the way courtesy of his background in engineering. Missy handles the marketing and continues to homeschool their four kids, each of whom works in the kitchen part-time. Her favorite part of the business is the people and how their family-run brewery has become a true gathering space for the community.

Copper State Brewing Co.'s We Drink at Dawn! Beermosa Radler delivers a refreshing burst of tangerine, blood orange, and pineapple. It's an easy-drinking sour offering the perfect balance of sweet and tart.

LAND MANAGER

Baird Creek Preservation Foundation
P.O. Box 824
Green Bay, WI 54305
(920) 328-3505
bairdcreek.org
bairdcreek.org/trails-maps-pets

BREWERY/RESTAURANT

Copper State Brewing Co.
313 Dousman Street
Green Bay, WI 54303
(920) 489-8575
copperstate.beer

Distance from trailhead: 5.2 miles

EAGLE TRAIL

HIKE BELOW SOARING CLIFFS AND EXPLORE LIMESTONE CAVES

STARTING POINT	DESTINATION
EAGLE TOWER	NIAGARA ESCARPMENT
BREWERY	**HIKE TYPE**
DOOR COUNTY BREWING COMPANY	MODERATE
DOG FRIENDLY	**SEASON**
YES (LEASH REQUIRED)	MAY–OCTOBER
FEES	**DURATION**
YES	1 HOUR 30 MINUTES
MAP REFERENCE	**LENGTH**
PENINSULA STATE PARK	2.4 MILES (LOOP)
HIGHLIGHTS	**ELEVATION GAIN**
OBSERVATION TOWER, CLIFFS, LAKE VIEWS	205 FEET

6.2%
ALCOHOL CONTENT

VACATIONLAND IPA

PALE YELLOW

TROPICAL, PEACH

GRAPEFRUIT, DARK STONE FRUIT

BITTERNESS **SWEETNESS**

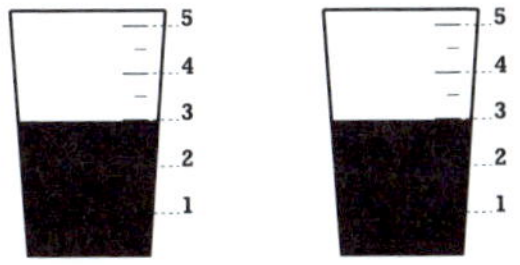

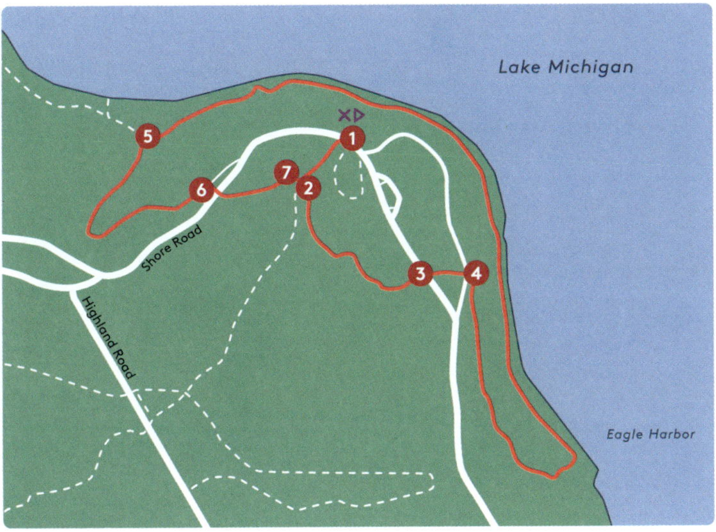

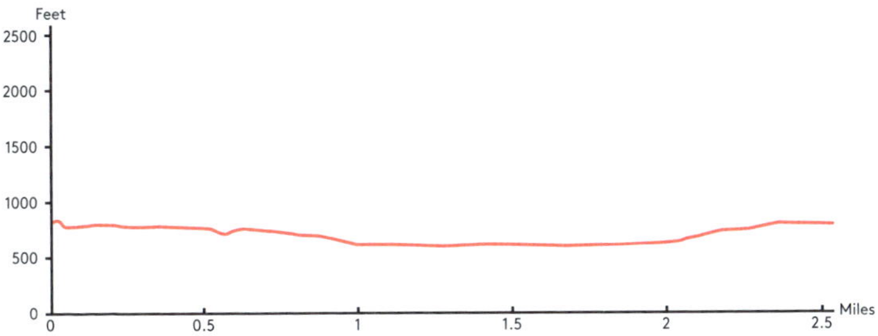

HIKE DESCRIPTION

Explore the limestone bluffs, caves, and natural springs along the Eagle Harbor shoreline. Extend your adventure with a trip to Door County Brewing for a thirst-quenching pint of Vacationland IPA.

Peninsula State Park encompasses a small peninsula on the western side of Door County along Lake Michigan's Green Bay. A mix of forest types covers the park, from densely packed cedars and hemlocks along the shoreline to oaks, maples, beech, and pines across much of the inland region. With this variety, the state park is known for having a vibrant display of color in the fall. It also stands out as a recreation space with something for just about everyone, such as camping, beach access, hiking and biking trails, a golf course, a theater, a lighthouse, and an observation tower.

Your adventure starts at the observation tower, Eagle Tower, with a climb to the top for a panoramic view of Eagle Harbor. The original tower, built by hand in 1914, started as a fire tower. As the area received increased visitors, it became more of a tourist attraction for its spectacular overlook of the harbor. A new iteration, built with the help of horses and machines, replaced the original in 1932. Then, in 2021, the park constructed the current 60-foot tower that includes two ways to reach the observation deck: a 100-step spiraling staircase or a 850-foot fully accessible canopy walk. Dogs can't join you on the tower, but they are welcome on the hiking trails.

Once you've taken in the sights from up top, it's time to head into the forest. You'll pick up the Sentinel Trail across the road from the tower and turn onto the Eagle Trail at the first junction. The trail is

well-signed and easy to track with trail names at each junction and trail markers along the way (a picture of an eagle on a yellow square). Your first half mile follows a wide, flat path meandering through a predominately beech and maple forest. However, once you cross the parking area for Eagle Terrace, a "Difficult Trail" sign signals an upcoming change. Before heading onto the "Difficult Trail" though, you'll hop on the spur for Eagle Terrace, a former limestone quarry. It's a quick trip down a couple of flights of stone stairs to a stone terrace overlooking Eagle Harbor.

Back on the main trail, you'll descend on a path of tangled roots and rocks as the forest transitions to cedar trees and you wind around several rock outcroppings. Once you reach the lake, the trail parallels the shoreline with emerging cliffs on your left. The cliffs, part of the Niagara Escarpment, start low and gradually increase in height until they tower more than 150 feet above you. The escarpment stretches from Niagara Falls through Ontario, Canada, and down to east-central Wisconsin. Here, you can see the cliffs up close as the trail cuts right along the base. You may have to climb over fallen rocks and large tree roots, so step carefully. Some interesting features to look for along the cliffs include caves, ferns growing from the cracks and ledges, and spring water flowing near the base. Many of the cracks and layers seem so straight it almost looks like someone built the wall out of geometric blocks. Once the trail departs from the base of the cliff, you'll begin the trek back to the top. The forest shifts back to mostly maple and beech, and the rocky path smooths out for an easy finish to your journey.

TURN-BY-TURN DIRECTIONS

1. From the base of Eagle Tower, climb to the top for a panoramic view. Once back at the base, cross the parking lot to begin hiking on the signposted Sentinel Trail.
2. At 0.1 miles, at a junction, turn left onto the signposted Eagle Trail.
3. At 0.4 miles, cross a paved road. In 250 feet, cross a parking lot and continue on the signposted Eagle Trail.
4. At 0.5 miles, reach a T-junction. Turn left to follow the sign for Eagle Terrace. Admire the overlook, then return to the junction and continue straight.
5. At 1.8 miles, at a T-junction, turn left to continue on the signposted Eagle Trail.
6. At 2.1 miles, cross a parking lot and continue on the signposted Eagle Trail. In 60 feet, cross a paved road.
7. At 2.3 miles, reach the junction from Step 2. Turn left to return to the trailhead.

FIND THE TRAILHEAD

From Baily's Harbor at County Highway F and Highway 57, head northwest on County Highway F. After 0.9 miles, turn right to stay on County Highway F. After 3.6 miles, continue straight onto Maple Grove Road. After 2.4 miles, turn right onto Water Street S. After 0.2 miles, turn left onto Shore Road. After 1.2 miles, reach the Eagle Tower parking spaces along both sides of the road. Eagle Tower is on the right, and the trail begins at the map on the left.

DOOR COUNTY BREWING COMPANY

John and Angie McMahon dreamed up Door County Brewing as a business that could bring their grown kids back home. At the time, the area didn't offer many options for year-round jobs or businesses; it's a summer tourist destination where many businesses close or significantly reduce hours from Labor Day to Memorial Day. One of their sons was already producing beer with a home brewing kit, and that sparked an idea—if they built a brewery, would he come home to be the brewmaster? The answer was yes, and the McMahons launched their family business in 2013.

Door County Brewing started strong with a porter as their first brew. Next came a Belgian-style wheat beer, then a variety of saisons and farmhouse beers to honor the strong Belgian presence in Door County. They've expanded to focus on a variety of traditional styles, including Vacationland IPA. It's a crushable beer with a light fruit flavor and a creamy mouthfeel.

LAND MANAGER

Peninsula State Park
9462 Shore Rd.
Fish Creek, WI 54212
(920) 868-3258
dnr.wisconsin.gov/topic/parks/peninsula
dnr.wisconsin.gov/topic/parks/peninsula/maps

BREWERY/RESTAURANT

Door County Brewing Co.
8099 WI-57
Baileys Harbor, WI 54202
(920) 239-8181
doorcountybrewingco.com

Distance from trailhead: 8.5 miles

LYND POINT LOOP

ESCAPE TO A SERENE BOREAL FOREST ALONG LAKE MICHIGAN

STARTING POINT	DESTINATION
NEWPORT PARKING LOT #3	LYND POINT
BREWERY	**HIKE TYPE**
PEACH BARN FARMHOUSE AND BREWERY	EASY
DOG FRIENDLY	**SEASON**
YES (LEASH REQUIRED)	MAY–OCTOBER
FEES	**DURATION**
YES	1 HOUR
MAP REFERENCE	**LENGTH**
NEWPORT STATE PARK	2.4 MILES (LOOP)
HIGHLIGHTS	**ELEVATION GAIN**
BOARDWALK, NEWPORT BAY	7 FEET

6.0% ALCOHOL CONTENT

SILO SISTERS PEACH SOUR

AMBER

FRESH PEACH

SWEET, SOUR, PEACH

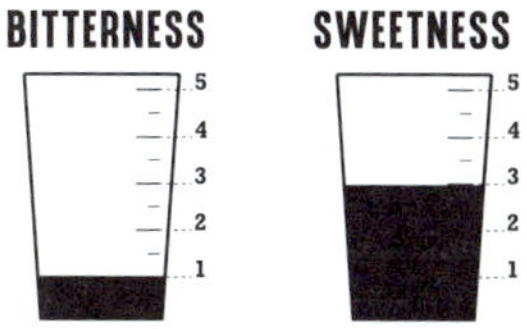

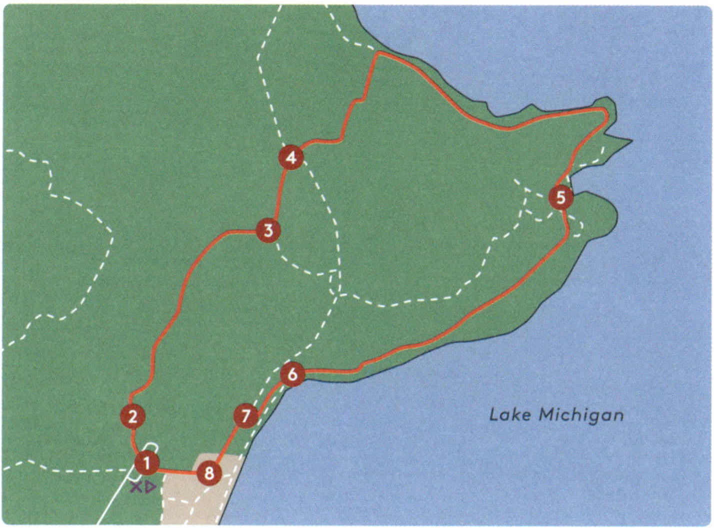

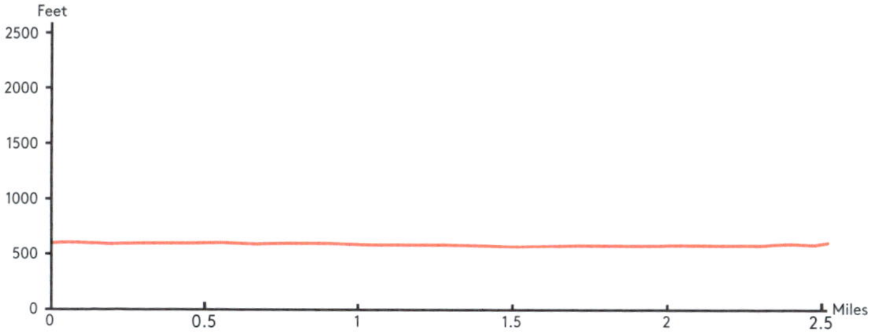

HIKE DESCRIPTION

Ramble through a lush forest to the rugged shoreline and sandy beaches of Newport Bay. After, wander into town for a juicy pint of Peach Barn's Silo Sisters Peach Sour.

Newport State Park sits at the northern end of the Door Peninsula, tucked away from the hubbub of the popular Door County towns. For anyone seeking the quiet solitude of nature, this is the place to be. Newport State Park received a Dark Sky Park designation in 2017, a testament to its seclusion along Lake Michigan's western shore and the resulting lack of artificial light. The park offers 30 miles of hiking trails (26 for winter activities) through a thick boreal forest. While the land here is rough, the trails are generally easy to moderate in difficulty, making it an excellent space for adventurers of varying abilities and experience.

The loop around Lynd Point is a short but diverse trek through Newport's wilderness. You'll begin your adventure on the Fern Trail, a wide, crushed-limestone path meandering through a mature forest of large cedar trees and mixed hardwoods. As the path transitions to a long boardwalk, the undergrowth becomes denser with ferns until you reach an opening in the trees where a sea of ferns has completely taken over the space. This section of the trail often floods in the spring, making it impassable for hikers. In 2023, the Newport Wilderness Society built the raised, 1,800-foot, accessible boardwalk crossing for a better, more inclusive hiking experience. Just over a half mile into your walk, shortly after departing the boardwalk, you'll reach a junction with the Europe Bay Trail where the accessible path continues to the right. For this route, however, you'll continue straight onto the

Lynd Point Trail. Here, the understory and forest floor open up under a high tree canopy. As you near the shoreline and the understory fills back in, you'll wind through a section of mossy, layered rock formations. Small varieties of ferns sprout from the tops of the rocks and amongst the rocks' cracks and crevices. Trees also started growing in these nooks long ago, and you'll see where the roots have pried apart the layers of rock.

Once you reach the shoreline, about a mile into your journey, you'll loosely follow it for the remainder of the hike. The seam where Lake Michigan meets the land is rough, rocky, and dotted with cedar trees. Watch your footing as you travel over the rooted path, and be sure to pause whenever you catch an opening in the trees to take in this magnificent lake. As you start to round Lynd Point, you'll pass by a couple of the seventeen backcountry campsites that Newport State Park has to offer. Many of the sites sit close to the shoreline, offering great opportunities for star-gazing. As you head into your last half mile of hiking, you'll catch sight of the sandy beach along Newport Bay, a distinct change from the rocky ledges you encountered earlier.

TURN-BY-TURN DIRECTIONS

1. From the trailhead kiosk, cross the parking lot to the signposted Fern Trail.
2. At 0.1 miles, continue straight, ignoring a trail spur on the right.
3. At 0.5 miles, keep left at the fork to remain on the signposted Fern Trail.
4. At 0.6 miles, reach a junction. Continue straight, transitioning onto the signposted Lynd Point Trail.
5. At 1.5 miles, continue straight, ignoring a trail spur on the right. In 100 feet, continue past a second spur on the right.
6. At 2.1 miles, continue straight, ignoring a trail spur on the left.
7. At 2.2 miles, turn left onto an unmarked gravel path.
8. At 2.3 miles, turn right onto a paved path to return to the trailhead parking lot.

FIND THE TRAILHEAD

From Sister Bay at WI-42 and WI-57, head northeast on WI-42. After 7.7 miles, turn right onto County Road NP. After 2.5 miles, turn right onto Newport Lane. After 0.5 miles, reach the park entrance and continue on Newport Park Road for 1.1 miles. Parking Lot #3 will be on the right, marked with a small sign. The trailhead kiosk is on the right side of the lot toward the beach. The trail begins on the left side of the lot at the sign for the Fern Trail.

PEACH BARN FARMHOUSE AND BREWERY

Jason and Sarah White didn't set out to open a brewery in northern Wisconsin. Sure, they had chatted about opening a brewery before, but just something small that would be more of a hobby in their retirement years—not mid-pandemic in a new-to-them town across the country. In 2020, they were living in Colorado and purchased the Sister Bay, Wisconsin, property with intentions to live closer to Sarah's family and offer a summer farmer's market featuring Colorado

peaches. In grad school, Jason had started a peach distribution company, bringing peaches grown in Palisade, CO, on the Rocky Mountains' western slope, to the front range and Denver area. When they first proposed the farmer's market idea to Sister Bay, the city council declined it due to property and business regulations. The same happened with their next couple of backup options. As they were leaving the city council meeting, Jason tossed out the notion of opening a brewery, half-joking because it seemed more unlikely than the previous requests—the city council loved it.

Peach Barn offers a range of beers to meet the diverse tastes that Door County tourism brings to town. Jason, however, has a soft spot for Belgian beer. As tourists themselves, Jason and Sarah loved exploring Brussels and Brugge in Belgium. They've tried to incorporate some of that vibe in their outdoor seating areas, and Jason tries to always have at least one Belgian beer on tap. A peach-based brew is, of course, another regular option available. Silo Sisters Peach Sour tastes like a sip of fresh peaches with a touch of tartness.

LAND MANAGER

Newport State Park
475 Cty Hwy NP
Ellison Bay, WI 54210
(920) 854-2500
dnr.wisconsin.gov/topic/parks/newport
dnr.wisconsin.gov/topic/parks/newport/maps

BREWERY/RESTAURANT

Peach Barn Farmhouse and Brewery
2450 S Bay Shore Drive
Sister Bay, WI 54234
peachbarnbrewing.com

Distance from trailhead: 12.1 miles

MICHIGAN

LAKE MARY PLAINS PATHWAY

DEVOUR THIS SPREAD OF STATELY PINES AND WILD BLUEBERRIES

STARTING POINT	**DESTINATION**
GLIDDEN LAKE	CRYSTAL FALLS STATE FOREST
BREWERY	**HIKE TYPE**
ALPHA MICHIGAN BREWING COMPANY	MODERATE
DOG FRIENDLY	**SEASON**
YES (LEASH REQUIRED)	MAY–OCTOBER
FEES	**DURATION**
YES	3 HOURS
MAP REFERENCE	**LENGTH**
POSTED AT TRAILHEAD	7.1 MILES (LOLLIPOP LOOP)
HIGHLIGHTS	**ELEVATION GAIN**
WILD BERRIES, TALL PINES, LAKE VIEWS	123 FEET

6.7%
ALCOHOL CONTENT

BRULE RIVER RED AMERICAN AMBER ALE

AMBER

MALTY,
LIGHT HOPS

CARAMEL,
MALT

BITTERNESS

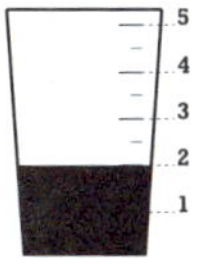

SWEETNESS

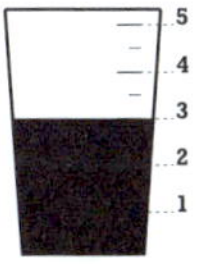

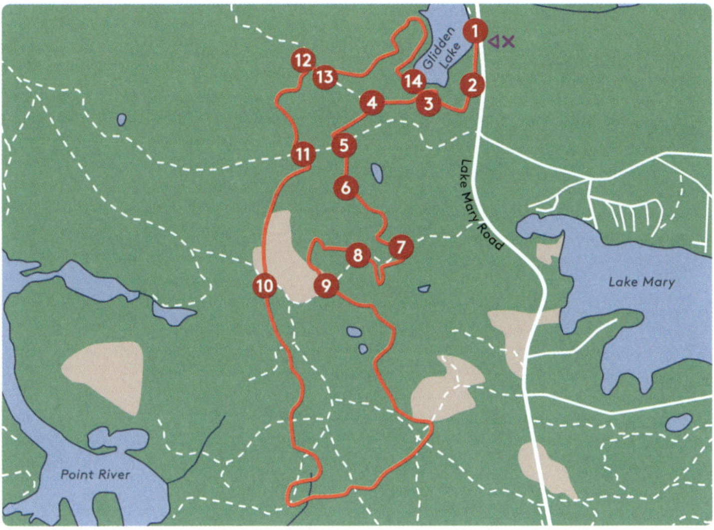

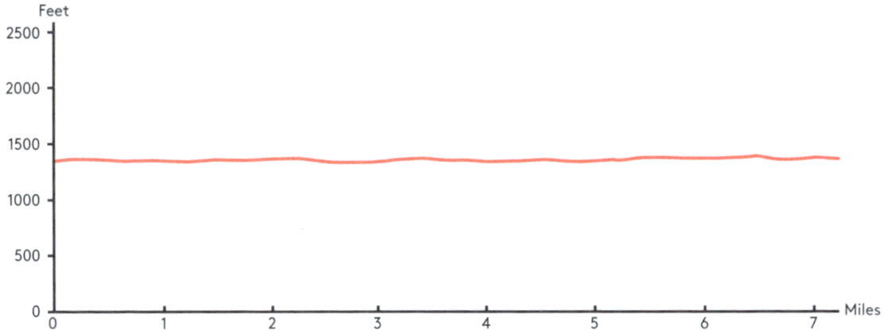

HIKE DESCRIPTION

Amble through a sea of pines, a swarm of blueberry bushes, and an overall stunning state forest. Then, swing down to Alpha Michigan Brewing Company for a taste of their Brule River Red.

Embark on a journey where the world slows down and nature takes center stage. With a well-marked trail that invites you to leave your phone behind, the Lake Mary Plains Pathway beckons you to immerse yourself in its beauty. This tranquil loop weaves through the Crystal Falls State Forest, meandering alongside the sparkling waters of Glidden Lake.

Blue triangles mark the Pathway trail system, and each intersection includes a number and a map. A series of off-highway vehicle (OHV) trails meanders through this same area, but they're generally dirt and often wider than the mowed-grass Pathway trails. Wherever these two trails cross paths, it'll be at a nearly perpendicular angle, and you'll see hiking markers and "No Vehicles" signs on the Pathway trail. The only potentially confusing part of this trail is that you won't encounter Lake Mary, as the name may imply, just Glidden Lake. Now, it's time to lace up your boots and let the adventure unfold.

From the Glidden Lake Campground, you'll enter a predominately pine forest sprawled with wildflowers and wild blueberries. If you time your visit just right—between late July and early September—you can treat yourself to these sweet, juicy gems for a delicious trailside snack. Continuing your journey over the rolling hills, the forest floor transforms into a lush carpet of ferns. Red pines, the primary type here, get their name from their bark, which grows as large, reddish-brown scales. They typically grow to reach heights of 60–80 feet—quite a difference from the low ferns growing at their base in this forest.

After wandering for several miles under the towering pines, you'll reach a recently logged section of forest at Intersection 6. Here, with the open landscape, you'll enjoy another burst of wildflowers and a great opportunity to look for eagles, hawks, and sandhill cranes. The last stretch of the trail weaves through a tapestry of mixed forests, gently hugging the shores of Glidden Lake as you make your way back to the campground and trailhead. At the time of writing, the trail section from Intersection 7 to 8 was closed for repairs on the boardwalk cutting through the bog on the northern side of the lake. If that segment is open when you visit, consider adding it for additional views of Glidden Lake and to create a full loop rather than a lollipop route.

TURN-BY-TURN DIRECTIONS

1. From the trailhead parking lot, follow the dirt road back to the campground entrance and continue along the campground road. In 300 feet, keep left at the fork.
2. At 0.2 miles, reach Intersection 1 at the back of the campground. Bear left onto the mowed-grass path.
3. At 0.5 miles, at Intersection 2, bear left onto the trail signposted as the Loop 2 & 3, Middle and Long Loops.
4. At 0.7 miles, reach Intersection 4. Turn left, following the arrow for Intersection 5.
5. At 0.9 miles, cross a dirt OHV trail, following the blue trail marker.
6. At 1.1 miles, bear left at the fork.
7. At 1.5 miles, cross a dirt OHV trail.
8. At 1.8 miles, cross another dirt OHV trail.
9. At 2.2 miles, reach Intersection 5. Cross a dirt OHV road to continue straight on the trail signposted as the Loop 3 Long Loop. Over the next 2.4 miles, continue straight across 9 more OHV trails.
10. At 4.6 miles, at Intersection 6, continue forward, following the arrow on the "Return" sign.
11. At 5.2 miles, cross a dirt OHV trail.
12. At 5.6 miles, at Intersection 7, turn right, following the arrow to Intersection 3.
13. At 5.7 miles, reach Intersection 3 and turn left.
14. At 6.6 miles, reach Intersection 2 from Step 3. Turn left to return to the campground and trailhead parking lot.

FIND THE TRAILHEAD

From Crystal Falls at N 5th Street and US Hwy 141/Crystal Avenue, head south on N 5th Street. In 377 feet, turn left onto Superior Avenue/M-69. After 4.5 miles, turn right onto Lake Mary Road and proceed for 1.1 miles. At the sign for Glidden Lake Campground, turn right into the campground entrance. Just ahead is the information kiosk with self-pay permits for day use. To the right is the entrance for the day-use and trailhead parking lot. The trail map is posted at the far end of the parking area.

ALPHA MICHIGAN BREWING COMPANY

Mike Bjork grew up in the town of Alpha, Michigan, at a time when about 500 people called the place home. After leaving to join the military, he met his wife, Mary, in language school. Eventually they both transitioned to careers with the CIA before retiring and returning to Alpha. By then, however, the town had dwindled to about 120 people. When the opportunity to open a brewery presented itself, Mike and Mary, along with their partners, saw it as a way to help elevate the town and give back to the community. They brew with a purpose—to donate a portion of their sales to support local charities, schools, and community projects.

Alpha Michigan Brewing Company is veteran-owned and offers a variety of styles to suit a range of beer lovers. Alpha's Brule River Red, an American amber ale, delivers a malty caramel flavor with a light hop aroma.

LAND MANAGER

Michigan Department of Natural Resources
Forest Resources Division
P.O. Box 30452
Lansing, MI 48909
(517) 284-5900
www2.dnr.state.mi.us/parksandtrails/Default.aspx
www2.dnr.state.mi.us/parksandtrails/Details.aspx?id=83&type=SFPW#-map-tab

BREWERY/RESTAURANT

Alpha Michigan Brewing Company
303 E Center Street
Alpha, MI 49902
(920) 358-9551
alphamibeer.com

Distance from trailhead: 10.7 miles

MANISTIQUE BOARDWALK

A BEACHSIDE STROLL THROUGH HISTORY

STARTING POINT	DESTINATION
FISHING PIER	MANISTIQUE LIGHTHOUSE
BREWERY	HIKE TYPE
FLATIRON BREWING	EASY
DOG FRIENDLY	SEASON
YES (LEASH REQUIRED)	YEAR-ROUND
FEES	DURATION
NONE	1 HOUR 45 MINUTES
MAP REFERENCE	LENGTH
POSTED AT TRAILHEAD	3.6 MILES (ROUND TRIP)
HIGHLIGHTS	ELEVATION GAIN
LIGHTHOUSE, BEACH, LAKE MICHIGAN	7 FEET

5.0%
ALCOHOL CONTENT

CZECH UP LAGER

DARK RED

ROASTED MALTS

ROASTED MALTS, SMOOTH

BITTERNESS

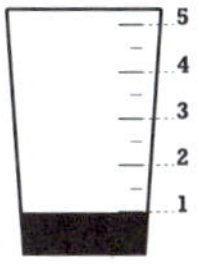

SWEETNESS

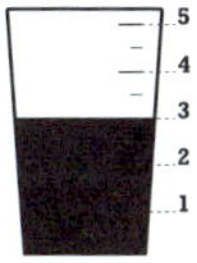

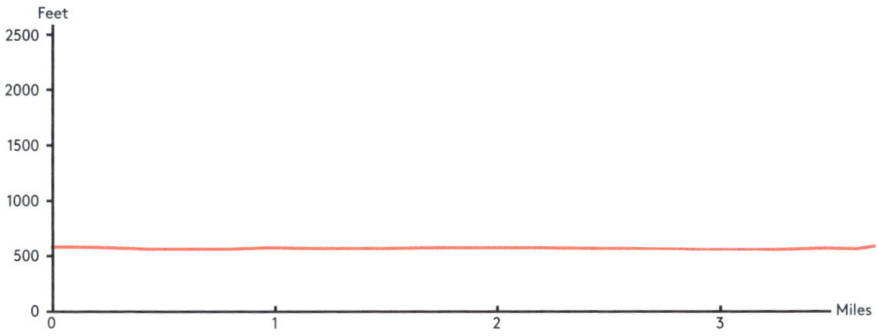

HIKE DESCRIPTION

Explore Manistique's history, beaches, and lighthouse with a leisurely stroll on the boardwalk. Jump to the present with a trip to Flatiron Brewing for a thirst-quenching flight of their tasty brews.

Winding along Lake Michigan's north shore, the Manistique Boardwalk serves as a blend of leisure and education, with interpretive signs detailing the area's rich history in logging and pig iron (or crude iron, which is used to make steel) along the scenic walkway. First constructed in 1991, the boardwalk provides access to a fishing pier, the east breakwater lighthouse, several picnic areas, and sandy beaches. The trail is a mix of pavement and wooden boardwalk, with a couple of sandy sections along Manistique Beach.

From the fishing pier, you'll head east on the boardwalk trail toward the beach and lighthouse. To get to the lighthouse, you'll have to cross about 250 feet of sand and rocks as you head down Manistique Beach to the breakwater. The path on top of the breakwater, however, is smooth blocks of concrete and easy to traverse. In the early 1900s, Manistique was thriving with the success of shipping products from the logging and iron industries. The town leaders recognized that a safe harbor protected from waves was key to the town's continued business and their aging wooden crib pier (timber stacked like a log house) couldn't keep up. So, they rallied support from the government to construct a new concrete breakwater and lighthouse. Construction of the east breakwater was completed in 1915, and the lighthouse reached operational status in 1916. Originally, a station keeper ran the lighthouse, but an automated system took over in 1969. The 35-foot-tall lighthouse still stands guard at the harbor entrance of the Manistique River.

After exploring the breakwater and lighthouse, you'll head back to the main path, where you'll continue along the top of the beach on a 500-foot wooden boardwalk. Due to the ever-changing landscape of this dune-like segment, portions of the walkway may be fully engulfed by sand. Just over a mile into your hike, you'll reach the Carl D. Bradley Lakeview Park, named after the Great Lakes freighter that sank 23 miles out from this point. On November 18, 1959, the ship encountered a storm during which the hull split in half and sank to the bottom of the lake. Only 2 of the 35 men on board survived the wreck. Because of this shipwreck and many similar stories, along with the lake's popularity, Lake Michigan is often considered the deadliest of the Great Lakes.

From the park, you'll dive into a few lightly wooded stretches of trail with scatterings of wildflowers in between. Several benches dot this section where you can take in the expansive views of the lake. Lake Michigan is the third largest of the Great Lakes (by area) and the only one of the five that lies completely within the United States—all the other Great Lakes share a partial border with Canada. You'll cross two more wooden boardwalks, one over a boggy section of land and another over a small stream, before reaching the trailhead and parking at the east end of the trail. Appreciate the beach, then turn around and enjoy the casual stroll back to the fishing pier when you're ready.

TURN-BY-TURN DIRECTIONS

1. From the trail map at the fishing pier parking lot, bear left onto the paved Boardwalk Trail.
2. At 0.2 miles, turn right to depart the Boardwalk Trail. Continue across the beach to the breakwater platform.
3. At 0.5 miles, reach the Manistique Lighthouse. Take in the view, then return to the Boardwalk Trail.
4. At 0.9 miles, reach the boardwalk and then turn right to continue on the boardwalk.
5. At 1.3 miles, reach Lakeview Park on the left. Continue straight on the Boardwalk Trail.
6. At 2.2 miles, reach the parking lot at the east end of the Boardwalk Trail. Enjoy the beach, then return to the fishing pier the same way you came.

FIND THE TRAILHEAD

From Manistique at Main Street and Maple Street, head south on Maple Street. After 0.3 miles, turn left onto E Lake Shore Drive/US Highway 2. In 300 feet, turn right on Harbor View Drive. After 450 feet, turn left onto S Cedar Drive and follow the road into the parking lot. The trail begins on the left.

FLATIRON BREWING

Adam Popour, Nick Powers, Jake Boudreau, and Ben Pineau started Flatiron Brewing out of their love for beer and for Manistique, the town where they all grew up. The group found their future brewery a home in a building that previously served as an auction house, an event center, and a gymnasium/recreation center. Now, as one of the largest venues in town, Flatiron still offers up its space for community and large-group events.

Despite the town's small size at just 2,800 residents, it has a spirited history with alcohol (no pun intended). In the late 1800s, a lumber company controlled all of Manistique except for one flatiron-shaped property (between Pearl, Water, and Main Streets). The company tried to force the town to remain "dry" (no alcohol), though many found a way around the rules by visiting whisky ships anchored just offshore. That is, until one man, Daniel Heffron, had a new idea. He purchased that flatiron-shaped property and built a saloon. Soon, others saw the success and purchased land from Heffron until nearly 30 saloons covered what became known as the "notorious Flat Iron Block." Today, Flatiron Brewing continues the tradition of serving up beer to the community, but in a more welcoming and family-friendly environment. Flatiron's Czech Up Lager is a smooth, dark lager with a warm, roasted flavor.

LAND MANAGER

City of Manistique
300 N. Maple St.
P.O. Box 515
Manistique, MI 49854
(906) 341-2290
cityofmanistique.org
visitmanistique.com/boardwalk.shtml

BREWERY/RESTAURANT

Flatiron Brewing
375 Trader's Point Drive, Stop 4
Manistique, MI 49854
(906) 286 4470
flatiron-brewing.com

Distance from trailhead: 1.2 miles

BUSH BAY

AN ENCHANTING FOREST STROLL ALONG LAKE HURON

STARTING POINT	DESTINATION
JOHN ARTHUR WOOLLAM PRESERVE TRAILHEAD	BUSH BAY

BREWERY	HIKE TYPE
LES CHENEAUX DISTILLERS	MODERATE

DOG FRIENDLY	SEASON
NO	APRIL-OCTOBER

FEES	DURATION
NONE	2 HOURS

MAP REFERENCE	LENGTH
ALLTRAILS	4.6 MILES (ROUND TRIP)

HIGHLIGHTS	ELEVATION GAIN
LAKE HURON, BOULDER FORMATIONS	15 FEET

6.4%
ALCOHOL CONTENT

VERA B'S HONEY BROWN

AMBER BROWN

HONEY,
NUTTY

HONEY,
NUTTY

BITTERNESS

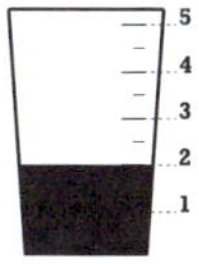

SWEETNESS

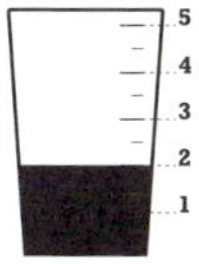

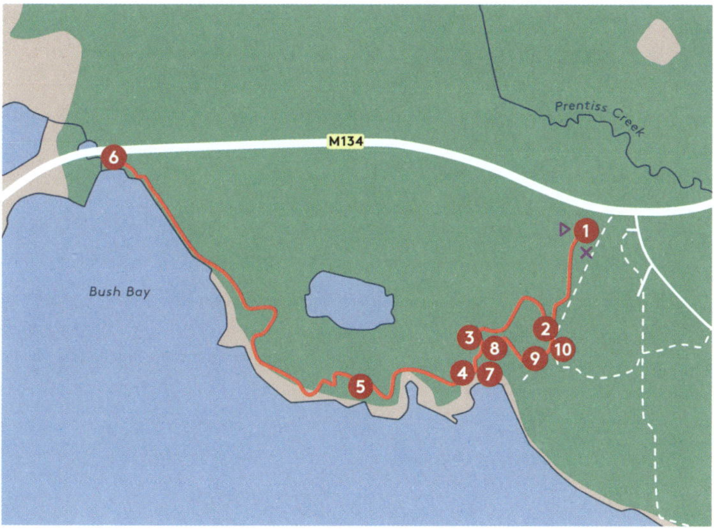

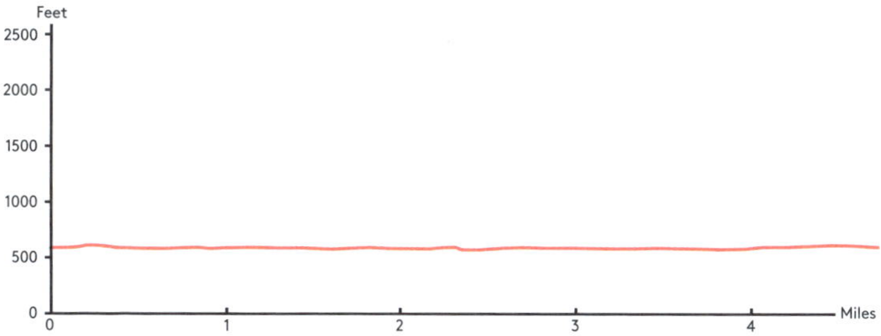

HIKE DESCRIPTION

Ramble through a thick forest along Lake Huron's craggy shoreline to explore an exquisite environment of boulders layered in tangled roots, plush moss, and delicate ferns. Wind down posthike with a crisp pint of Vera B's Honey Brown from Les Cheneaux Distillers.

The Nature Conservancy's John Arthur Woollam Preserve encompasses 185 acres of coastal wetlands and mixed forests along the northern end of Lake Huron, the third largest of the Great Lakes by volume. One of the preserve's top priorities includes safeguarding the 4,300 feet of lake shoreline within its boundaries. The Bush Bay Trail sweeps through the preserve to continue up the eastern side of Bush Bay. The Nature Conservancy still manages the trail, though more than half of the route winds through privately owned land outside the preserve's boundary.

Your adventure begins on the eastern end of the trail, where you'll head into the preserve on a wide path. Take advantage of this spacious stretch to admire the wildflowers and lush forest. After around a third of a mile, you'll turn onto the Bush Bay Trail, a single-track path marked with red arrows. Here, the trees squeeze in closer as you weave your way toward Lake Huron.

Around this point, you'll start to see boulders dotting the forest floor, from couch-sized up to that of a tall cargo van. Still following the arrows, you'll slip through a short corridor between two extra-large

boulders to emerge in a cove of these jumbo stones. Many are rough and pitted with small holes. Gnarled tree roots lace over their moss-covered surfaces. Tiny ferns sprout from some of the pockets and holes while the tops are layered in a mix of grasses and small shrubbery. The whimsical ambiance of this space brought on a popular nickname for the hike, "The Narnia Trail." In line with that, you'll see a lamppost and "Narnia" sign posted near two of the largest rocks.

Wandering on, the forest opens along the lake, offering space to admire the rocky shore. Jagged boulders dot the waters up close, while off in the distance you might see some of the Les Cheneaux Islands, or freighters traversing to or from Port Dolomite, a limestone and dolomite mine across Bush Bay. You'll trek along the rocky and rooted path for another mile until you reach the western end of the trail and a small dirt parking lot.

From here, you'll retrace your steps through the forest to the preserve boundary and pick up a short trail spur to head down to a sandy beach along Lake Huron. Stroll across the sand, dip your toes in the water, or just soak up the view. When you're ready, you'll head back to the Bush Bay Trail to catch the Woollam Shortcut Trail, marked with yellow arrows. You'll enjoy an easy stroll through the woods for the remainder of your adventure back to the trailhead.

TURN-BY-TURN DIRECTIONS

1. From the trailhead, pass through the gate to follow the two-track trail into the forest.
2. At 0.3 miles, turn right following the red arrow onto the Bush Bay Trail.
3. At 0.7 miles, continue straight following the red arrow for the Bush Bay Trail.
4. At 0.8 miles, turn right to stay on the Bush Bay Trail, following the red arrow. In 400 feet, continue straight past the trail map marking the preserve's boundary and where the trail continues onto private property.
5. At 1.2 miles, reach a lamppost and a "Narnia" sign. Continue following the arrows.
6. At 2.3 miles, reach the parking lot at the western end of the trail. Return to the T-junction at Step 4.
7. At 3.9 miles, reach the junction from Step 4. Turn right and continue for 80 feet to reach a beach. Enjoy the view, then return to the junction and continue straight.
8. At 4.0 miles, reach the junction from Step 3. Turn right onto the Woollam Shortcut Trail, following the yellow arrow.
9. At 4.1 miles, reach a T-junction. Turn left to follow the orange arrow.
10. At 4.3 miles, reach the T-junction from Step 2. Continue straight to return to the trailhead.

FIND THE TRAILHEAD

From Cedarville at M-134 and M-129, head east on M-134 and proceed for 6.2 miles. At the John Arthur Woollam Preserve sign, turn right onto the dirt road. After 250 feet, the road dead-ends at a small gravel parking lot. The trail begins at the gate at the far end of the lot.

LES CHENEAUX DISTILLERS

The idea for Les Cheneaux Distillers sparked from a fun conversation around the campfire: What would we do if the apocalypse happened? Jay Bowlby wanted to make booze. Over the next few years, good friends and co-owners Jay and Sue Bowlby and Jay and Kirsten Bohn transformed that idea into a full-fledged business plan. Katie and Pete Duman were living in Marquette when Katie's parents, the Bowlbys, asked if they wanted to help run the business. They were excited about the idea and moved back to join the team; Katie jumped into the marketing side of the business, and Pete started brewing with Katie's dad. Katie loves being part of a family-owned-and-operated company that makes their own product, and it feels extra special when customers return for more.

Les Cheneaux Distillers launched in 2017, and the second location, the Tipper Room, opened in 2022. While the Bowlbys and Bohns initially dreamed up Les Cheneaux Distillers as just a distillery, their plans quickly morphed to include a brewery and restaurant. With an average of ten beers on tap at all times, they have a style and flavor for just about everyone. Vera B's Honey Brown, made with local honey, delivers a warm honey flavor with a hint of nuttiness.

LAND MANAGER

The Nature Conservancy of Michigan
101 E. Cesar E. Chavez Avenue
Lansing, MI 48906
(517) 316-0300
nature.org/en-us/get-involved/how-to-help/places-we-protect/john-arthur-woollam-preserve
alltrails.com/trail/us/michigan/john-arthur-woollam-preserve-trail

BREWERY/RESTAURANT

Les Cheneaux Distillers
172 S Meridian Street
Cedarville, MI 49719
(906) 484-1213
lescheneauxdistillers.com

Distance from trailhead: 6.4 miles

TAHQUAMENON FALLS

MAJESTIC WATERFALLS AND A RIVERSIDE TREK

STARTING POINT	DESTINATION
UPPER FALLS TRAILHEAD	LOWER FALLS
BREWERY	**HIKE TYPE**
TAHQUAMENON FALLS BREWERY & PUB	MODERATE
DOG FRIENDLY	**SEASON**
YES (LEASH REQUIRED)	MAY–SEPTEMBER
FEES	**DURATION**
YES	2 HOURS 45 MINUTES
MAP REFERENCE	**LENGTH**
POSTED AT TRAILHEAD	5.7 MILES (POINT TO POINT)
HIGHLIGHTS	**ELEVATION GAIN**
WATERFALLS, TAHQUAMENON RIVER	270 FEET

5.0%
ALCOHOL CONTENT

BLACK BEAR STOUT

RICH BROWN

CHOCOLATE

CREAMY, CHOCOLATE

BITTERNESS

SWEETNESS

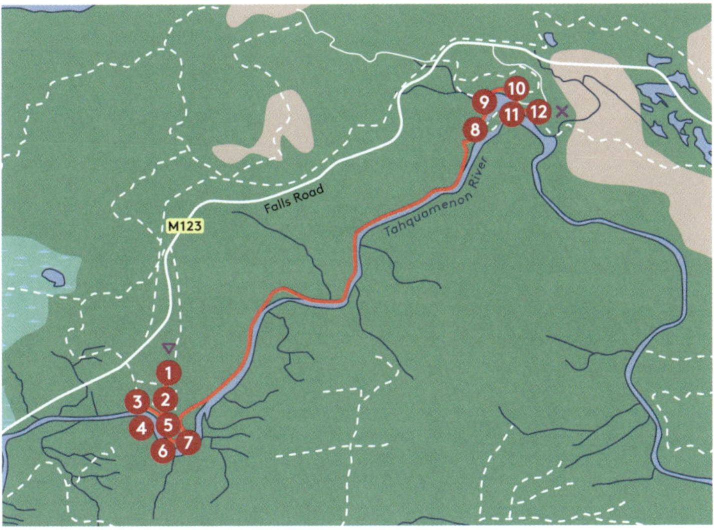

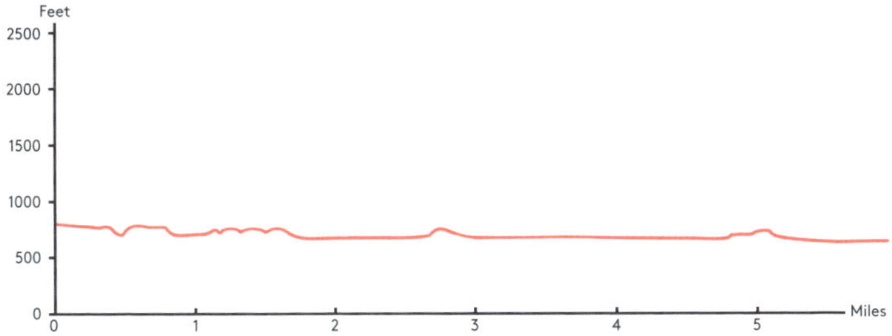

HIKE DESCRIPTION

Trek along the Tahquamenon River from its mighty 200-foot-wide Upper Falls to the quieter but equally captivating Lower Falls. Then, head back upriver for a tasty pint of Black Bear Stout at Tahquamenon Falls Brewery and Pub.

Tahquamenon Falls State Park resides in the quiet forests of the Upper Peninsula's northeastern corner, quite a few miles from any moderately sized town. While this park's remote setting might be a drawback for some, the awe-inspiring waterfalls on the Tahquamenon River make any length of drive worth the effort.

This point-to-point route runs from Upper Falls to Lower Falls. A fee-based, dog-friendly shuttle runs between the upper and lower parking lots during the summer; check with the park for a current schedule and fees. Alternatively, you can set up your own travel or hike back the way you came for a longer adventure.

You'll set out on a paved path heading to the Upper Falls viewing platforms. Your first major viewpoint is at the brink, or top of the waterfall. You'll descend a 94-step staircase to reach an outstanding panorama of the river as it plunges 50 feet into the gorge. After marveling at this wonder, you'll head back to the paved trail and downriver to the Gorge View. Here, you'll descend 181 steps and cross a boardwalk for a fantastic view of the gorge and the front of the falls.

Back up top, you'll leave the pavement behind to journey alongside the Tahquamenon River for the next four miles. This well-trodden but rocky and root-laced path winds through a lush forest with grand hemlocks and bursts of wildflowers dotting the riverbank. You'll cross boardwalks and bridges over boggy terrain and seasonal streams.

As you head into your fifth mile, the river splits around an island, and you'll pass by a metal bridge leading to an optional one-mile loop around the island (not included in the turn-by-turn directions). From here, you'll continue along the river to a viewing platform for a portion of Lower Falls. Take in this series of drops, then meander further downriver toward the visitor center for another platform showcasing the cascades on the opposite side of the island. When you've soaked up all this picturesque river has to offer, wrap up your hike with a short walk to the parking lot to catch a ride back to your starting point and the Tahquamenon Falls Brewery and Pub.

TURN-BY-TURN DIRECTIONS

1. From the trailhead, follow the paved path, passing the bathrooms and heading into the forest.
2. At 0.2 miles, reach an Upper Falls trail map and bear right at the fork. In 150 feet, reach a trail sign. Keep right to follow the arrow for "Falls Brink Viewing Areas."
3. At 0.4 miles, at the "Attention: 94 Steps to the Brink" sign, turn left to go down the stairs to a viewing platform. Enjoy a closer look at Upper Falls, then retrace your steps back to the trail sign from Step 2.
4. At 0.6 miles, reach the trail sign from Step 2. Keep right to follow the arrow for Falls Gorge Viewing Areas.
5. At 0.7 miles, continue straight, ignoring an unmarked trail spur on the right. In 250 feet, continue straight, ignoring the signposted Nature Trail on the right.
6. At 0.8 miles, reach a junction with a trail map. Turn right at the "Gorge View 181 steps" sign to go down the stairs and continue on the boardwalk. Once you've reached the end, return to the top of the stairs.
7. At 1.1 miles, reach the junction from the previous step. Turn right, leaving the pavement to continue on the dirt trail.
8. At 5.1 miles, continue straight past a bridge on the right.
9. At 5.2 miles, reach a viewing platform on the right. Enjoy the view of Lower Falls, then return to the trail. In 150 feet, continue straight, ignoring an unmarked trail spur on the left.
10. At 5.5 miles, reach a trail map and bathrooms on the left. Continue straight.
11. At 5.6 miles, reach a viewing platform on the right and the visitor center on the left. Check out the final view of the river, then continue straight.
12. At 5.7 miles, reach the end of the trail at the Lower Falls trailhead and parking lot.

FIND THE TRAILHEAD

From Paradise at M-123 and Whitefish Point Road, head northwest on M-123/Tahquamenon Scenic Byway and proceed for 14 miles. Turn left at the sign for Upper Falls Tahquamenon Falls State Park. After 0.2 miles, the road ends at the Upper Falls parking lot. The trail begins by the Fact Shack at the southwest corner of the lot.

TAHQUAMENON FALLS BREWERY & PUB

In 1949, Lark Ludlow's grandfather, John Barrett, a resident of Newberry, purchased 164 acres next to Tahquamenon Falls. He gave it all to the State of Michigan, except for two acres, which is where the Tahquamenon Falls Brewery and Pub now sits. John, an entrepreneur at heart, started out with buildings that he leased to people selling souvenirs and refreshments to park visitors. Over time, the property and business passed down through the family until it landed with Lark and her youngest brother in 1987.

In the early 1990s, as they started making plans to build an indoor dining facility, Lark noted the recent rise in microbreweries. She decided this was the perfect time to start one herself along with the dining. She learned everything she needed to know from other brewers, particularly from the folks at The Vierling, the UP's first microbrewery, who she's remained friends with.

Tahquamenon Falls Brewery and Pub opened in 1996, and Lark still loves to see visitors marvel at a brewery housed within a state park. She's found there's no better compliment than hearing how much a guest enjoyed their beer. The brewery's Black Bear Stout, often compared to Guinness, boasts a smooth, creamy body and a medium chocolate flavor.

LAND MANAGER

Tahquamenon Falls State Park
41382 W. M-123
Paradise MI, 49768
(906) 492-3415
www2.dnr.state.mi.us/parksandtrails/details.aspx?id=428&type=SPRK
www2.dnr.state.mi.us/parksandtrails/details.aspx?id=428&type=SPRK#-map-tab

BREWERY/RESTAURANT

Tahquamenon Falls Brewery & Pub
24019 Upper Falls Drive
Paradise, MI 49768
(906) 492-3300
tahquamenonfallsbrewery.com

Distance from trailhead: 350 feet

CHAPEL LOOP

EXPLORE WATERFALLS, SANDY BEACHES, AND DRAMATIC CLIFFS

STARTING POINT	**DESTINATION**
CHAPEL FALLS TRAILHEAD	CHAPEL FALLS
BREWERY	**HIKE TYPE**
EAST CHANNEL BREWING COMPANY	STRENUOUS
DOG FRIENDLY	**SEASON**
NO	MAY–OCTOBER
FEES	**DURATION**
NONE	5 HOURS
MAP REFERENCE	**LENGTH**
POSTED AT TRAILHEAD	10.7 MILES (LOOP)
HIGHLIGHTS	**ELEVATION GAIN**
SANDSTONE ARCHES, WATERFALLS, LAKE SUPERIOR	575 FEET

7.6%
ALCOHOL CONTENT

OLD TRU'S IPA

LIGHT AMBER

CITRUS,
PINE

CITRUS,
PINE,
MALT

BITTERNESS **SWEETNESS**

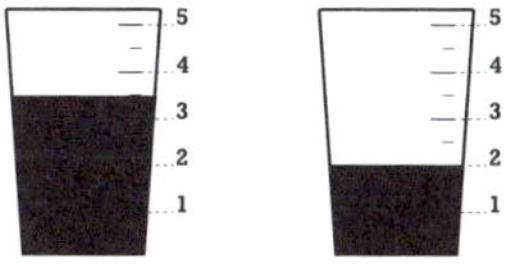

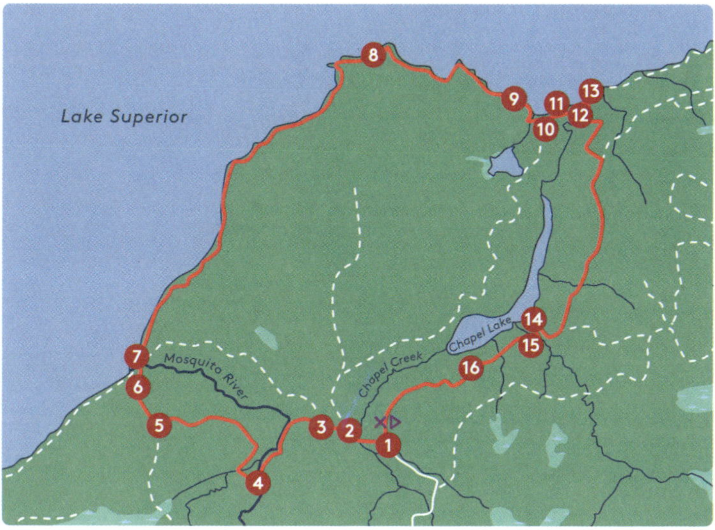

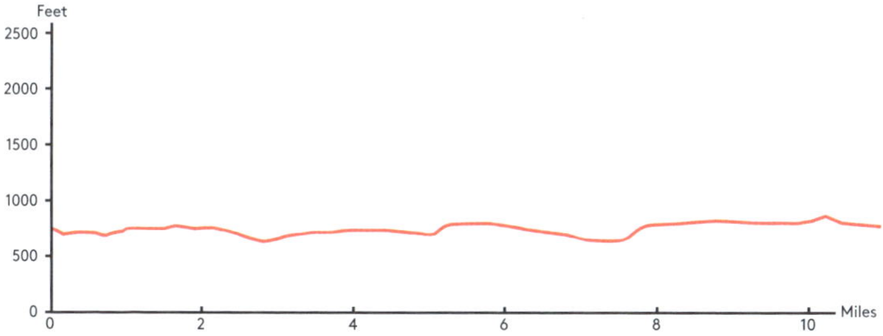

HIKE DESCRIPTION

Hike this classic circuit within Pictured Rocks National Lakeshore to experience some of the park's top waterfalls and geologic wonders. Then, head into town for an ice-cold brew at East Channel Brewing.

Pictured Rocks National Lakeshore gets its name from 15 miles of cliffs along Lake Superior. The rock face features horizontal striping from varying sediment layers, as well as vertical stripes where minerals seep out and stain the rock. Iron creates lines of orange and red, manganese is black, and copper develops blues and greens. Wind and water have carved an array of features into the sandstone, such as arches, sea caves, and spires.

Your hike begins a couple of miles inland amidst a mixed forest of hemlocks and hardwoods. The first scenic stop is just one mile in at Mosquito Falls, a series of two drops along the Mosquito River. After another mile and a half, you'll reach Mosquito Beach and your first

glimpse of the scenic Pictured Rocks cliffs. Here, you'll cross a bridge over the Mosquito River and continue along the top of the cliffs for about four miles to Chapel Beach. In this stretch, you'll catch views of Lover's Leap, a 250-foot arch, and Grand Portal, a 300-foot arch. Grand Portal partially collapsed in the 90s, so you'll see a pile of sandstone blocking the lower portion of the opening. The water used to be deep enough that some ships could pass under the arch.

You'll reach Chapel Beach about seven miles into your journey. Two sets of stairs lead down to the beach if you want to explore (optional, not included in the mileage or map). At the far end of the beach, you'll see Chapel Beach Falls, where Chapel Creek cascades over the rocks down to Lake Superior. Cross the bridge and continue to Chapel Rock, a grand sandstone formation with a solitary pine tree balancing on it. From here, you'll turn right, heading back inland through a maple forest to Chapel Falls (different from Chapel Beach Falls). It's an easy two-mile stroll along a wide dirt path to this last waterfall, which boasts an impressive, almost 60-foot drop in the river. A half mile past the falls, you'll catch the spur on your right for the final viewpoint, an overlook of Chapel Lake. After admiring the beauty, return to the main trail to finish the last stretch of your hike back to the trailhead.

TURN-BY-TURN DIRECTIONS

1. From the trailhead, bear left on the path signposted for Mosquito Falls.
2. At 0.3 miles, bear left at the fork, signposted for Mosquito River.
3. At 0.4 miles, bear left at the fork, signposted for Mosquito Falls.
4. At 1.0 miles, reach Mosquito Falls on the right.
5. At 2.3 miles, reach an unmarked T-junction and turn right.
6. At 2.6 miles, keep right, ignoring the trail spurs for a backcountry campground on the left.
7. At 2.7 miles, keep right to cross a wooden bridge over a river. Then, continue straight, following the "Chapel Beach" sign. In 300 feet, pass by the signposted Mosquito Campground on the right and Mosquito Beach on the left.
8. At 5.5 miles, keep right to follow the trail past a beach on the left.
9. At 6.8 miles, bear left at the fork to follow the trail along the cliff. The right spur continues slightly inland and reconnects 0.1 miles ahead.
10. At 7.0 miles, reach a four-way junction, signposted for Chapel Beach on the left and Chapel Beach Trail on the right. Continue straight, ignoring both signposted trails.
11. At 7.1 miles, continue straight, ignoring the Chapel Beach Campground on the right and several social spurs on the left and right.
12. At 7.2 miles, cross the bridge over the river.
13. At 7.3 miles, reach Chapel Rock. Turn right at the junction onto the signposted Chapel Falls Trail.
14. At 9.2 miles, reach a viewing platform for Chapel Falls.
15. At 9.3 miles, reach a set of stairs on the right. Hike down for an alternate view of the waterfall, then return to the trail.
16. At 9.7 miles, reach a spur on the right. Follow the spur for 200 feet to view Chapel Lake. Then, return to the main trail and continue straight to the trailhead to close the loop.

FIND THE TRAILHEAD

From Munising at Munising Avenue and Elm Avenue, head southeast on Munising Avenue. After 0.3 miles, at the traffic circle, continue straight on Munising Avenue. After 2.7 miles, continue straight onto Adams Trail. After 11.3 miles, turn left onto Chapel Drive and proceed for 1.1 miles. Turn left onto Camp Road/Chapel Road. After 1.1 miles, bear right onto Chapel Road and continue for 2.9 miles until the road dead-ends at the Chapel Falls Trailhead parking lot. This is a popular trailhead, and the parking lot fills up fast, so you may have to park along the road and walk back. The trail begins at the top of the parking lot.

EAST CHANNEL BREWING COMPANY

One of brewery owner Joe DesJardins's favorite parts of operating East Channel Brewing is the sense of community within Munising and among the local breweries. It's not just that the neighborhood shows up to support charities and events that East Channel hosts; they also carry a sense of pride in helping the brewery put its best foot forward with little things like helping new taproom staff talk through the beer options or straightening a beer display at the liquor store while passing through.

And while some might see multiple breweries in a town and think they're competitors, Joe feels that it's anything but. He doesn't hesitate to reach out to the neighboring brewers if he's running short on an ingredient or needs help, and he happily returns the sense of support whenever he can. He sees it as the community's success, not just one business. East Channel has two locations: the original cozy brewery on Maple Street (highlighted here), and a small beer garden at the production facility on Superior Street. Both offer Old Tru's, a West Coast IPA with a malty backbone and a hint of citrus and pine.

LAND MANAGER

Pictured Rocks National Lakeshore
1505 Sand Point Road
Munising, MI 49862
(906) 387-3700
nps.gov/piro
nps.gov/piro/planyourvisit/upload/Chapel-Beaver-Day-Hikes-Map-508.pdf

BREWERY/RESTAURANT

East Channel Brewing Company
209 Maple Street
Munising, MI 49862
(906) 387-3006
eastchannelbrewery.com

Distance from trailhead: 19.3 miles

MOUNT MARQUETTE LOOP

ALL-ENCOMPASSING VIEWS OF MARQUETTE'S RUGGED BEAUTY

STARTING POINT	DESTINATION
NTN SOUTH TRAILHEAD	SUMMIT OVERLOOK

BREWERY	HIKE TYPE
BLACKROCKS BREWERY	MODERATE

DOG FRIENDLY	SEASON
YES (LEASH REQUIRED)	MAY–OCTOBER

FEES	DURATION
NONE	2 HOURS 15 MINUTES

MAP REFERENCE	LENGTH
POSTED AT TRAILHEAD	4.5 MILES (LOOP)

HIGHLIGHTS	ELEVATION GAIN
PANORAMIC VIEW, FALL COLORS	599 FEET

4.8% ALCOHOL CONTENT

SUPER DELUXE HELLES LAGER

GOLDEN YELLOW

MALTY, ORANGE

FLORAL, SPICY, ORANGE

BITTERNESS

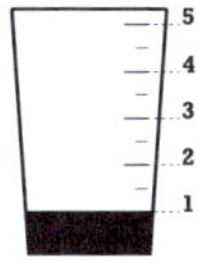

SWEETNESS

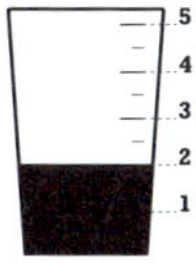

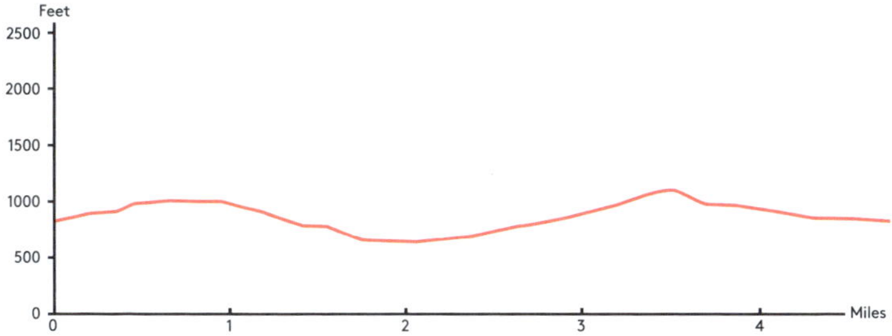

HIKE DESCRIPTION

Hustle your way to the top of Mount Marquette for an outstanding panorama of Lake Superior and the surrounding forest. Wind down afterward with a fresh pour of Super Deluxe at Blackrocks Brewery.

Sandwiched between Lake Superior and the southern tip of the Huron Mountains, Marquette is a hub for outdoor enthusiasts. Mount Marquette, at the southern end of town, is home to a maze of trails for hikers and bikers of varying abilities. One of the most scenic routes, the Mount Marquette Loop, brings adventurers to an outlook at the top of the mountain. From this vantage point, you get a spectacular view of the town from Hogback Mountain to the ore docks on Lake Superior. It's also a great spot to take in the fall colors (the Upper Peninsula is known for fantastic fall foliage) or watch the northern lights.

From the Noquemanon Trail Network (NTN) South Trailhead, you'll head into the forest on the Gurly Trail Section to begin your loop along the south side of Mount Marquette. While quite a few trails crisscross along the way, it's easy to stay on track thanks to the NTN's detailed signage, including both the overall route (Mount Marquette Loop) and the specific trail name (like Trail Section "Gurly").

About a half mile in, you'll cross Mount Marquette Road (for the first of several times), a dirt road with a less fun but more direct route to the overlook. The oak, maple, and pine forest is gorgeous and worthy of a more rambling exploration that this hike provides. You'll descend about 350 feet over the next mile until you reach a smaller, secondary

trailhead at map kiosk 13. Then, you'll climb about 450 feet over a mile and a half as you hike along the north side up to the overlook. You'll cross a couple of seasonal streams and wind up a few short switchbacks along the way.

Around the three-mile mark, you'll reach a sign directing you up a short trail spur to the Mt. Marquette Overlook. The outlook is a partially exposed rock dome with plenty of space if you want to relax for a bit to enjoy the view. When you're ready, you'll make your way back down the trail spur to continue your loop. The last mile of your journey winds around a few ravines as you make your way down to the trailhead.

TURN-BY-TURN DIRECTIONS

1. From the trailhead, follow the signposted Mount Marquette Loop Trail (Blue Loop).
2. At 0.1 miles, at a junction, turn right to continue on the Blue Loop, signposted as Trail Section "Gurly."
3. At 0.6 miles, cross a dirt road and continue on the Blue Loop signposted as Trail Section "Doctors."
4. At 0.9 miles, continue straight at a junction.
5. At 1.0 miles, continue straight, ignoring a trail spur on the right. In 250 feet, continue straight, ignoring a second trail spur on the right.
6. At 1.6 miles, reach a T-junction and turn right onto the trail signposted as "More Difficult." In 250 feet, reach a junction and turn left to continue on the Blue Loop signposted as Trail Section "Forget Me Not."
7. At 1.8 miles, cross a dirt road and reach map kiosk 13 immediately on the left. Continue straight onto the Blue Loop signposted as Trail Section "Up A Creek."
8. At 2.0 miles, continue straight, ignoring a trail spur on the left. Ignore several unsigned trail spurs on the right over the next 0.5 miles.
9. At 2.5 miles, reach a junction at map kiosk 15. Turn left to stay on the Blue Loop signposted as Trail Section "Secrets."
10. At 2.8 miles, reach map kiosk 16. Continue straight on the Blue Loop signposted as Trail Section "Goat."
11. At 3.1 miles, reach a T-junction; turn left for the signposted Mt. Marquette Overlook Trail. In 300 feet, bear right at the fork to continue on the signposted "Scary Trail."
12. At 3.2 miles, cross the dirt road. In 300 feet, bear right at the fork.
13. At 3.3 miles, cross the dirt road again and continue straight. Reach the overlook in 200 feet. Enjoy the view, then return to the T-junction from Step 11.
14. At 3.6 miles, reach the T-junction from Step 11; turn left onto the signposted Split Tree Trail.
15. At 3.8 miles, continue straight, ignoring a spur on the right.
16. At 4.1 miles, bear left at the fork.
17. At 4.3 miles, bear left at the fork, ignoring the trail spur on the right signposted as "Less Difficult."
18. At 4.6 miles, reach the junction from Step 2; turn right to return to the trailhead.

FIND THE TRAILHEAD

From Marquette at 3rd Street and Washington Street, head south on 3rd Street. After 0.3 miles, turn left onto Fisher Street. After 250 feet, turn right onto Champion Street. After 0.3 miles, turn right onto Jackson Street. After 300 feet, turn left onto Division Street. After 1.5 miles, turn left onto M-553 South and proceed for 0.2 miles until you reach the parking lot on the left. The trail begins at the top of the lot by the map kiosk.

BLACKROCKS BREWERY

David Manson and Andy Langlois started brewing to challenge their brains in ways that their corporate jobs couldn't. They worked as pharmaceutical reps and, when the industry faced economic downsizing, they used the opportunity to launch their beer production from a hobby to a full-time brewery. In December 2010, they poured their first official beer.

The Blackrocks team has grown quite a bit since then, many of whom, including David and Andy, take full advantage of the outdoors, which practically begins at their doorstep. With this in mind, the brewery donates to the local non-profit, NTN, who manages a bulk of the local trails.

Blackrocks Brewery crafts a variety of beers, including Super Deluxe, a German Helles lager. It's brewed with Saphir and Tettnang hops, delivering a crisp and refreshing taste with just a hint of sweetness.

LAND MANAGER

City of Marquette
300 W Baraga Avenue
Marquette, MI 49855
(906) 228-0435
marquettemi.gov
noquetrails.org/south-trails

BREWERY/RESTAURANT

Blackrocks Brewery
424 N 3rd Street
Marquette, MI 49855
(906) 273-1333
blackrocksbrewery.com

Distance from trailhead: 2.7 miles

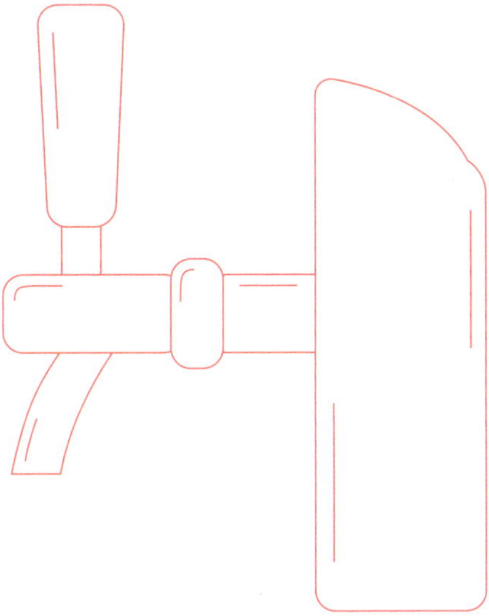

HOGBACK MOUNTAIN

SENSATIONAL VIEWS AT THE TOP OF A ROCKY PEAK

STARTING POINT	DESTINATION
HOGBACK NORTH TRAILHEAD	HOGBACK SUMMIT
BREWERY	**HIKE TYPE**
BARREL + BEAM BREWERY	STRENUOUS
DOG FRIENDLY	**SEASON**
YES (LEASH REQUIRED)	MAY–OCTOBER
FEES	**DURATION**
YES	1 HOUR 30 MINUTES
MAP REFERENCE	**LENGTH**
POSTED AT TRAILHEAD	3.6 MILES (ROUND TRIP)
HIGHLIGHTS	**ELEVATION GAIN**
MOUNTAIN VISTA, FALL COLORS	655 FEET

6.5%
ALCOHOL CONTENT

SAISON TERRE A TERRE

GOLDEN YELLOW

SPICE,
FRUIT

FRUITY,
SPICY,
DRY

BITTERNESS

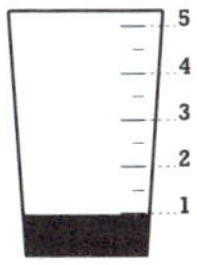

SWEETNESS

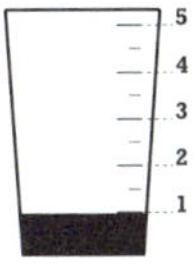

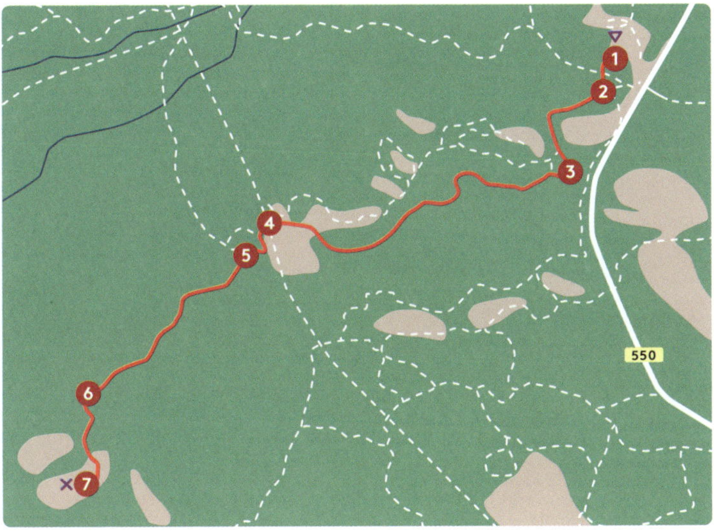

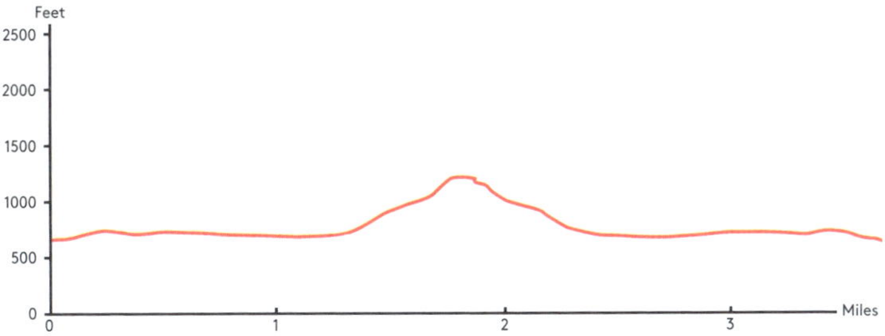

HIKE DESCRIPTION

Scramble up this rocky, mountain trail for fantastic views overlooking Lake Superior and the surrounding forests. When you've finished, make your way back to Marquette for a crisp farmhouse ale at Barrel + Beam Brewery.

Hogback Mountain sits at the southern end of the Huron Mountains, just north of Marquette. The Huron Mountains are a particularly rugged section of Upper Peninsula terrain and home to the state's highest peak, Mount Avron (1,979 feet). Hogback itself is the fourth highest peak, topping out at 1,220 feet. A thick boreal forest blankets the range, hiding granite peaks, wild lakes, rivers, and waterfalls. While much of the Huron Range is challenging to access beyond the rough and minimally maintained logging roads, the southern foothills sport a variety of opportunities for almost any type of adventure. This area, known as the Little Presque Isle Multiuse Pathway System, includes Top of the World, Harlow Lake, Wetmore Landing, and Hogback Mountain.

There are two popular routes up Hogback: One trail climbs the mountain from the southeast side, whereas our route leads you up the north side. The trail is well-signed with "Hogback North" trail markers, particularly near the beginning, where you'll pass several trail junctions. At the first junction, you'll reach a large, yellow "Caution" sign with a

reminder of the trail's challenges—rugged terrain and no cell service—to ensure you're prepared for the trek. While the first mile has relatively minimal elevation gain, don't let that trick you into thinking the hike to the top will be easy. The footpath is a mix of packed dirt, jagged rocks, and mazes of gnarled roots. You'll encounter steep terrain that requires a bit of scrambling using both your hands and feet.

The surrounding forest is a mix of pines and northern hardwoods dotted with boulders and rock outcroppings hidden among the trees. After the first mile, the trail begins to climb toward the summit; the outcroppings get larger and the trail gets rockier. Just as you emerge from the forest, you'll reach a rock wall. Follow the spray-paint trail markers to scramble your way up the rock face. The natural grooves and cracks in the rock can serve as hand- and footholds until the surface angle lessens enough to walk directly up the textured rock to the wide, flat top of Hogback. Looking east, you'll enjoy an expansive view of Lake Superior with Sugarloaf Mountain to the northeast and Marquette to the southeast. As you spin to the west, a thick forest blankets the land, with the Huron Range rising to the northwest. You'll head in this direction to cross through the small cluster of trees just below the summit. Beyond the trees, the mountaintop opens up again with bare rock and an alternate perspective of this western spread. In the fall, the maple, beech, and birch trees light up these views with yellows, oranges, and reds. It creates a stunning contrast with the green pines and deep blue of Lake Superior. The Upper Peninsula is known for its fantastic display of fall foliage, and this hike will certainly deliver.

TURN-BY-TURN DIRECTIONS

1. From the trail map, follow the path leading into the woods. In 250 feet, continue straight across a two-track dirt road and pass a large "Caution" sign on the left.
2. At 0.1 miles, continue straight to follow the "Hogback North" trail marker, ignoring a trail spur on the left.
3. At 0.3 miles, continue straight, ignoring a second trail spur on the left.
4. At 1.0 miles, continue straight to cross a wooden bridge over a stream.
5. At 1.1 miles, continue straight, following the "Hogback North" trail marker and ignoring a trail spur on the right.
6. At 1.5 miles, keep left at the fork, following the "Summit" sign.
7. At 1.7 miles, reach the summit. Take in the views, then return to the trailhead.

FIND THE TRAILHEAD

From Marquette at 4th Street and Washington Street, head north on 4th Street and proceed for 0.7 miles where the road becomes Presque Isle Avenue. After 0.2 miles, at the traffic circle, take the second exit to continue straight. After 1.0 miles, turn left onto Hawley Street and continue for 0.5 miles where the road turns into Big Bay Road. After 4.6 miles, turn left onto Beagle Club Road where a large dirt parking lot will be on the left in 250 feet. The trail begins at the far end of the lot.

BARREL + BEAM BREWERY

Nick VanCourt and Marina Dupler, Barrel + Beam's owners, met while attending Marquette's Northern Michigan University before moving to Wisconsin to begin their careers. Nick enjoyed his job, but loved beer more. So, he returned to school to take the brewing program at the World Brewing Academy, a partnership between Siebel Institute of Technology in Chicago, Illinois, and Doemens Academy in Munich, Germany. Part of the curriculum included hands-on brewing experience in Germany, during which Nick discovered a great appreciation for the process and styles of German and Belgian beers. Back in the U.S., he built up his brewing experience with a couple of breweries around Wisconsin until a brewing opportunity with a Marquette brewery brought him and Marina back home to Michigan.

As Nick's experience grew, he honed in on what he enjoyed most: farmhouse ales. In 2016, he and Marina decided to build their own brewery with that focus in mind. They purchased the old lodge building that had housed the Northwoods Supper Club, a dining and social club operating from the 1930s to 2006. The expansive lodge required significant renovations after sitting vacant for 10 years, but Nick and Marina preserved the heavy wooden beams and rustic charm. Barrel + Beam Brewery launched in 2018 and specializes in barrel-aged beers, farmhouse ales, meads, and ciders. Saison Terre A Terre is a classic saison with a light body and crisp carbonation. The flavor starts with a hint of spice and tartness finishing smooth and dry.

LAND MANAGER

Michigan Department of Natural Resources
Parks and Recreation Division
P.O. Box 30257
Lansing, MI 48909
(517) 284-7275
dnr.state.mi.us/parksandtrails/Details.aspx?id=87&type=SFPW#overview
michigandnr.com/Publications/PDFS/RecreationCamping/little_presque_isle_harlow_lake.pdf

BREWERY/RESTAURANT

Barrel + Beam Brewery
260 Northwoods Road
Marquette, MI 49855
(906) 273-2559
barrelandbeam.com

Distance from trailhead: 9.3 miles

MT. BALDY

A STEADY CLIMB TO TANGLED MOUNTAINTOP TERRAIN

STARTING POINT	**DESTINATION**
HELMUT AND CANDIS STERN PRESERVE TRAILHEAD	MT. BALDY
BREWERY	**HIKE TYPE**
BRICKSIDE BREWERY	STRENUOUS
DOG FRIENDLY	**SEASON**
NO	MAY–OCTOBER
FEES	**DURATION**
NONE	3 HOURS
MAP REFERENCE	**LENGTH**
POSTED AT TRAILHEAD	6.3 MILES (ROUND TRIP)
HIGHLIGHTS	**ELEVATION GAIN**
SUMMIT VIEWS, KEWEENAW PENINSULA	764 FEET

4.5%
ALCOHOL CONTENT

SUMMER WIT

DARK STRAW

CINNAMON, ORANGE

CINNAMON, GINGER

BITTERNESS

SWEETNESS

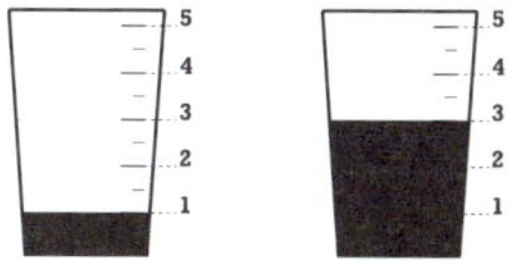

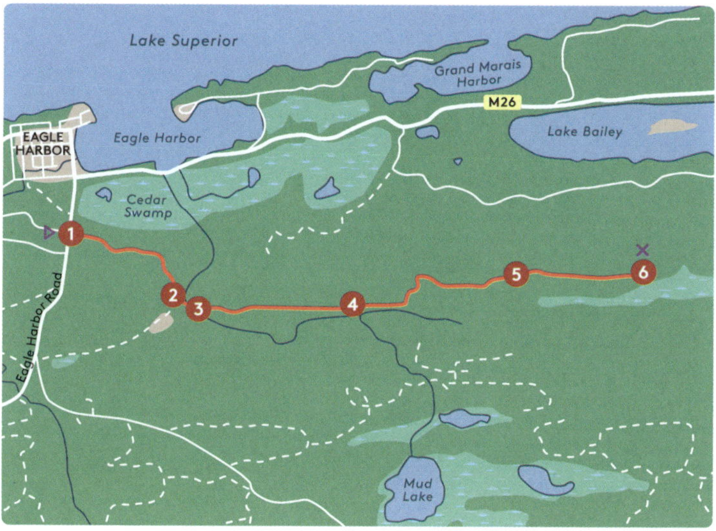

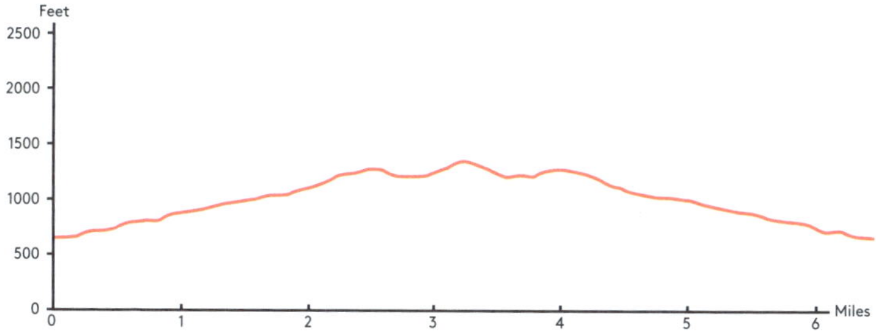

HIKE DESCRIPTION

Hop across a creek and wander through a stunted forest as you trek to the top of Mt. Baldy. After soaking up a panorama of the Keweenaw Peninsula, head north to Copper Harbor, where Brickside Brewery serves up ice-cold craft beers.

In 2001, The Nature Conservancy purchased the land for the Helmut and Candis Stern Preserve to protect rare plant communities, a half mile of shoreline along Lake Bailey, and the striking Mt. Baldy—also known as Lookout Mountain. Mt. Baldy's name comes from its bald appearance at the summit, with wide patches of exposed bedrock. Strong winds cut across Lake Superior and whip over this high point, creating an environment that's too severe for many plants to survive. The trees that manage to take root here are undersized and gnarled, with permanently windblown branches.

Your ascent to this warped landscape begins on private property on a wide, two-track trail heading into the forest. The footpath quickly transitions from dirt to sand as you make your way past a sand pit. The deep sand in combination with the gentle incline is enough to get your heart pumping across this short stretch. Nearly a half mile past

the sand, the trail dips down to Cedar Creek. This wide but generally shallow stream requires good footwork if you want to cross it without getting wet. There's no bridge, so you'll have to hop across strategically placed rocks. If the water is higher, your only option may be to walk directly through the stream. Once across, you'll weave through the woods for another mile as you steadily hike higher.

Halfway to the peak, you'll reach three yellow steel pillars stationed across the trail to allow only foot traffic for the remainder of the route. This is where you leave private property and enter The Nature Conservancy's Mt. Baldy preserve. This last section of trail is also known as the Nicole Bloom Memorial Trail, a tribute to a Michigan Tech student and passionate environmentalist who lost her life in a mountain climbing accident.

About two and half miles into your journey, you'll emerge from the thick forest to a false summit—an open stretch of rocky terrain that many mistake as the highest point. You're at about 1,250 feet here, so you still have a short climb across the next half mile to reach the 1,332-foot summit. However, this false summit is where you'll be treated to your first views of Lake Superior. You'll continue along the path as it briefly dips back into the trees before your final ascent.

As you move up the ridgeline, the landscape shifts to a mix of stunted trees twisted by the wind and low juniper shrubs creeping across the bedrock. You'll hike up a rocky path to the bare dome of Mt. Baldy's summit. This vantage point offers sweeping vistas of the Keweenaw Peninsula. On the southern side of the summit, the cliff plunges an impressive 230 feet. Perch here for views of Mount Bohemia across the peninsula. On the northern side, the mountain slopes gently down toward Lake Bailey. Sprawl out on the bedrock to settle in and savor the lake views. From either direction you can marvel at the immensity of Lake Superior. Your return hike follows the same trail back down.

TURN-BY-TURN DIRECTIONS

1. From the trailhead, head out on the trail to the left of the trail map.
2. At 0.7 miles, continue straight, ignoring an unmarked trail spur on the right.
3. At 0.8 miles, reach Cedar Creek. Continue straight across the creek by hopping on rocks or wading through the water.
4. At 1.6 miles, reach a series of steel pillars crossing the trail. Continue straight between the pillars to transition onto the signposted Nicole Bloom Memorial Trail.
5. At 2.6 miles, continue straight as you emerge from the trees to a false summit.
6. At 3.2 miles, reach the end of the trail at the summit. Enjoy the 360-degree view, then retrace your steps back to the trailhead.

FIND THE TRAILHEAD

From Mohawk at US-41/Mohawk Street and 6th Street, head northeast on US-41/Mohawk Street and proceed for 10.2 miles. Turn left onto Eagle Harbor Cutoff Road. After 5.2 miles, immediately after passing by the Eagle Harbor Fire Department on the right, turn right into the gravel parking lot for the Helmut and Candis Stern Preserve at Mt. Baldy. The parking lot is located on Eagle Harbor Township property. Do not park in the neighboring Eagle Harbor Fire Department lot or block any access roads. The trail begins at the far end of the lot.

BRICKSIDE BREWERY

Jason Robinson opened Brickside Brewery, Michigan's northernmost brewery, in 2012. After enjoying the results of his homebrewing, Jason knew he wanted to make it about more than just a tasty hobby—he wanted to bring great beer to the residents and tourists of Copper Harbor and the Keweenaw Peninsula. Now, many years later, brewing is still his favorite part of the business. Jason loves creating his own recipes. He also enjoys the freedom of the process in that once he's set up a fresh batch to brew, he can step away until it's ready.

Brickside Brewery's Superior Wit is a Belgian-style wheat beer highlighting coriander and orange. Over the years, Jason has tweaked this recipe's ingredients to create new spin-offs like Wilkins Wit, featuring lemongrass and orange, and Summer Wit, the featured beer, still with the orange but also a bit of cinnamon and a hint of ginger.

LAND MANAGER

The Nature Conservancy of Michigan
Helmut and Candis Stern Preserve at Mt. Baldy
Eagle Harbor Cut Off Road
Eagle Harbor, MI 49950
(517) 316-0300
nature.org/en-us/get-involved/how-to-help/places-we-protect/helmut-candis-stern-preserve-at-mt-baldy/
visitkeweenaw.com/listing/helmut-%26-candis-stern-preserve-at-mt-baldy/7/

BREWERY/RESTAURANT

Brickside Brewery
64 Gratiot Street
Copper Harbor, MI 49918
(906) 289-4772
bricksidebrewery.com

Distance from trailhead: 14 miles

GREAT CONGLOMERATE FALLS

TRACE THE BLACK RIVER TO A 40-FOOT SPLIT WATERFALL

STARTING POINT	DESTINATION
NCT ALGONQUIN FALLS TRAILHEAD	GREAT CONGLOMERATE FALLS

BREWERY	HIKE TYPE
COLD IRON BREWING	MODERATE

DOG FRIENDLY	SEASON
YES (LEASH REQUIRED)	MAY-OCTOBER

FEES	DURATION
NONE	2 HOURS 30 MINUTES

MAP REFERENCE	LENGTH
POSTED AT TRAILHEAD	6 MILES (ROUND TRIP)

HIGHLIGHTS	ELEVATION GAIN
WATERFALL, BLACK RIVER	404 FEET

5.0%
ALCOHOL CONTENT

DRIFT SOUTH JALAPEÑO ALE

GOLDEN YELLOW

JALAPEÑO

JALAPEÑO, SWEET PEPPER

BITTERNESS

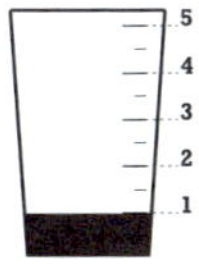

SWEETNESS

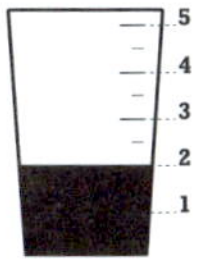

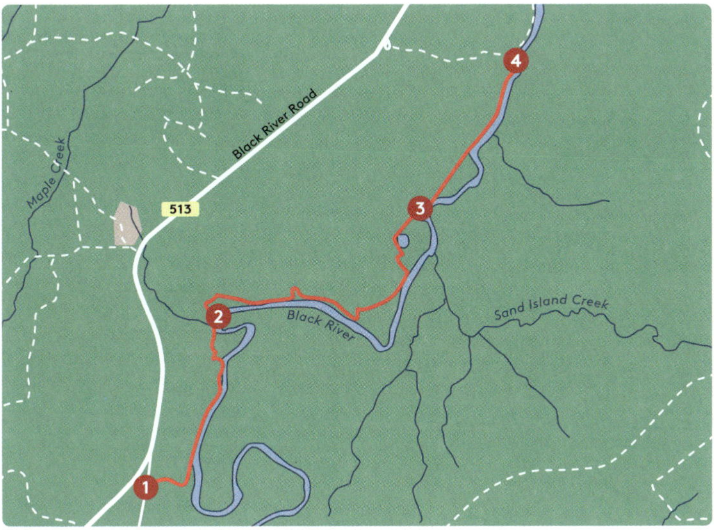

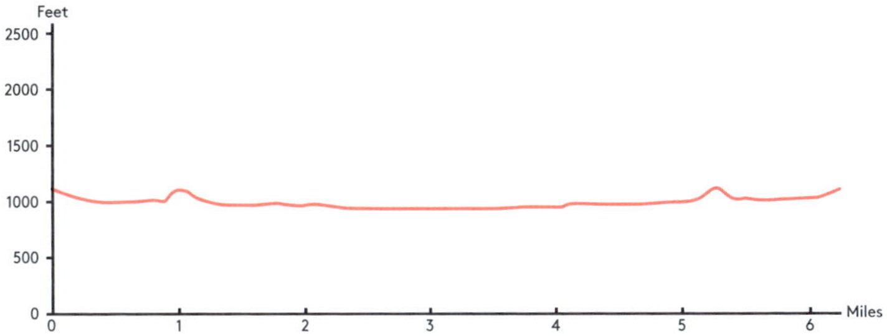

HIKE DESCRIPTION

Stretch your legs on the North Country Trail (NCT) as it follows the Black River to a split waterfall. Keep the river vibe going strong with a stop at Cold Iron Brewing for an invigorating pint of their Drift South Jalapeño Ale.

The Ottawa National Forest, located in the western portion of Michigan's Upper Peninsula, is a marvelous expanse of wilderness covering approximately one million acres. With its diverse landscapes of dense forests, winding rivers, and sparkling lakes, this national forest is a paradise for outdoor enthusiasts. Among its many wonders, the Black River stands out, offering dramatic waterfalls, rocky shorelines, and a remarkable stretch of hiking trails. Originating in Wisconsin, the Black River cuts through the western end of the national forest before emptying into Lake Superior. While nearby attractions like the Porcupine Mountains Wilderness draw large crowds, the Black River region provides a more tranquil experience and is a must-visit for any hiker traveling through the area.

Our route explores the Ottawa National Forest and the Black River via the North Country Trail (NCT). The NCT dives into the heart of the North American wilderness across 4,800 miles of trail through eight states. From the NCT Algonquin Falls trailhead, you'll step into a lush hardwood forest carpeted in ferns and moss. The well-worn path is easy to follow as you make your way down to the Black River. Overall, the trail descends about 200 feet from the trailhead to the Great Conglomerate Falls overlook. The only major break in the descent is a ridgeline that you'll reach about three-quarters of a mile in. Here, you'll have to ascend about 100 feet up the ridge to get around a ravine and continue along the river. As you trek along the NCT, you'll weave through patches of old-growth hemlock and cross several small streams, enhancing the serene atmosphere of your hike. This forest is not only beautiful, it's also alive with wildlife. Keep your eyes peeled for deer, foxes, and even bears, which can sometimes be spotted roaming the woods.

Every so often, the trees will part to reveal glimpses of the Black River. Although its waters may not possess the classic blue hue many expect, the river's brown color—often compared to root beer—adds a unique charm. The coloration is a result of tannins leaching into the water from the surrounding hemlocks and decaying plant material. A little over two miles into your adventure, you'll reach an opening in the trees overlooking a large marsh along the river. From here, the trail temporarily veers away from the water before returning to hug the shoreline for the remaining half mile to the Great Conglomerate Falls overlook. The waterfall gets its name from the large mound of conglomerate rock that splits the river. Conglomerate is a sedimentary rock made up of rounded, gravel-sized stones surrounded by finer sediments, like sand, cemented together by iron oxide, silica, or calcite.

The halved river cascades down about 40 feet on each side of the rock before rejoining to form one waterway. Several more falls dot the Black River as it descends to Lake Superior, but Great Conglomerate is the largest. Our route returns to the trailhead from here, though the NCT continues on to include Potawatomi Falls, Gorge Falls, and Rainbow Falls before heading west into the Porcupine Mountains.

TURN-BY-TURN DIRECTIONS

1. From the trailhead, follow the dirt trail into the forest.
2. At 0.9 miles, the trail takes a sharp left to climb up and over a ridgeline.
3. At 2.2 miles, reach a break in the trees on the right overlooking a marsh along the left side of the river.
4. At 3.0 miles, turn right at a junction, continuing down the rock steps to the waterfall overlook. Take in the incredible view, then return to the trailhead the way you came.

FIND THE TRAILHEAD

From Ironwood at Lowell Street and Highway 2, head east on Highway 2. After 4.6 miles, turn left onto Powderhorn Road. After 3.0 miles, turn left onto Black River Road/Black River National Forest Scenic Byway. After 7.1 miles, make a sharp right onto Copper Peak Road. Continue for 0.1 miles, and the trailhead parking area will be on the left. The trail begins near the left side of the parking area.

COLD IRON BREWING

Co-owner and brewmaster Andy Warren considers Cold Iron Brewing to be a community effort. He and the seven other owners came together to create not just a brewery but a gathering space for the town and its visitors. Ironwood serves as the gateway to the Upper Peninsula's western end, so all the people funneling through to experience the Northwoods needed a place to regroup and hang out post-adventure.

The Cold Iron building originated as office space for the Ottawa National Forest, dating back to the 1960s. During renovations, Andy and the team uncovered gorgeous wooden rafters that look as if they were specially designed for a Northwoods brewery, bringing the outdoors vibe inside. Cold Iron Brewing is a family-friendly space with a range of beers on tap and mixable six-packs to bring your favorites home. Drift South Jalapeño Ale delivers a pepper flavor without the jalapeño heat. This pale ale's malt backbone pairs well with the fresh, jalapeño taste.

LAND MANAGER

Ottawa National Forest
E6248 US 2
Ironwood, MI 49938
(906) 932-1330
fs.usda.gov/ottawa
fs.usda.gov/Internet/FSE_DOCUMENTS/fseprd530082.pdf

BREWERY/RESTAURANT

Cold Iron Brewing
104 S Lowell Street
Ironwood, MI 49938
(906) 285-7020
coldironbrewing.com

Distance from trailhead: 15.5 miles

DEDICATION AND ACKNOWLEDGEMENTS

This book is dedicated to my mom and dad, Robbie and David Radaich. Thank you for looking after Frank and Bernard, and for always advocating for my pets and adventures. You raised me to be a strong, independent woman who can do whatever she puts her mind to, but you've also made me feel safe to ask for help whenever I need it, and I'm forever grateful for that.

To my friends Jeff and Olivia Love, thank you for being fantastic friends, great beer buddies, pit-bull advocates, and all-around solid human beings. I miss our brew crew adventures and hope that we can fit in a few more during my next trip back to Arizona.

Shout out to everyone at the breweries for welcoming me and sharing your stories, despite my aura of bug spray and sweat. I often arrived directly from the trails, and that's likely how many readers will walk through your doors as well. It warms my heart to know everyone will be invited in as friends to explore your delicious creations.

Cheers to the land managers, park and forest rangers, Department of Natural Resources staff, and other protectors of these wonderful outdoor spaces. I greatly appreciate the knowledge, tips, and feedback you shared, and especially the work you put into educating visitors, preserving nature, and crafting an array of trails for all to enjoy.

Much gratitude to my brothers, Neil and Lee Radaich, for answering my calls and texts from the road. You humored my vague mechanical questions about whatever the latest clunk was coming from my van, and helped me feel safe to continue on.

To my niece, Naomi Radaich, thank you for taking care of my house and yard while I was on the road. You worked hard, and it's wonderful to see how responsible and considerate you've become.

To Jane Getting and Karie and Greg Yurick, thank you for welcoming me and the tornado that is Lu into your homes with little notice, even if just for one night. You likely received more Lu licks than would be considered respectable, but it's probably safe to assume Lu cherished every single one, and I appreciate you accepting both of us as we are.

Thank you to all the Beer Hiking authors who came before me to make this fantastic series what it is today. Extra thanks to Johanna Flashman, Jason Friedman, Philip Vondra, and Carey Kish—your books were the ones I looked to for examples and inspiration. The pages are worn and the spines creased, and I hope to open them all again for their intended purpose in the future.

Last but not in any way least, thank you to the Helvetiq team for offering me this opportunity and supporting it along the way. A special thanks to Richard Harvell for reaching out and sharing the vision for this project, Daniel Malak for the beautiful design and artwork, and the sales team for location tips and advice. And especially to my editor, Johanna Flashman: Thank you for all of your work and patience, even as I put everything off until the very last moment and sent through some tragically rough first drafts. I'm incredibly grateful for your expertise in both editing and the outdoors, and the compliment sandwiches when you'd send back edits on a particularly challenging draft.

This project required so much more of everything than I anticipated, and I couldn't have done it without each and every one of you.